SECOND EDITION

UNDERSTANDING YOUR COLLEGE EXPERIENCE

Strategies for Success

John N. Gardner

President, John N. Gardner Institute for Excellence in
    Undergraduate Education
Brevard, North Carolina

Distinguished Professor Emeritus, Library and Information Science
Senior Fellow, National Resource Center for The First-Year Experience
    and Students in Transition
University of South Carolina, Columbia

Betsy O. Barefoot

Senior Scholar
John N. Gardner Institute for Excellence in Undergraduate Education
Brevard, North Carolina

Negar Farakish

Associate Vice President for Academic Affairs/Dean of American Honors
Union County College, New Jersey

bedford/st.martin's
Macmillan Learning

Boston | New York

For Bedford/St. Martin's
Vice President, Editorial, Macmillan Learning Humanities: Edwin Hill
Publisher for College Success: Erika Gutierrez
Senior Executive Editor for College Success: Simon Glick
Developmental Editor: Jennifer Jacobson of Ohlinger Publishing Services
Assistant Production Editor: Erica Zhang
Media Producer: Sarah O'Connor
Production Manager: Joe Ford
Marketing Manager: Kayti Corfield
Associate Editor: Bethany Gordon
Editorial Assistant: Mary Jane Chen
Copy Editor: Steve Patterson
Indexer: Steve Csipke
Photo Researcher: Sue McDermott Barlow
Senior Art Director: Anna Palchik
Text Design: Jerilyn Bockorick, Cenveo Publisher Services
Cover Design: William Boardman
Cover Photo: Mature students sitting at a table in a university library. © Digital Vision/
    Getty Images
Composition: Cenveo Publisher Services
Printing and Binding: LSC Communications

Manufactured in the United States of America.

1 0 9 8 7 6
f   e   d   c   b   a

For information, write: Bedford/St. Martin's, 75 Arlington Street, Boston, MA 02116
    (617-399-4000)

ISBN 978-1-319-02918-0 (Student Edition)
ISBN 978-1-319-06445-7 (Loose-leaf Edition)

Acknowledgments
Acknowledgments and copyrights appear on the same page as the text and art selections they cover; these acknowledgments and copyrights constitute an extension of the copyright page.

Chapter Opening Images: Chapter 1: p. 3, T. Dallas/Shutterstock.com; Chapter 2: p. 27, FlatDesign/Shutterstock.com; Chapter 3: p. 47, lisboaimagelab/Shutterstock.com; Chapter 4: p. 77, Introwiz/Shutterstock.com; Chapter 5: p. 105, VoodooDot/Shutterstock .com; Chapter 6: p. 127, WonderfulPixel/Shutterstock.com; Chapter 7: p. 153, Kraphix/ Shutterstock.com; Chapter 8: p. 171, Introwiz1/Shutterstock.com; Chapter 9: p. 197, Domofon/Shutterstock.com; Chapter 10: p. 223, Introwiz1/Shutterstock.com; Chapter 11: p. 241, Happy Art/Shutterstock.com; Chapter 12: p. 271, Introwiz1/Shutterstock.com.

At the time of publication all Internet URLs published in this text were found to accurately link to their intended website. If you do find a broken link, please forward the information to collegesuccess@macmillan.com so that it can be corrected for the next printing.

Dear Student,

More than ever before, a college education is an essential step in preparing you for almost any career. In the past, many well-paying jobs required only a high school diploma, but most employers today require that job applicants have some form of education beyond high school. This can be a college degree or a certificate in a particular vocation.

As higher education is becoming more expensive, some people are questioning whether a college degree is worth the cost. Yes, college is expensive, but the benefits of a college education are well worth the price tag. A college-educated person receives a better salary and enjoys a healthier life, more confidence, and a greater future for his or her children. All the research shows that in the long run, you'll be better off with a college degree. If you're reading this, it means you're on a good path.

While you might have many reasons for being in college, we hope your primary goal is graduation. And you will be more likely to graduate if you have a successful first year. When we were in our first year of college, there were no college success courses. New students had to sink or swim. As a result, some students did well, some struggled, and some dropped out or flunked out.

Today, most colleges offer first-year seminars or college success courses to help students make it through the first year and continue on their way toward graduation. As college professors, researchers, and administrators with many years of experience working with first-year students, we understand the challenges of starting college. We know what tools and strategies you need to meet these challenges, and you'll find them in this book, *Understanding Your College Experience*, which you are likely reading because you are enrolled in a college success course. Although this book might seem different from your other textbooks, we believe that it could be the most important book you read this term because it's all about improving your chances for success in college and in your career. This information will help you discover your own strengths and your needs for improvement. We know that if you apply the ideas in this book to your everyday life, you are more likely to enjoy your time in college, graduate, and achieve your life goals. Welcome to college!

John N. Gardner

Betsy O. Barefoot

Negar Farakish

About the Authors

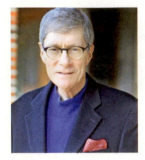

John N. Gardner brings unparalleled experience to this authoritative text for first-year seminar courses. His first college teaching experience was at a two-year public college in a small, rural town in South Carolina. That experience was so inspiring that he made a lifetime commitment to continue serving such students. He is the recipient of the University of South Carolina's highest award for teaching excellence. He has 25 years of experience directing and teaching in the most respected and most widely emulated first-year seminar in the country, the University 101 course at the University of South Carolina. He is recognized as one of the country's leading educators for his role in initiating and orchestrating an international reform movement to improve the beginning college experience. He is also the founding leader of two influential higher education centers that support campuses in their efforts to improve the learning and retention of beginning college students: the National Resource Center for The First-Year Experience and Students in Transition at the University of South Carolina (**sc.edu/fye**) and the John N. Gardner Institute for Excellence in Undergraduate Education (**jngi.org**) based in Brevard, North Carolina. The experiential basis for all of John Gardner's work is his own miserable first year of college on academic probation, an experience that he hopes to prevent for this book's readers.

Betsy O. Barefoot is a writer, researcher, and teacher whose special area of scholarship is the first year of college. During her tenure at the University of South Carolina from 1988 to 1999, she served as codirector for research and publications at the National Resource Center for The First-Year Experience and Students in Transition. She taught University 101, in addition to special-topics graduate courses on the first-year experience and the principles of college teaching. She conducts first-year seminar faculty training workshops around the United States and in other countries, and she is frequently called on to evaluate first-year seminar outcomes. She currently serves as Senior Scholar in the Gardner Institute for Excellence in Undergraduate Education. In her Institute role she led a major national research project to identify institutions of excellence in the first college year. She currently works with both two- and four-year campuses in evaluating all components of the first year.

Negar Farakish is an educator and administrator with years of experience in teaching and working with community college students from diverse backgrounds and academic abilities. In her various roles, she has taught and assisted wide-ranging groups of students from the academically underprepared to those pursuing highly competitive majors and careers at these institutions. She currently serves as the Associate Vice President for Academic Affairs and Dean of American Honors at Union County College in New Jersey and teaches as an Adjunct Assistant Professor at Teachers College, Columbia University.

Brief Contents

v

Contents

PART ONE

WELCOME TO YOUR COLLEGE EXPERIENCE

start

finish

4   Discovering How You Learn   77

PART TWO   SUCCEEDING IN COLLEGE

5   Getting the Most Out of Class   105

Contents   **ix**

PART THREE **YOUR PATH TO SUCCESS IN COLLEGE AND BEYOND**

Preface

Anyone who teaches beginning college students knows how much they have changed in recent years. Today's students are increasingly job-focused, skilled in using technology, and concerned about the future. And more than ever, students worry about how they will pay for college. Recently, popular media sources such as the *Wall Street Journal* and *USA Today* have raised doubts about college's worth, concerns about how student debt delays Millennials from starting families and businesses,[1] and questions about whether money spent on a college degree would be better invested in a start-up business or travel.[2] While it is tempting to focus on the few individuals who can find an alternate path to a successful future, we know, for the overwhelming majority of individuals, a college degree is more essential than ever before.

Understanding Your College Experience is designed specifically for institutions with high proportions of open-enrollment, nonresidential, and returning students. Thus it will work well at traditional two-year or community colleges, colleges that serve the same populations as traditional open-enrollment institutions but have growing numbers of selective admissions four-year programs particularly in health care, and four-year schools with many open-enrollment students. We've created this new edition of *Understanding Your College Experience* with also the underprepared students who need the most support in mind.

All of these students matter, and we've devoted our professional lives to them. To ensure that this new book speaks to as many of them as possible, we've labored to represent as many of them as possible in its pages. We want students who read *Understanding Your College Experience* to see themselves and their lives represented. Please see the list below for some of the student populations and situations we've worked to represent—we think you'll see many of your students here as well:

- Students entering college directly from high school
- Returning students
- Students retraining for a new career
- Students who are still in high school
- First-generation college students
- Online and hybrid learners
- Diverse students
- Students who are working parents

[1]"Recent Grads Doubt College's Worth." *The Wall Street Journal* online, September 29, 2015, Douglas Belkin (author).
[2]"Kids Skip College—Not Worth the Money." *USA Today* online, April 22, 2013, Oliver St. John (author).

- Students who manage a household
- Students who are on active military duty or are veterans
- Students concerned about affording college
- Commuter students
- Full-time students who work extensive hours on or off campus
- Part-time students working part-time or full-time jobs
- Students with mental health issues
- Students with learning differences
- ESL students
- Transfer students—those who have just transferred or plan to transfer
- Students with varying levels of experience with digital media

Each chapter of *Understanding Your College Experience* is designed to give students the practical help they need to gain self-knowledge, set goals, succeed, and persist so that their hopes and dreams have a better chance to become realities. *Understanding Your College Experience* offers skills and strategies in areas where first-year students often need the most support. These skills, such as academic and career preparation and planning, time management, and information literacy, are important for college courses and for the workplace. At a time when institutions are mainstreaming developmental education students and increasing class sizes, students will need more, not less, individual attention and skills so that they can ask for the help they need. Of course, concerns about student retention remain, as do pressures on college administrators to do more with less. These realities of college life mean that students need strategies they can use immediately.

This edition of *Understanding Your College Experience* is based on feedback from generations of users and our collective experience in teaching current students. It is grounded in the growing body of research on student success and retention and includes many valuable contributions from leading experts in the field. Most of all, it is a text born from our devotion to students and to their success: We simply do not want even a single student to fail.

Our writing style in this text is intended to convey respect and admiration for students while recognizing their continued need for challenge and support. The language and reading level are appropriate for first-year students. We have addressed topics that our experience, our research, and our reviewers tell us are concerns for students of many different educational backgrounds. We have also embedded various reading and writing strategies to scaffold students' efforts to comprehend the material and apply the skills presented in each chapter. And we have included technology tools and tips that can enhance students' studying experience.

Part One of *Understanding Your College Experience*, Welcome to Your College Experience, sets the stage with a significantly revised introductory chapter, The Essentials for College Success, challenging students to explore their purpose for attending college, by helping them learn how to apply that purpose to short- and long-term goal setting, and by understanding how critical academic planning is. A new Chapter 2 offers expanded and early coverage of Cultivating Motivation, Resilience, and Emotional

Intelligence; emphasis on these topics reoccurs throughout the book. Students are armed with solid time, energy, and money management strategies in Chapter 3, and then they explore how they learn in Chapter 4. Part Two, Succeeding in College, enumerates essential study skills like reading, note taking, and test taking, and guides students in collecting, evaluating, and then using information in writing and speaking. Part Three, Your Path to Success in College and Beyond, emphasizes thinking in college and practical and realistic considerations such as maintaining wellness and relationships in the diverse environments where students live and work. Part Three also includes a comprehensive chapter on majors and careers.

Whether you are considering this textbook for use in your college success course or your first-year seminar, we thank you for your interest. We hope this book will guide you and your campus in understanding the broad range of issues that can affect student success.

KEY FEATURES OF THIS EDITION

- **Powerful LaunchPad course space now available.** When it comes to retaining new information, research shows that self-testing with small, bite-sized chunks of information works best. *LearningCurve for College Success,* a new adaptive online quizzing program, helps students focus on the material they need the most help with. With LearningCurve, students receive as much practice as they need to master a given concept and are provided with immediate feedback and links back to online instruction. A personalized study plan with suggestions for further practice gives your students what they need to thrive in the college success course, in their college, career, and beyond!

- **An increased focus on technology and learning.** Tech Tips in every chapter ask students to apply many of the technology skills they likely already have and use in their personal lives in an academic setting. For some readers, the Tech Tips teach new skills. This application-based feature appears at the end of the chapter so as not to disturb the flow of the main narrative.

- **A carefully executed design and art program** keep students focused on the content while keeping them engaged by including images that reflect the reality of the broad range of students in the course to help make them feel comfortable and connected. Captions invite students to think critically.

- **Models (including digital models) let students see principles in action.** Because many students learn best by examples, full-size models—more than in any competing book—show realistic examples of annotating a textbook, creating a mind map, multiple styles of note taking, managing time, and other strategies for academic success. In most cases, digital models are included to reflect the tools students will be using in their everyday lives. For example, digital sample calendar templates reflect the schedules of students balancing multiple priorities—work, family, and college.

- **Features and pedagogy built to help students engage in the material.**
  - **A pre-reading activity** kicks off each chapter to get students thinking about and looking at the content that is to come.
  - **Chapter-opening profiles** help students see themselves in the text. Each chapter of the text opens with a story of a first-year student who has used the strategies in the chapter to succeed. The profiled students come from diverse backgrounds and attend all kinds of colleges around the country.
  - **Your Turn activities** in each chapter encourage students to build communication, collaboration, critical thinking, organization, and self-assessment skills by asking them to reflect on or apply content introduced in the chapter. Your Turn activities are broken into four types: Try It, Discuss It, Work Together, and Stay Motivated.
  - **Key terms** are boldfaced and defined within the narrative so as not to disturb the flow of reading. In addition, a glossary of key terms appears at the end of the book.
  - **Chapter-ending activities** encourage reflection, communication, critical thinking, organization, application, and self-assessment skills by asking students to THINK, WRITE, and APPLY concepts introduced in the chapter.
  - **Use Your Resources** sections at the end of each chapter connect the text to student experiences at their specific institutions. To help students take more control of their own success, every chapter includes a quick overview of college and online resources for support, including learning centers, library, websites, professional staff, and fellow students. The box ends with a prompt for students to write in their own ideas and resources at their colleges.

KEY CHAPTER-BY-CHAPTER CONTENT

Chapter 1, The Essentials for College Success, discusses the benefits of the course and the textbook and resources available at the students' academic institution to make a successful transition to college. The chapter emphasizes the benefits of a college education and introduces students to the concepts of purpose and goal setting with dedicated attention to academic planning.

Chapter 2, Cultivating Motivation, Resilience, and Emotional Intelligence, is new to this edition; it begins by exploring motivation and resilience and then offers expanded coverage of emotional intelligence (formerly covered in one short section in what had been Chapter 11 in the first edition). By presenting these topics in the second chapter of the book, students get the opportunity to explore them at a point early in the term when this self-awareness is critical and encounter them throughout the book.

Chapter 3, Managing Time, Energy, and Money, presents students with strategies to coordinate the use of these valuable resources. The chapter starts with time-management techniques and continues to offer suggestions for managing energy and money in conjunction with time. Multiple worksheets are provided in the chapter to help students map their use of these resources.

Chapter 4, Discovering How You Learn, begins with a new and very approachable section on learning theories; introduces students to learning theories of Maslow, Bandura, and Schlossberg; and features a new figure, "Maslow's Hierarchy of Needs Pyramid." Chapter 4 introduces students to the VARK Learning Styles Inventory, to help them identify their preferred learning styles, and discusses MBTI and multiple intelligences. The chapter also includes an updated section, discussing learning disabilities that affect many students in college.

Chapter 5, Getting the Most Out of Class, presents students with engagement strategies they can apply through listening, participating, and note taking before class, in class, and after class.

Chapter 6, Reading to Learn from College Textbooks, offers tips and tools for active reading, increasing comprehension, and understanding the differences in math, science, and social science textbooks. The chapter focuses on strategies for improving academic reading and vocabulary development.

Chapter 7, Studying, Understanding, and Remembering, provides memory improvement techniques and study skills that promote deep learning. The chapter includes a new tool for students to use to consider changes they are willing to make so that study time is more efficient.

Chapter 8, Taking Tests Successfully, is filled with strategies students can apply as they prepare for tests in various courses. In particular, the emotional aspect of test taking is discussed, and a test anxiety quiz is provided, allowing students to evaluate how serious an issue this is for them and to create a plan to overcome it. The chapter concludes with a discussion of academic honesty.

Chapter 9, Collecting, Evaluating, and Using Information, combines topics like information literacy and using the library (formerly in Chapter 8) with writing and speaking (formerly in Chapter 9) in a single streamlined and logically organized chapter. The authors have broadened the presentation of the "library" to heighten awareness of how central the library or a learning commons is to student life today.

Chapter 10, Thinking in College, has been significantly revised to give students a better understanding of what is involved in college-level thinking and to include practical strategies on how to achieve it. Students are clearly shown how concepts like fast and slow thinking, problem solving, creativity, and collaboration all relate to critical thinking. The chapter features a helpful visual guide to Bloom's Taxonomy, which is important for students to understand as they develop insights into their own learning in college.

Chapter 11, Maintaining Wellness and Relationships in a Diverse World, discusses multiple aspects of wellness—stress management, nutrition, exercise, sleep, emotional health—as well as caffeine, alcohol, and tobacco use; cyberbullying; and protecting oneself and others against sexual assault. The chapter offers strategies to help students effectively function within their diverse college communities and for getting involved in campus life, managing relationships, and appreciating diversity.

Chapter 12, Making the Right Career Choice, serves as a step-by-step guide to selecting a major and exploring careers; it presents strategies for career planning, enhancing marketability, developing the right mindset for creating a strong future, conducting industry and company research, gaining experience while in college, and job searching.

EXTENSIVE RESOURCES FOR INSTRUCTORS

To help you meet the challenges of engaging and retaining today's students, we have created a complete package of support materials:

- **LaunchPad for *Understanding Your College Experience*.** LaunchPad combines an interactive e-book with high-quality multimedia content and ready-made assessment options, including LearningCurve adaptive quizzing. Pre-built units are easy to assign or adapt with your own material, such as readings, videos, quizzes, discussion groups, and more. LaunchPad also provides access to a grade book that tracks performance for your whole class, for individual students, and for individual assignments.

- **Unique to LaunchPad: *LearningCurve for College Success.*** *LearningCurve for College Success* is an online, adaptive, self-quizzing program that quickly learns what students already know and helps them practice what they haven't yet mastered. LearningCurve motivates students to engage with key concepts before they come to class so that they are ready to participate; it also offers reporting tools to help you discern your students' needs. An updated version of LearningCurve available with LaunchPad for *Understanding Your College Experience* features a larger question pool with new multiple-choice questions and new questions on motivation, mindset, and resilience.

- **Ordering information.** LaunchPad for *Understanding Your College Experience* is available to package at a significant discount. To package the paper text with LaunchPad, use ISBN 978-1-319-10213-5. To package the loose-leaf edition with LaunchPad, use ISBN 978-1-319-10217-3. To order LaunchPad standalone, use ISBN 978-1-319-06430-3.

- **The Academic and Career Excellence System (ACES).** This instrument measures student strengths in twelve critical areas and prompts students to reflect on their habits, behaviors, attitudes, and skills.

Norm-referenced reports indicate whether students are at a high, moderate, or low skill level in particular areas. For more information, go to **macmillanhighered.com/ACES**.

- **Instructor's Annotated Edition.** A valuable tool for new and experienced instructors alike, the Instructor's Annotated Edition includes the full text of the student edition with abundant marginal annotations, chapter-specific exercises, and helpful suggestions for teaching, fully updated and revised by the authors. The author-written instructor annotations are organized into several categories: **Retention** strategies help students persist in the first year. New **Online Learning** annotations provide special guidance for instructors teaching in the online environment. New **Motivation** annotations offer ideas to keep students motivated about the content being covered. **In Class** annotations provide activities for students to do alone or in groups in the classroom setting. **Outside Class** annotations offer ideas and specific assignments for students to do between class meetings. **FYI** annotations provide additional bits of information or inspiration related to the narrative.

  In addition, an **Active Learning Strategies** insert at the beginning of the IAE includes chapter-specific exercises and activities designed as retention strategies to support writing, critical thinking, working in groups, planning, reflecting, and taking action.

- **Instructor's Manual.** The Instructor's Manual includes chapter objectives, teaching suggestions, an introduction to the first-year experience course, a sample lesson plan for each chapter, sample syllabi, final projects for the end of the course, and various case studies that are relevant to the topics covered in the text. The Instructor's Manual is available online.

- **Computerized Test Bank.** The Computerized Test Bank contains more than 700 multiple-choice, true/false, short-answer, and essay questions designed to assess students' understanding of key concepts. This edition features over 150 new questions and more challenging scenario-based questions that ask students to apply their understanding to concepts in the text. An answer key is included. A digital text file is also available.

- **Lecture Slides.** Available online for download, lecture slides accompany each chapter of the book and include key concepts and art from the text. Use the slides as provided to structure your lectures, or customize them as desired to fit your course's needs.

- ***French Fries Are Not Vegetables.*** This comprehensive instructional DVD features multiple resources for class and professional use. This video is also available with our LaunchPads. ISBN 978-0-312-65073-5.

- **Curriculum Solutions.** Our new Curriculum Solutions group brings together the quality and reputation of Bedford/St. Martin's content with Hayden-McNeil's expertise in publishing original custom print and digital products. With our new capabilities, we are excited to deliver customized course solutions at an affordable price. Make *Understanding Your College Experience*, Second Edition, fit your course and goals by integrating your own institutional materials, by including only the parts of the text you intend to use in your course, or both. Please contact your local Macmillan Learning sales representative for more information and to see samples.

- **CS Select custom database.** The CS Select database allows you to create a textbook for your college success course that reflects your course objectives and uses just the content you need. Start with one of our core texts, then rearrange chapters, delete chapters, and insert additional content—including your own original content—to create just the book you're looking for. Get started by visiting **macmillanhighered.com/csSelect**.

- **TradeUp.** Bring more value and choice to your students' first-year experience by packaging *Understanding Your College Experience*, Second Edition, with one of a thousand titles from Macmillan publishers at a 50 percent discount from the regular price. Contact your local Macmillan Learning sales representative for more information.

STUDENT RESOURCES

- **LaunchPad for *Understanding Your College Experience*, Second Edition.** LaunchPad is an online course solution that offers our acclaimed content, including e-book, videos, LearningCurve adaptive quizzes, and more. For more information, see the Extensive Resources for Instructors section.

- **Unique to LaunchPad: *LearningCurve for College Success*.** *LearningCurve for College Success* is an online, adaptive, self-quizzing program that quickly learns what students already know and helps them practice what they haven't yet mastered.

- **Ordering information.** LaunchPad for *Understanding Your College Experience* is available to package at a significant discount. To package the paper text with LaunchPad, use ISBN 978-1-319-10213-5. To package the loose-leaf edition with LaunchPad, use ISBN 978-1-319-10217-3. To order LaunchPad standalone, use ISBN 978-1-319-06430-3.

- **E-book Options.** E-books offer an affordable alternative for students. You can find PDF versions of our books when you shop online at our publishing partners' sites. Learn more at **macmillanhighered.com /ebooks**.

- ***The Bedford/St. Martin's Planner.*** Everything that students need to plan and use their time effectively is included, along with advice on preparing schedules and to-do lists, as well as blank schedules and calendars (monthly and weekly) for planning. Integrated into the planner are tips and advice on fixing common grammar errors, taking notes, and succeeding on tests; an address book; and an annotated list of useful websites. The planner fits easily into a backpack or purse, so students can take it anywhere. To order the planner standalone, use ISBN 978-0-312-57447-5. To package the planner, please contact your local Macmillan Learning sales rep.

- *Bedford/St. Martin's Insider's Guides.* These concise and student-friendly booklets on topics that are critical to college success are a perfect complement to your textbook and course. One Insider's Guide can be packaged with *any* Bedford/St. Martin's textbook. Additional Insider's Guides can also be packaged for additional cost. Topics include:
  - **New!** *Insider's Guide for Adult Learners*
  - **New!** *Insider's Guide to College Etiquette*, Second Edition
  - **New!** *Insider's Guide for Veterans*
  - **New!** *Insider's Guide to Transferring*
  - *Insider's Guide to Academic Planning*
  - *Insider's Guide to Beating Test Anxiety*
  - *Insider's Guide to Building Confidence*
  - *Insider's Guide to Career Services*
  - *Insider's Guide to College Ethics and Personal Responsibility*
  - *Insider's Guide to Community College*
  - *Insider's Guide to Credit Cards*, Second Edition
  - *Insider's Guide to Getting Involved on Campus*
  - *Insider's Guide to Global Citizenship*
  - *Insider's Guide to Time Management*, Second Edition

  For more information on ordering one of these guides with the text, go to **macmillanhighered.com/collegesuccess**.

- *Journal Writing: A Beginning.* Designed to give students an opportunity to use writing as a way to explore their thoughts and feelings, this writing journal includes a generous supply of inspirational quotes placed throughout the pages, tips for journaling, and suggested journal topics. To order the journal standalone, use ISBN 978-0-312-59027-7.

ACKNOWLEDGMENTS

Special thanks to the reviewers who helped develop *Understanding Your College Experience*, Second Edition.

Lois Andre, Cape Cod Community College

Laura Bowen, Athens Technical College

Andrea Dance, College of the Abermarle

Rebecca Davis, Hudson County Community College

Sheryl Duquette, Erie Community College

Maryann Errico, Georgia Perimeter College

Linda Gannon, College of Southern Nevada

Paula Hood, Coastal Carolina Community College

Jennifer Graham, Northern Maine Community College

John Kester, Richmond Community College

Edwin Kroll, Kalamazoo Valley Community College

Sheila Lau, Diablo Valley College

Priscilla MacDuff, Suffolk County Community College

Martha Madigan, Lansing Community College

Malinda Mansfield, Ivy Tech Community College

Melissa Nicholas, Florida Keys Community College

Casey Reid, East Central College

Hailey Sheets, Southwestern Michigan College

Eric-Gene Shrewsbury, Patrick Henry Community College

Betty Taylor, Cleveland Community College

Kim Thomas, Polk State College

Carol Warren, Georgia Perimeter College

Rhonda Wilkins, Georgia Perimeter College

Christi Young, Southwestern Michigan College

Yingfan Zhang, Suffolk County Community College

In addition, we want to thank **Mark Hendrix**, formerly of Palm Beach State College, for his contributions to the Tech Tip features.

We continue to be grateful to the reviewers from the first edition, as they helped to shape the text you see today.

First Edition: Torris Anderson, Jr., Ocean County College; Cynthia Armster, City Colleges of Chicago; Sherry Ash, San Jacinto College-Central; Diego Baez, Harry S. Truman College; Beverly Brucks, Illinois Central College; Richard Conway, Nassau Community College; David Ferreira, Broward College; Maria Galyon, Jefferson Community and Technical College; Jo Ann Jenkins, Moraine Valley Community College; Jill Loveless, Mohave Community College; Gail Malone, South Plains College; Patrick Peyer, Rock Valley College; Claudia Swicegood, Rowan-Cabarrus Community College; Susan Taylor, North Florida Community College; Kim Toby, Somerset Community College.

As we look to the future, we are excited about the numerous improvements to this text that our creative Bedford/St. Martin's team has made and will continue to make. Special thanks to Edwin Hill, Vice President of Editorial, Humanities; Erika Gutierrez, Publisher for Communications and College Success; Simon Glick, Senior Executive Editor for College Success; Jennifer Jacobson, Development Editor of Ohlinger Publishing Services; Bethany Gordon, Associate Editor; Mary Jane Chen, Editorial Assistant; Kayti Corfield, Marketing Manager; and Erica Zhang, Assistant Production Editor. Most of all, we thank you, the users of our book, for you are the true inspirations for our work.

CONTRIBUTORS

Although this text speaks with the voices of its three authors, it represents contributions from many other people. We gratefully acknowledge those contributions and thank these individuals whose special expertise has made it possible to introduce new students to their college experience through the holistic approach we deeply believe in.

Amber Manning-Oullette provided guidance on revising the chapter "Maintaining Wellness and Relationships in a Diverse World." Amber is currently a lecturer at Iowa State University. She holds a B.S. in Psychology, an M.S. in Counselor Education, and a Ph.D. in Educational Administration and Higher Education.

Lea Susan Engle was an essential contributor to the coverage of information literacy. Lea is a former Assistant Professor and first-year experience librarian at Texas A&M University and is currently a Training and Outreach Coordinator in Learning Sciences at the University of Texas at Austin. Lea earned a B.A. in Women's Studies from the University of Maryland, College Park, and holds an M.S. in Information Studies and an M.A. in Women's and Gender Studies from the University of Texas at Austin.

Casey Reid was a vital contributor to the chapter that discusses time management. She holds a B.A. in Anthropology and Professional Writing and an M.A. in Writing from Missouri State University. She is now a Ph.D. candidate in English from Old Dominion University. For seven years, she was an English faculty member at Metropolitan Community College in Kansas City. She is currently employed at East Central College in Missouri, where she has overhauled the first-year experience course and started a peer coaching program.

The chapter "Making the Right Career Choice" was shaped by **Heather N. Maietta**, the former Associate Vice President of Career and Corporate Engagement at Merrimack College. Heather has presented or co-presented nationally on topics related to career and professional preparation and is a Certified Career Development Facilitator Instructor through the National Career Development Association. Heather has authored articles and research reports in several publications, including *About Campus, Career Convergence*, and *ESource*.

Chris Gurrie is Assistant Professor of Speech at the University of Tampa. Gurrie is an active public speaker and participates in invited lectures, workshops, and conferences in the areas of faculty development, first-year life and leadership, communicating effectively with PowerPoint, and communication and immediacy. He contributed the first generation of Tech Tips that were adapted for this new text and wrote the *Guide to Teaching with YouTube*, available as part of the Instructor's Manual and Test Bank.

PART ONE

WELCOME TO YOUR COLLEGE EXPERIENCE

 THE ESSENTIALS FOR COLLEGE SUCCESS

 CULTIVATING MOTIVATION, RESILIENCE, AND EMOTIONAL INTELLIGENCE

3 MANAGING TIME, ENERGY, AND MONEY

STUDENT GOALS

4 DISCOVERING HOW YOU LEARN

STUDENT GOALS

1 The Essentials for College Success

PRE-READING ACTIVITY: Before you start reading, take a few minutes to look through this chapter. As you look at the headings of the different sections, pick three topics that interest you. Why do you think that learning about these topics might help you in college?

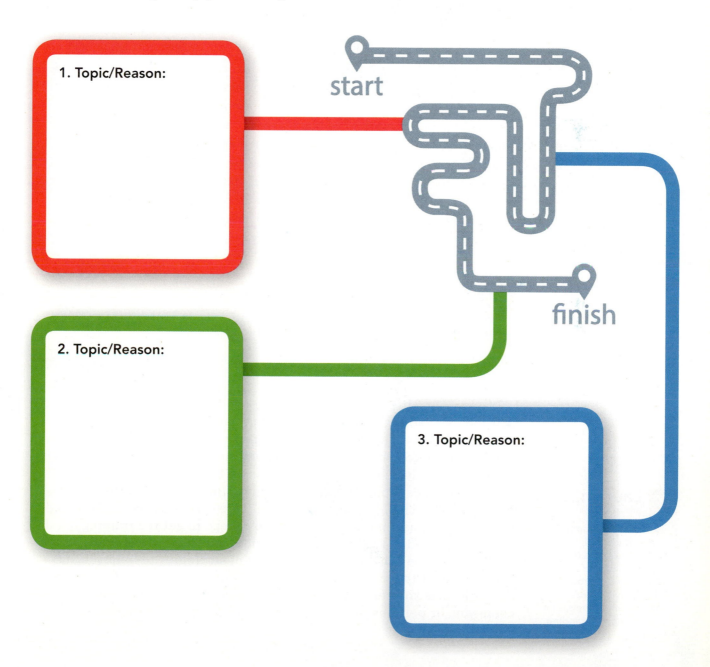

1. Topic/Reason:

start

2. Topic/Reason:

finish

3. Topic/Reason:

📁 PROFILE

Maria Lopez, 18

Early Childhood Education Major, *Lone Star College, North Harris*

arek_malang/Shutterstock.com

Maria Lopez always knew she was going to college even though no one else in her family had ever attended any college or university. For Maria, going to Lone Star College was an easy choice, and she is very happy that she chose to attend this college. "The North Harris campus is close to home," she explains, "so I can still help my family, keep my part-time job, and continue my education with some of my high school friends."

Now that her first year is under way, Maria has learned there are some key differences between high school and college, specifically the amount of time she spends studying. "In high school, I studied maybe five hours a week," she explains. "Now I study many more hours, something I learned was important right away in my first-year-experience course. I also quickly learned the importance of organizing, managing my time, and staying on top of my assignments. Setting goals and finding a purpose for being in college have also led to my success."

> **"[I]n my first-year-experience course . . . I . . . quickly learned the importance of organizing, managing my time, and staying on top of my assignments."**

Maria enjoys attending her college. "Here everyone guides you," she says. "You can ask for help from your instructors, other students, and a lot of other people like tutors or counselors. I think I would be lost at a university in my first year, not having anyone to teach me about the rules of the college and how it is different from high school."

To access the Learning-Curve study tool, Video Tools, and more, go to LaunchPad for *Understanding Your College Experience.* macmillanhighered.com /gardnerunderstanding

Do you hope to graduate from college and find a good job? If so, you have something in common with Maria and many other college students. Today, the workplace is changing so much that most people will need some education beyond high school to support themselves and their families properly. In the United States, more than 67 percent of high school graduates (approximately 21 million students) attend college. As the job market changes, people of all ages are constantly changing career directions and beginning or returning to college to get the training or education they need to further their aspirations and reach their goals.

This book will present you with a set of strategies to help you succeed at one of the most important things you'll ever do—get a college education. As you settle into your new college routine, we want to welcome you, or perhaps welcome you back, to the world of higher education.

THE COLLEGE EXPERIENCE

Depending on who you are, what your life situation is, and why you decided to enroll, college can mean different things. Some students choose to attend college to learn a specific set of skills, receive training for specific careers, and earn a certificate or diploma that allows them to get jobs in their field of interest after graduation. Some attend college to complete their associate degree perhaps close to home and at a lower cost and then, if their college does not offer the higher degree they wish to obtain, to transfer to a four-year college or university for a bachelor's degree. Some come to college after a major life event or personal transition, such as divorce or loss of life partner. Others start or return to college after retirement for the sheer love of learning.

College is some students' top priority; for others, it can be an additional priority on top of family or work obligations. Some students already have jobs but want to change their careers or improve their chances for a promotion. Some students come to the United States from other countries just to study. College is really far more than any single image you might carry around in your head about why students attend and what the college experience actually involves.

Whether you have just graduated from high school or are an older student with a job and a family, college will be a time when you take some appropriate risks, learn new things, and meet new and different people—all in a supportive environment.

Did You Make the Right Choice to Attend College?

You have joined more than 20 million other students enrolled in about 4,400 colleges and universities in the United States. American society values higher education because receiving a college degree gives you opportunities for success regardless of your race or ethnic background, national origin, immigration status, family income level, family history, or personal connections. One marker of success is the amount of money that you earn both immediately after earning a degree and over a lifetime. What you earn in the future will depend on what you learn and do now. As Figure 1.1 shows, the more education you have, the more likely you are to be employed and the higher your earnings will be.

In addition to increasing your earning power, college is about helping you become a better thinker and a leader in your community, company, or profession. In short, college can change your life for the better.

FIGURE 1.1 > Education Pays

Note: Data are for persons age 25 and over. Earnings are for full-time wage and salary workers.

Data from: *Current Population Survey*, U.S. Department of Labor, U.S. Bureau of Labor Statistics, 2015. U.S. Department of Labor.

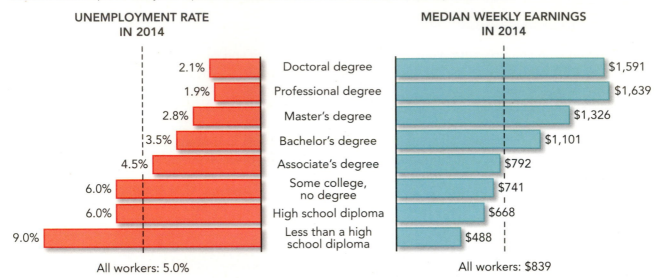

UNEMPLOYMENT RATE IN 2014

2.1%	Doctoral degree
1.9%	Professional degree
2.8%	Master's degree
3.5%	Bachelor's degree
4.5%	Associate's degree
6.0%	Some college, no degree
6.0%	High school diploma
9.0%	Less than a high school diploma

All workers: 5.0%

MEDIAN WEEKLY EARNINGS IN 2014

$1,591	Doctoral degree
$1,639	Professional degree
$1,326	Master's degree
$1,101	Bachelor's degree
$792	Associate's degree
$741	Some college, no degree
$668	High school diploma
$488	Less than a high school diploma

All workers: $839

What Opportunities Does College Provide?

Two-year colleges and some four-year institutions offer certificates, associate in arts (AA), associate in science (AS), associate in applied science (AAS), and bachelor in arts (BA) or science (BS) degree programs (see Table 1.1). These institutions play an important role in providing students with educational opportunities because they accept and work with all students regardless of their past academic performance. In addition, students can get a great education at a much lower cost than at a college or university that awards only four-year degrees. The education that you receive will help you start, restart, and be successful in your future career and life.

> **Explore Your Options**

College is a great place to connect with others, take some risks, and explore careers such as business, law enforcement, or nursing.

Steve Debenport/E+/Getty Images

TABLE 1.1 › Guide to Degree Programs

Degree	Refers to the type of diploma students receive after graduation and differs based on the number of credit hours students complete.
Credit Hours	Represent the number of clock hours you spend in each class every week during a term and the number of credits you will earn if you satisfactorily complete a course. For example, a one-credit course generally meets once a week for 50 to 60 minutes.

Degree Programs

Certificate Program	Certificate programs include a set number of courses (usually 30 credits) that prepare students to complete a specific task or educate them about one particular aspect of a field to be able to obtain entry-level positions. For example, an Emergency Medical Technician certificate program prepares students to enter the field of emergency medicine and start working as first responders.
Associate in Arts (AA) or Associate in Science (AS)	These programs carry about 60 credits and allow students to transfer to four-year programs to obtain bachelor's degrees.
Associate in Applied Science (AAS)	These programs carry about 60 credits focused on training students for a specific profession or career. The AAS degree has fewer transferable credits than the AA or AS degrees.
Bachelor of Arts (BA) or Bachelor of Science (BS)	Four-year programs that carry about 120 credits.

In addition to being a pleasant experience, college is a lot of work. Being in college means studying for hours each week, staying up late or getting up early to complete assignments and prepare for class, going to class, taking exams, and possibly working harder than you ever have. For many students, college becomes like a job with defined duties, expectations, and obligations. If you already have a job, this will be your second one. And if you have a family of your own, college will be your third job!

Getting involved in campus life improves your college experience and your chances for a good job, so make sure to take advantage of student activities on your campus. For example, some clubs are related to professions; an education club may include students who plan to become teachers, or a business club may give students an opportunity to learn more about companies in their area and to interact with business professionals and leaders. The most important type of involvement, however, is with fellow students who you can get to know, study with, and share mutual support.

College will also provide you with numerous opportunities to

- complete the basic skills training you didn't master in high school.
- develop social networks both in person and online.
- explore student organizations and take advantage of leadership opportunities.
- participate in many exciting activities and events.
- network for improved employment opportunities.
- go to college after serving in the military.

What Is Your Purpose for Attending College?

Having a purpose for going to college is essential. Without a purpose, you won't know where you're going or how to get there. While some students come to college with a clear sense of purpose, others do not. For many students a strong sense of purpose builds over time. College will be a set of experiences that will help you to clarify your purpose and achieve your own goals. It is possible that as you discover more about yourself and your abilities, your reasons for coming to college will change. In fact, a majority of college students change their academic plans at least once during the college years, and some students find they need to transfer to another college or university to meet their academic goals.

Here are some questions to ask yourself about your purpose for being in college:

- Am I here to study a subject that interests me?
- Am I here to develop new knowledge and ideas?
- Am I here to complete a certificate, a diploma, or an associate or bachelor's degree?
- Am I here to prepare myself for employment or to improve my skills in a job I already have?
- Am I here to meet new people?
- Am I here so I can better serve my community and country?
- Am I here to better understand myself and society?

Your honest answers to these questions will drive most of the decisions that you make in college, decisions that will likely impact the rest of your life. Because knowledge expands all the time, college classes won't teach you everything you will ever need to know, but college, as a process of formal education, will teach you how to think and how to keep learning throughout your life.

YOUR TURN ❯ WORK TOGETHER

Ask a couple of your classmates why they decided to attend this college and what they expect college to be like. Compare your reasons and expectations with theirs. Do you find similarities or differences?

How Is Your College Committed to Helping You Succeed?

Each college has two main objectives: to help its students graduate and to support them in becoming successful in their future careers. To do that, colleges provide support services to students at no additional cost. For example, most colleges have academic advisers who provide students with information about their courses and help them register in the appropriate courses every term. These advisers are available to students throughout the term to provide guidance and support and to answer questions students might have. Colleges also have financial aid advisers who can assist students and their families in understanding how to pay for college.

Additionally, most colleges have learning centers, providing free tutoring to students in nearly all subjects, and career centers that help students with career planning and job hunting. Remember that the faculty and staff of a college are there to serve students and meet their needs and help students to become successful, so do not be shy—ask for help. To assist you in identifying and using your college resources, at the end of each chapter in this book, we provide a list of resources typically available at colleges— resources that offer additional help related to chapter topics. Students who seek help are the ones who are the most successful, so take advantage of the support available to you.

What Will You Get Out of Your College Success Course and This Textbook?

Research shows that college success courses, such as this one, will help you and other first-year students avoid some of the mistakes—both academic and personal—that many beginning students make, such as not taking advantage of the helping services and resources, not developing certain college-level study skills, and making choices that you would have made differently if you had the knowledge you really needed.

This course will provide a safe place for sharing your successes and your challenges, getting to know other first-year students, beginning a lasting relationship with your instructor and other students, developing your academic plan based on your strengths and interests, and shaping or reshaping your career after graduation.

As individuals with many years of experience working with first-year students, we know that starting college can be challenging. However if you apply the ideas in this book to your everyday life, you are more likely to enjoy your time in college, graduate, and achieve your goals. In this textbook, we cover a lot of topics. For instance, you'll read about managing your time, taking notes, making the most of the way you learn, preparing for tests, building relationships, and planning for your future career.

⌃ It's an Adjustment
You may feel alone during the first few weeks in college. You may not immediately meet others who look, dress, or think like you, but your college will offer many ways for you to connect with other students.
©Will&Deni McIntyre/McIntyre Photography, Inc/Terra/Corbis

SETTING GOALS FOR ACHIEVING YOUR PURPOSE

Of all the components of college success, the most essential is having a purpose. You may be very clear on why you are in college and what you hope to achieve, or you may still be trying to figure that out. Wherever you are, the road to achieving your purpose requires that you set goals along the way.

For most students, a central component of purpose is being successful. So what does success mean to you? Is success about money, friendship, or power? Is it about achieving excellence in college, employment, or life in general? For most people, success is a combination of all of these factors and more. While luck or "who you know" may play a role, first and foremost, success will be the result of your planning, your decisions, and your hard work.

Consider Your Strengths

To achieve your purpose and become successful, where do you begin? First, you need to think carefully about your strengths. Everyone is good at doing something, and your strengths, whatever they are, can help you choose the path that is right for you. Your strengths might be in these areas:

- Intrapersonal: You make friends easily.
- Mechanical: You have always been able to figure out how to fix things around the house.
- Organizational: You keep your family on track with their duties and chores.
- Leadership and persuasion: You are able to convince others that you are right.
- Persistence: When you want something, you never give up.

All of these characteristics and many others are strengths that you can apply to your college experience. You should also use your strengths for excelling in college while you work on the areas you need to improve. For instance, if you have good interpersonal skills but need to improve your organizational skills, make friends with students who have excellent organizational skills and ask them to help you improve yours.

Get Started with Goals

It is important to establish goals—personal and career goals for today, this week, this month, this term, this year, and beyond. Students who prefer to go with the flow and let life happen to them are more likely to waste their time and less likely to achieve success in college or in a career. They are more likely to get distracted and not stay focused. So instead of simply reacting to what college and life present to you, think about how you can take more control over the decisions and choices you make now, literally every day, to achieve your goals. While it is easy to make general plans, you need to determine which short-term steps are necessary if those plans are to become a reality. A short-term goal might be to read 20 pages from your history text twice a week to prepare for an exam that will cover the first hundred pages of the book. An intermediate-term goal might be to begin predicting which elective college courses you could choose that would help you attain your career goals. A long-term goal would be to make a decision about a degree program and to make plans for what are you going to do with your degree after you graduate.

Follow the SMART Goal-Setting Guidelines

You'll read about academic planning in the next section of this chapter, which will help you map out how to turn your goals into your reality. But first, here are guidelines that break down the aspects of goal setting so that you are smart about how you approach it. In fact, these are the SMART goal-setting guidelines—to set goals that are *Specific*, *Measurable*, *Attainable*, *Relevant*, and *Timely* (SMART):

1. Be **specific** about what you want to achieve, why, and when.

2. State your goal in **measurable** terms. That means how many steps you should take to obtain your goal and how you know when each step is complete.

3. Be sure that the goal is **attainable**. If you don't have the necessary skills, strengths, and resources to achieve your goal, change it. Be sure you really want to reach the goal. Don't set out to work toward something only because you want to please others. Plan your steps carefully and within a reasonable timeframe.

4. Know how the goal is **relevant** to your life and why the goal matters. Make sure your goal helps your larger plan and gives you a sense of moving forward.

5. Consider whether the goal is achievable within the **timeframe** you desire and what difficulties you might have. Plan for ways you might deal with problems. Decide which goal comes next and how you will begin. Create steps and a time line for reaching your next goal.

For instance, let's assume that after you graduate you might want to get a good job or advance in the job you currently have. This goal isn't very specific, however, nor does it state a particular time period. A much more specific goal would be to decide which program of study you want to complete to prepare you for the job or position you are interested in obtaining after you graduate. What are some short-term goals that would help you reach this goal? Once you choose your program of study, the next goal might be to look through the course catalog to identify the courses that you need to take to complete the program to prepare for the career of your choice or for advancement. An even more specific goal would be to prepare your academic plan and identify which courses you should take each term. You might discover that the job(s) that interest you most will require a four-year degree. If so, one long-term goal would be to prepare for transfer. You can see an academic adviser who can help you create a program plan, specifying which courses you need to take and in what order. Remember that dreaming up long-term goals is the easy part. To reach your goals, you need to be specific and systematic about the steps you will take; understanding the fundamentals of academic planning by working with an academic adviser will help you plan these steps. Use Figure 1.2 on the next page to set SMART goals for this term. Think through this exercise and then return to it so that you can apply what you learn in the section on academic planning.

FIGURE 1.2 › Practice Setting SMART Goals

What are your goals for this term? Using the SMART goal-setting guide, try to set one goal in each of the four areas listed: academic, career, personal, and financial. Follow the goal through time, from immediate to long-term. An example is provided for you.

	S	M	A	R	T
Type of Goal	SPECIFIC goal	How many MEASURABLE steps?	Why can I ATTAIN the goal?	How is this RELEVANT to me?	What TIMEFRAME do I desire? What potential difficulties will arise, and how will I deal with them to stay on track?
Academic	Complete my academic plan this term based on my chosen program of study.	1. In the next 2 weeks, review the college catalog to select a program of study or major that interests me and prepares me for my future job/career. 2. Select my required courses and map every term. 3. Choose my elective courses. 4. Meet with an academic adviser to make sure my academic map makes sense.	I am organized. I have a manageable range of interests.	I can't use my time in college well if I don't know where I am headed. An adviser can give me ideas for how I can apply my interests to a program of study.	• Meet with an academic and a career adviser by the middle of the term. • Obtain all the necessary signatures to finalize my academic plan. • Have the plan all ready to go by Thanksgiving break. **Potential Difficulties:** • I do not know an academic or career adviser. • I have not made a decision about the major I want to study. **How to Deal with Difficulties:** • Visit the academic and career advising centers to work with advisers. • Discuss my academic and career goals with the advisers and ask for their advice regarding the major I should select.
Academic					
Career					
Personal					
Financial					

ACADEMIC PLANNING

Now that you have had some practice with goal setting, we'll turn to the topic of academic planning, which will provide you with a roadmap to achieving your goals. Some students come to college with clear direction; they know what they want to study, what jobs and careers they would like to enter after college, or whether they want to transfer. Others enter college as undecided (sometimes also called "undeclared" or "exploratory"), understanding that their experience with different academic subjects will help them make an academic choice. Still others start a program of study but are uncertain how that program can help them find a job later. Each of these situations is normal.

Programs of Study

Even before you have figured out your own purpose for college, you might be required to select a program of study, sometimes referred to as a **major,** in an area of study like psychology, engineering, education, or nursing. Every program of study includes required courses and electives. Required courses are the ones directly related to the area of study as well as general education courses such as college-level math and English courses. Electives are courses that you get to choose because they interest you. An electrical engineering major, for example, would be required to take courses related to that area of study, like Circuits and Systems, and general education courses like English and world history. The student can also choose electives such as music appreciation and fine arts. Although it's hard to see the direct connection between some of the required courses and what you want to do with the rest of your life, you may discover potential areas of interest that you have never considered before, discover a new career path, and find a new sense of purpose.

Many students change their majors or programs of study as they better understand their strengths and weaknesses, learn more about career options, and become interested in different areas of study. Some colleges allow you to be undecided for a while or to select liberal arts as your major until you make a decision about what to study. An early selection does allow you to better plan which courses you need to take and with which instructors and students within your program to connect. An academic adviser or counselor can provide you with proper information and guidance to help you make the right academic decisions.

Even if you are ready to select a major, it's a good idea to keep an open mind and consider your options. You might learn that the career you always dreamed of isn't what you thought it would be at all. Working part-time or participating in co-curricular activities such as joining a student organization can help you make decisions and learn more about yourself in the process.

Transfer Considerations

If you are planning to transfer to another college or university, it makes sense to choose your major early and select your courses based on the requirements of the college or university of your choice for transfer. Completing courses that you can transfer will help you save time and money. Most colleges that award associate degrees have a transfer center or, at the very least, a transfer counselor whose job is to provide academic advisement and prepare students for a successful transfer to another institution. All two-year colleges have agreements with four-year colleges and universities to ensure that their students can transfer their credits without difficulty. Some of the four-year colleges or universities even offer their degrees on the two-year college campus.

When you begin college, if you know that you will need to transfer, make sure that the courses you take will be transferable—that is, will be accepted for credit at the new college or university. Good academic planning involves an awareness that your major and career ultimately have to fit your interests, life preferences, personality, and overall life goals.

Connecting Programs of Study with Careers

Earlier in the chapter, we asked questions about why you are in college. Many students would immediately respond, "So I can get a good job or education for a specific career." Yet some academic programs or majors do not lead directly to a particular career path or job. You actually can enter most career paths from any number of academic majors. Only a few technical or professional fields—such as accounting, nursing, and engineering—are tied to specific majors.

Exploring your interests is the best first step to identifying an academic major as well as career paths or jobs that are right for you. Here are some helpful strategies:

- **Know your interests, skills, values, and personality.** Assessing your skills and personality is particularly important if you have no idea what you are interested in studying or what career paths are related to your choice of major. For example, if you like science and helping sick people, you may want to consider a career in health care like nursing, physical therapy, or dental hygiene. If you like to talk, read, solve problems, and stand up for yourself and others, you may want to consider a career in the legal profession as a paralegal or a lawyer. If you like to work with computers and design games, you may want to think about computer science or game design. Your campus career center can help you discover your unique strengths—and weaknesses—that can influence your direction as you explore career choices.

- **Pay attention to grades.** Employers and four-year colleges and universities want candidates with good grades. Good grades show that you have the necessary knowledge and skills and a strong work ethic.

- **Explore career paths.** Talking to or observing professionals in your areas of interest is an excellent way to try before you buy. Participation in "job shadowing" or "a-day-in-the-life" programs is time well spent. Many college graduates enjoy being career mentors for current students. This is also a great way to network with those working in your area of interest. Ask your career center about scheduling one of these opportunities.

- **Develop computer skills.** Most of today's college students are comfortable with technology; however, not all technology experience is equal. As you begin to make decisions about your career path, become familiar with technologies used in your field. Take advantage of the computer courses and workshops your college offers, or learn by experimenting with different software programs on your own.

- **Build communication skills.** The ability to communicate verbally and in writing with people inside and outside an organization is one of the most important skills that employers look for in new graduates. Take every available opportunity to practice communicating, whether through classroom presentations or group work or on the job.

- **Take advantage of experiential learning.** Experiential learning is learning by doing and from experience. Internships and service-learning courses are two common forms of experiential learning, but they are not the only ways to gain experience in your area of study. Find opportunities to apply what you learn in your courses to what you do outside the classroom.

YOUR TURN > STAY MOTIVATED

With two or three other students, discuss where you imagine working after college. Will you be employed in an office, a hospital, a studio, or a lab? Or will you be working outdoors? How can you use the environment in which you desire to work as motivation to get into the career of your choice? If any of your classmates already have careers, find out why and how they chose those careers. How do they feel about their work settings?

Working with an Academic Adviser

Academic planning is a necessary step in your college career, and it should be an ongoing process that starts early in your first term. An **academic plan** lists the courses you need to take and complete in your program of study to graduate with a degree. Before you register for classes next term, meet with your academic adviser. Your academic adviser can help you choose courses that are required, weigh career possibilities, and map out your degree or certificate requirements. Advisers can also recommend instructors and help you simplify the different aspects of your academic life. Here are a few ways to make sure that your first meeting with your adviser is a valuable experience:

- **Look at your college course catalog and think about the available majors.** If you haven't already decided on a major, ask your adviser about opportunities for taking an aptitude test or a self-assessment to help you narrow down your options. Often these are administered free in your career center (Read more about self-assessments and self-exploration below).

- **Prepare materials to bring to the meeting. Even if you submitted your high school or other college transcripts with your college application, bring a copy of your transcripts to the meeting.** The transcript—your complete academic record that shows your major, when you took particular courses, your grades for each course, and your overall GPA—is an important tool; it shows your academic adviser where you've been, your academic strengths, and your interests. At some colleges, your adviser may also have access to all this information online, but even so, it is still a good idea to bring your own copies along for such conversations.

- **Make a list of majors that appeal to you.** Academic advisers love it when students come prepared—it shows that they're passionate and are taking their future seriously. Being prepared will encourage advisers to remember you and invest more time in working with you.

- **Map out your timeframe and goals.** Do you plan to enroll full-time or part-time? When do you plan to graduate, and with what degree? Do you plan to transfer to another college?

- **Know the right questions to ask.** Once you've chosen a major, you'll need to understand how to move forward in your academic program to meet the necessary requirements. You will have **prerequisites**—the basic courses you need to take before you can enroll in upper-level classes in your major. Your major may also have **co-requisites**—courses you have to take in conjunction with other courses during the same term (a chemistry lab alongside your chemistry class, for example). So, with this knowledge under your belt, here is what you need to find out:

  - How many credits must I take each term to graduate on time? (Note: If you are on financial aid, are doing work-study, or are a college athlete, you will have to take a minimum number of credits per term.)

- What are the prerequisites for my major? What are the co-requisites?

- Can I use AP (Advance Placement) credits, CLEP (College-Level Examination Program) credits, or placement exams to fulfill some requirements of my major?

- What career opportunities will I have once I graduate? What will the salary potential be?

- **Know what to take away from your meeting.** When you leave the meeting, take with you a printout of your current course schedule and plans for classes you might take in the next term and beyond.

- **Know these rules of thumb about selecting your classes:**

  - Decide which classes you want to take, find out which days and times they meet, and make sure they don't overlap. Most full-time students take four or five courses a term.

  - Make sure to register as early as possible—in person or online.

  - Resist the temptation to cram all of your classes into one or two days. Aim for a manageable workload by spreading your classes throughout the week.

  - Leave time between courses so that on exam days you can study immediately before the exam.

- **Go for a mix of hard and easy courses.** Especially at the beginning, you might not realize how challenging college courses can be or how much outside work they entail.

- **Know what to do if your academic adviser isn't the right match for you.** If you think you and your adviser are not a good match, go to the advising office or academic department office and ask to be assigned to a different adviser. Asking for alternative advising is one of your rights as a student. Academic planning is so critical to your success in college that it's worth persevering until you find an adviser with whom you feel comfortable. If you don't know where to start in finding a new adviser, talk to your college success instructor.

- **Set up subsequent meetings with your academic adviser.** Check in with your adviser at least once a term, if not more often. It's important to stay connected, especially if you plan to transfer or apply to graduate school. Programs change requirements occasionally, so it's smart to touch base with your adviser periodically in case you need to make any necessary adjustments.

YOUR TURN > TRY IT

Have you explored your college's career center? If you haven't made a visit, what are you waiting for?

MAKING THE TRANSITION BY CONNECTING WITH OTHERS

Colleges can seem to be like large cities, especially if you went to a small high school or grew up in a small town. To feel comfortable in the college environment, it is important for you to find places where you feel that you belong, but it will take some initiative on your part. We know that you have a lot going on, but the time you invest to make this happen now is time well spent.

How Is College Different?

If you just graduated from high school, were home-schooled, or completed your GED, you will soon find that college is different. For instance, in college you are probably part of a more diverse student body, not just in terms of race but also in terms of age, religion, political opinions, marital and family status, and life experiences. You have more potential friends; they may or may not be from your neighborhood, place of worship, or high school.

Also, you can choose from many more types of courses, but managing your time is sure to be more difficult because your classes will meet on different days and times. In high school, you may have had frequent tests and quizzes, but tests in college are sometimes given only twice or three times a term. You will probably be required to do more writing in college than in high school, and you will be encouraged to do original research and examine different points of view on a topic. You will be expected to study outside of class, prepare assignments, read different materials, and be ready for in-class discussions.

> ### ❯ Don't Be a Lone Ranger

You can develop learning relationships with other students in a study group, club or organization related to your major, or even in student activities. It's not wise to be a "lone ranger" as you approach studying; you will learn more deeply by studying with other students. You will also develop friendships that will last through your college experience.

The Washington Post/Getty Images

Your instructors might rely far less on textbooks and far more on lectures than your high school teachers did. They also might allow you more freedom and even push you to express views that are different from theirs. You may also have opportunities to apply some of your personal and work experience to what you are learning and to what is being presented and discussed in class.

Challenges for Online Learners. If you are taking courses online, your experience is going to be significantly different from students who attend classes at your college. Online courses require students to be more disciplined and able to manage their time and study more independently. Without in-person class meetings, you might find it more challenging to make connections with other students, so you might need to make an extra effort to do so. However, your online course will surely provide you with electronic means to "chat" with other students and the instructor. To increase your engagement in such a course, you do need to use such means to communicate, especially with other students. If your online course incorporates a few class meetings, it may provide more structure and allow students and instructors to meet periodically. Also remember that through social media platforms such as Facebook, Instagram, and Twitter many students do not need to be physically on campus to be involved in college life.

Issues for Returning Students. If you are a **returning student**—someone who is not a recent high school graduate and may have a job, a family, and who is "returning" to formal education after being out of the educational system for some period of time—you will find that college presents both opportunities *and* challenges. While college can be an opportunity for a new beginning, working full-time and attending college at night, on weekends, or both can mean extra stress, especially with a family at home.

Returning students often experience a lack of freedom because of many important competing responsibilities. You might have a difficult daily commute, or you might have to arrange and pay for child care. You might have to manage work and school responsibilities and still find time for family and other duties. You may also need to let your family know that attending college means that you have to spend time studying and that you may ask them for help or need their support more than ever. You also might find it difficult to relate to younger students whose interests may be different from yours.

In spite of your concerns, you should know that many college instructors value working with returning students because their life experiences have shown them the importance of an education. Your instructors will enjoy interacting with you because they believe you will be motivated, mature, and focused and have a broad range of experiences that will give you a unique and rich point of view about what you're learning in your classes.

Building Relationships with Your Instructors

One of the most important types of relationships you can develop in college is with your instructors. Frequent, high-quality interactions with your instructors can have a positive effect on how well you do academically. Your relationships with your college instructors are going to be very different from your relationships with your high school teachers. College students are expected to be more independent and seek the advice and assistance of their instructors; in other words, you should attempt to make connections with your college instructors and get to know them.

Knowing and Meeting Expectations. While instructors' expectations might be different from course to course, most instructors expect their students to attend class, arrive on time, do assigned work, listen and participate, and not give up when they have to learn difficult material. If you repeatedly arrive late or leave early, you are breaking the basic rules of etiquette and politeness, and you are intentionally or unintentionally showing a lack of respect for your instructors and your classmates.

Instructors also expect honesty and openness. Many instructors invite you to express your feelings about the course through one-minute papers or other forms of class assessment. In addition, college instructors expect you to be motivated to do your best.

The instructor-student relationship should be based on mutual respect and reasonable expectations. In college, it is your responsibility to meet the expectations of your instructors. In return, you should expect your instructors to be organized and prepared, to be knowledgeable about the subjects they are teaching, to provide comments on your papers and exams, and to grade your work fairly. You should be able to approach your instructors when you need academic help or if you have a personal problem that may make studying difficult.

To get a clear sense of the expectations of each of your instructors, pay close attention to the syllabus for each course (see Table 1.2). Make sure

> **Exchanging Ideas**

Most college instructors love to exchange ideas. Many successful college graduates can name a particular instructor who made a positive difference in their lives and influenced their academic and career paths. Develop meaningful relationships with your instructors. It could change your life for the better.

© John Stanmeyer/VII/Corbis

you review each syllabus carefully at the beginning of the term, refer to it through the term, and keep it in your course notebook with other course materials.

TABLE 1.2 ❭ The Syllabus and Grades

The Syllabus	
What is a syllabus?	A syllabus is a statement of the requirements of a given course and also a contract between the students and the instructor that the college must honor.
What is on a syllabus?	A syllabus includes basic information about the course, the instructor's office hours and contact information, expectations, and grading criteria for assignments, tests, papers, exams, or presentations. The syllabus will also include the attendance policy, a week-by-week plan for the course, and assignments, exams, papers, and projects and their due dates.
When do I get the syllabus?	Generally, instructors provide the syllabus to their students during the first class session and/or place it online.
Grades	
How are grades calculated?	Letter grades (A, B, C, D, F) are calculated in different ways. Often A = 95–100, A– = 90–94, B = 85–89, B– = 80–84, and so on.
What is a GPA?	The grades you earn will build your **grade point average (GPA)**. Your GPA is the average of points you receive based on your grades for each course. Generally, college GPAs range from 0 (F) to 4.0 (A or A+). This is referred to as a "4-point scale."
What are the other grade options?	"W" for "withdraw": requested by students who need to drop the course before the end of the term. This grade is typically used for students who have to leave the course because of emergencies or difficulties. "I" for "incomplete": given to students who may need additional time to complete the course because of an emergency. "P" for "pass" or "F" for fail: given in certain courses instead of letter grades.

Making the Most of Learning Relationships. You can visit your instructors anytime during the term, either face-to-face or online, to ask questions, seek help with a difficult topic or assignment, or discuss a problem. Some of your instructors will have private offices and keep regular **office hours**, the posted hours when they are in their offices and available to students. It's up to you to take the initiative to visit your instructors during their office hours or at whatever times and locations they determine, but it is their job to be available to assist students like you. Check with your instructors to find out if you need to make an appointment before going to their offices. Visiting an instructor may seem a little scary to some students, but most instructors welcome the opportunity to get to know them.

The relationships you develop with instructors can be valuable to you both now and in the future—you might find that one or more of them become lifelong mentors and friends. Instructors who know you well can also write that all-important letter of recommendation when you are applying for transfer or for a job after college. It is often these recommendations that make the ultimate difference in whether a student is accepted or rejected when applying for a new position. Many successful college graduates can name a particular instructor who made a positive difference in their lives and influenced their academic and career paths.

Instructors who teach part-time at your college might be called part-time instructors or **adjuncts**, and they may not have assigned offices. While adjuncts are not usually required to hold office hours, they often make themselves available to meet with their students before or after class or by appointment.

If you ever have a problem with an instructor, ask for a meeting to discuss your problem and see if you can work things out. If the instructor refuses, go to a person in a higher position in the department or college. If the problem is a grade, keep in mind that your instructor has the right to assign you grades based on your performance, and no one can force him or her to change those grades. However, you can always speak with your instructor about your grade, find out what mistakes you made, and see how you can improve your grade in the future. In addition, all colleges allow students to challenge a grade that they believe is incorrect through a formal "appeal" or "petition." Most important, don't let a bad experience change your feelings about college. Each instructor will probably be out of your life by the end of the term, so if there are problems, just do your best, focus on your studies, and get through the course.

HAVE NETIQUETTE

As you have been planning for college, you have probably heard how you'll use technology as a student. Activating your college e-mail and registering for text alerts allow you access to information regarding class cancellations, weather-related closings, student events, and other types of college-related communication such as campus emergencies. Your instructors may use e-mail to send you files and updates. Make sure you activate your college e-mail and check it daily.

THE PROBLEM

You communicate with your friends and family by e-mail, text, Skype, Facebook, and FaceTime, but you are not sure about the proper way to communicate with your college instructors.

THE FIX

Take a few minutes to figure out what exactly you need to ask, jot down your main points, and then compose a clear and concise e-mail or text message.

HOW TO DO IT

Whether your class is online or face-to-face, at some point you will need to communicate with your instructor using technology. Writing e-mails and text messages to your instructors is different from writing e-mails to your family and friends.

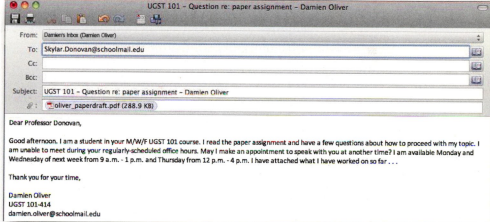

IF YOU ARE E-MAILING YOUR INSTRUCTOR, CONSIDER THE FOLLOWING:

1. Look at the example shown here, and follow its format. It's best to use your college e-mail address because it has your name, and it helps your instructor recognize you as a student.

2. Make the subject line informative. Your instructor might receive hundreds of e-mails every day, and a relevant subject like the name of the course or the assignment helps him or her respond faster. A subject line like "Class" or "Question" isn't helpful; a blank subject line usually goes to the spam folder.

3. Address your instructor with respect. Think about how you address your instructor in class, or look at your syllabus to see his or her proper title. If an instructor uses *Doctor*, then you should use *Dr.* If you don't know his or her title, you can never go wrong with *Dear Professor* plus your instructor's last name.

4. Sign every e-mail with your full name and course number.

5. When attaching files to your e-mail (a skill you should have), use widely accepted file formats like .doc, .docx, or .pdf. Also, be sure your last name is included in the file name you use. See the example shown.

IF YOU ARE USING ONLINE VIDEO FOR COMMUNICATION WITH YOUR INSTRUCTOR, KEEP THE FOLLOWING IN MIND:

1. Make sure that you contact your instructor during office hours or by appointment. You do not want to disturb your instructor with a live chat when he or she is teaching another class, having dinner, or spending time with his or her family.

2. Always choose an appropriate place to be before you get online. Inform the people around you about the videoconference so that they do not appear in the background, or you do not invade their privacy.

3. If you are home during the videoconferencing, ensure that children and pets do not interrupt your conversation with the instructor.

1

THINK
WRITE
APPLY

What you have learned in this chapter about why college is important to you and what motivates you to do your best in college?

_____

_____

_____

_____

_____

WRITE

Write a paragraph about what you found most useful or meaningful in this chapter. Include anything that was covered in this chapter that left you with more questions than answers.

_____

_____

_____

_____

_____

APPLY

It is absolutely essential that you have an academic plan in place during your first term at college. Using your college catalog, which lists the programs of study and the courses students must take, complete the chart on the opposite page, and make an appointment with an academic adviser to ensure that you have correctly mapped your courses and selected the right courses in the correct order to graduate on time.

Academic Plan for: _____ Program of Study: _____ Total Number of Credits: _____

Expected Graduation Date: _____ Adviser's Name and Contact Info: _____

Term	General Education Courses	Required Major Courses	Electives

USE YOUR RESOURCES

Below are suggestions for resources that are available at many colleges and the online resources that are available to everyone.

AT YOUR COLLEGE

VISIT . . .	IF YOU NEED HELP . . .
Academic Advising Center	selecting courses, obtaining information on degree requirements, and deciding on a major.
Learning Center	with memory skills and studying for exams.
Computer Center	using Word, Excel, PowerPoint, and e-mail.
Counseling Center	dealing with personal problems and stress management.
Math Center	improving your math skills.
Writing Center	writing your first paper or revising a first draft.
Career Center	with career interest assessments, counseling, finding a major, job and internship listings, interviewing with prospective employers, and preparing résumés and interview skills.
Transfer Center	finding information on transfer policies, requirements, and programs at four-year institutions that you can transfer to.
Adult Reentry Center	as a returning student, in making supportive contacts with other adult students, and gathering information about services such as child care.
Veterans Office	as a veteran, in managing financial aid and paperwork.
International Student Services	as an international student, in making the transition to a new country and culture as well as to the college.

ONLINE

GO TO . . .	IF YOU NEED HELP . . .
Brock University website: brocku.ca/webfm_send/1394	writing SMART goals.

MY COLLEGE'S RESOURCES

LaunchPad for *Understanding Your College Experience* is a great resource. Go online to master concepts using the LearningCurve study tool and much more. **macmillanhighered.com/gardnerunderstanding**

2 Cultivating Motivation, Resilience, and Emotional Intelligence

PRE-READING ACTIVITY: Your level of motivation, skills at managing difficult situations, and willingness to bounce back from frustrations will make a difference in your college success. For the following statements, mark whether you agree or disagree, and write down the reason for your response.

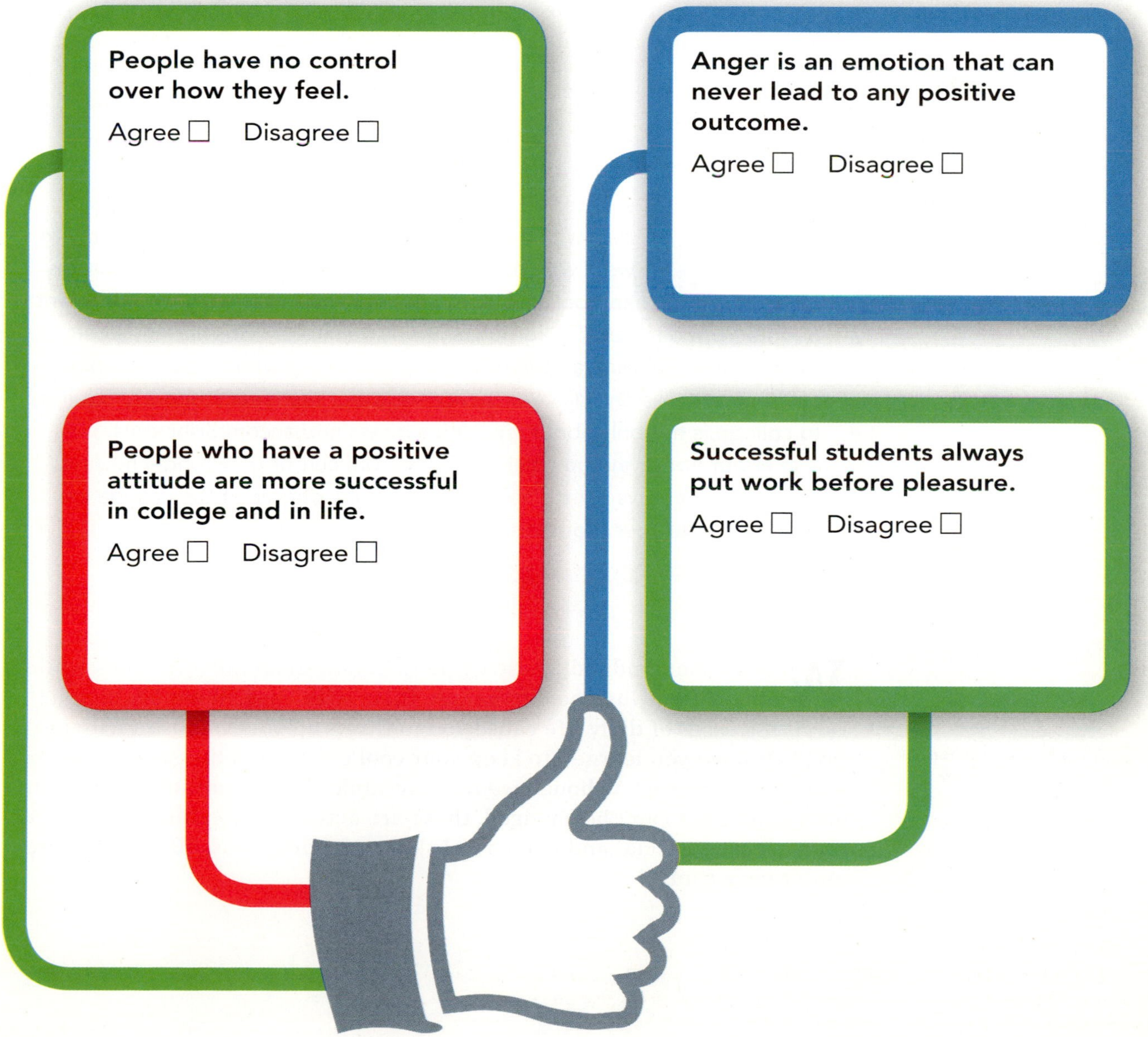

People have no control over how they feel.
Agree ☐ Disagree ☐
Anger is an emotion that can never lead to any positive outcome.
Agree ☐ Disagree ☐
People who have a positive attitude are more successful in college and in life.
Agree ☐ Disagree ☐
Successful students always put work before pleasure.
Agree ☐ Disagree ☐

Flat Design/Shutterstock.com

📁 **PROFILE** ✕

Gustavo Mejia, 20
Business Administration Major, *South Texas College*

When he was growing up in Turmero, Venezuela, Gus Mejia was encouraged by his family to attend college. "I see college as the path to the future," he says, "one that will help me build a better life for my family." Gus began college at Sinclair Community College in Dayton, Ohio, where he took classes full-time. He quickly learned a few things that helped him succeed. "As an international student, I left important parts of my life behind when I made the decision to go to college, such as family, friends, and my country. Being alone for almost a year taught me how important it is to have a positive attitude and an optimistic spirit." This realization didn't come without hard work and practice. One of the most important things Gus had to learn during his first year of college was how to deal with the stress of managing college and living in a new environment.

> "Going to college is not only about enjoying success and accomplishments, but also about not giving up when things get difficult or go wrong."

Gus figured out that understanding how these stresses affected him emotionally helped him better deal with difficult situations. He also had to learn how to work with other students, no matter what their customs and beliefs. "Being able to work efficiently with different people from different backgrounds is very valuable." Gus had the ability to understand himself and others and to get along with people in a new environment. His one piece of advice for other first-year students: "Going to college is not only about enjoying success and accomplishments, but also about not giving up when things get difficult or go wrong," he says. "You should always ask for help because many people at the college can help you solve your problems."

To access the Learning-Curve study tool, Video Tools, and more, go to LaunchPad for *Understanding Your College Experience.* macmillanhighered.com /gardnerunderstanding

Why do some individuals struggle to handle stressful situations while others, like Gus, seem to handle them with ease? What about you? Do the stresses of daily life cause you to throw up your hands in frustration? Or have you learned to keep your cool even when life seems crazy and out of control? Although we tend to think of these abilities as personality traits that can't be changed, these are actually a combination of attitudes, learned social and behavioral skills, and decisions, all of which are under your control.

THE IMPORTANCE OF MOTIVATION, ATTITUDE, AND MINDSET

If you're like most students, you will face big challenges every day, from studying for exams and making time for work and college to facing money troubles and taking care of family members. At some point in your college career, things *will* go wrong no matter how much you plan ahead and how hard you work. When you're facing such challenges, how you *think* and especially how you *feel* have a huge effect on your ability to keep going.

What if you have a work shift this afternoon, and a test tomorrow, and you haven't studied enough? What if your car breaks down on the way to pick up your kids and you have a paper due tomorrow? In these tough moments, how you think and feel will make all the difference. If you feel powerless and overwhelmed, you're more likely to give up—to skip studying, miss a shift at work, or may even leave your kids stranded! But if you *believe* you can overcome these challenges, you'll feel energized to keep going and figure out solutions.

The good news is that everyone faces tough moments like these and that you can learn the skills you need to handle them. And remember, you're not alone. Although your classmates might not admit it, many of them share your challenges and fears. In this section, we'll go over habits of mind, and we will give you strategies that will help you achieve your goals. These include staying motivated, keeping a good attitude, and developing a growth mindset, all of which we'll explain below.

Motivation

Among the most important factors that will help you to achieve college success is your **motivation**—your desire to make an effort. Motivation involves having a high level of commitment and energy that you will focus on a goal. When you are motivated, you are determined to follow a course of action. You keep making an effort, and when you hit obstacles, you make adjustments to work around them, or you deal with them head on. Sometimes being motivated involves pledging to yourself and to others to do your best to reach your goal.

Different people are motivated in different ways. You might need a better car and a bigger apartment or want to work in a career field that truly interests you. You might want to build a better life for yourself and your family so you need to earn a college degree to earn more income. Perhaps you can no longer meet the physical demands of your construction job, and you need to earn a bachelor's degree in order to qualify for a management position. Or perhaps you've enjoyed working as a physical therapy assistant and have decided to go to nursing school because you are truly committed to helping others and are ready for more responsibility. Whatever your motivation for attending college, you need to stay mindful of the goals you want to achieve, particularly when you face challenges on your path.

Components of Motivation

Think about how the words used in the word cloud relate to motivation.

Rob Wilson/Shutterstock.com

In general, there are two kinds of motivation. **Intrinsic motivation** comes from a desire inside yourself to make something happen, and the internal reward is the feeling you get inside when you achieve it—like the nursing student we just mentioned who wants to help others. **Extrinsic motivation** comes from the hope of an external reward or the fear of an undesirable outcome or a punishment—like the student training for a management position fearing that his days doing manual labor are coming to a close. In real life, intrinsic and extrinsic motivation work together. As the construction management student spends more time in classes, he enjoys getting to know his instructors and finds he has a lot in common with them. He feels less nervous about becoming a boss and no longer being "one of the guys." This excitement becomes the intrinsic motivation that will help him keep going over the long haul. The future nurse will not only be helping patients, but as she comes to appreciate the good salary she will earn, this hope of external reward becomes part of her motivation for becoming a nurse.

YOUR TURN > STAY MOTIVATED

Think about the goals—academic, personal, professional—that you are working toward now. Using the table below, select one goal in each category and write it down. What is motivating you to work toward each goal? Name one or more factors, and circle whether each is an intrinsic or extrinsic factor. You can expand on this exercise in a journal entry or in a group discussion.

My Goal	My Motivation	Extrinsic or Intrinsic?
Academic goal:	What motivates me to achieve this goal is _____.	Is my motivation extrinsic or intrinsic?
Personal goal:	What motivates me to achieve this goal is _____.	Is my motivation extrinsic or intrinsic?
Career goal:	What motivates me to achieve this goal is _____.	Is my motivation extrinsic or intrinsic?

Attitude

Attitude is the way you are thinking and feeling in relation to the events around you. Attitude has a lot to do with how well you can stay motivated, whether it's being motivated to land a better paying job, to do well in your college courses, or to get to the gym or the grocery store. Attitude is an important part of staying motivated because your attitude shapes your behavior. For instance, if you have a bad attitude about math because you've had trouble in math in the past, you will be likely to give up on your math courses before you even give yourself a chance to do well.

Whether positive or negative, attitudes often come from our previous environments and experiences with others. Have you ever wondered whether you were "college material"? Has anyone, a family member or teacher, ever told you that you aren't? How has a comment like this affected your attitude about starting college? Or maybe a friend or family member has told you how proud they are that you are in college, and this has made you feel determined to work hard.

A good starting place to developing a more positive attitude is to think honestly about the attitude you're likely to have in certain situations. How would you handle stressful or surprising situations such as these?

Situation	Describe your attitude: How would you react?
You ask for time off from work to study for a final exam, and your boss refuses your request.	
Your financial aid check doesn't arrive in time for you to purchase your books.	
Your babysitter doesn't show up before you need to leave for class.	
You lose a major paper or report because your computer crashes.	
You need to finish a paper the evening before the due date, and your child gets sick.	
As a non-native English speaker, you're struggling in many of your classes.	
Your commute to campus is taking twice as long due to major construction.	
You fail a pop quiz that caught you entirely by surprise.	
You lose your psychology notebook, and the final exam is next week.	
A group project isn't going well because other members of the group aren't doing their share of the work.	

Any of these things can and do happen to students just like you. Most college students have many responsibilities, which can make it hard to maintain a good attitude and stay motivated. When you face these kinds of frustrations, do you get really stressed or mad? Do you expect the worst? Do you stay relaxed, do your best, and keep going?

If you've been told by people who know you well that you're negative or pessimistic or you realize that you always expect the worst, maybe it actually is time for an attitude adjustment:

- Spend time thinking about what you can learn from difficult situations you faced and overcame.

- Give yourself credit for good choices that you made, and think about how you can build upon these successes.

- Recall experiences when things did not work out, and try to think through the mistakes that you made and how you could have done better.

- Seek out individuals, both on and off campus, who are positive. Ask them where their optimism comes from.

- Take advantage of the opportunities you will get in your college success course to explore the effect your attitude has on the outcomes you want.

- Be mindful of your attitude as you move through the weeks of this term.

Mindsets

Another way to look at motivation is to examine what are called "mindsets." **Mindsets** refer to what you believe about yourself and about your most basic qualities such as your personality, intelligence, or talents. If you have a fixed mindset, you are likely to believe that your characteristics and abilities—either positive or negative—*are not going to change* through any adjustments to your behavior or effort. A growth mindset, however, means that you are willing to try new approaches and that you believe that *you can change.*[1]

People with a fixed mindset are often trying to prove themselves, and they're very sensitive about being wrong or making mistakes. They also think that having to make an effort means they are not smart or talented. Many new college students are "fixed" in their beliefs about themselves and their abilities. People with a growth mindset believe that their abilities can be improved—that there is no harm in being wrong or making a mistake. They think that the effort they make is what makes them smart or talented. Some of us have a different mindset for different tasks. For instance, you may find that you have a fixed mindset for your athletic abilities but a growth mindset for music.

Consider Amber, a second-year college student. Amber was her high school's valedictorian, and before college she had never earned a grade lower than an A minus. Her high school was pretty small and lacked some advanced courses, but Amber assumed that she was prepared for college. During her first college year, however, Amber earned Bs, Cs, and even a D in college algebra. The extrinsic motivation that had come from good

---

[1]Based on Carol S. Dweck, *Mindset: The New Psychology of Success* (New York: Ballantine, 2006), p. 16.

grades was long gone, which turned her fixed-mindset world upside down. For several months, Amber was disinterested in almost everything; she completely lost her motivation to study and learn when earning an A had seemingly become impossible.

Slowly, though, Amber turned things around. She began watching how others studied and interacted with instructors. Not all the examples were good ones. Some students would brag about skipping class and staying up all night to study instead of managing their time better. But others had a deliberate plan that included taking really good notes, studying every day, trying to sit close to the front of the classroom, and talking with instructors after class. Amber started adopting these behaviors. Little by little, she practiced new study strategies, began to accept criticism without falling apart, and gained an understanding that sometimes she could learn more from her mistakes than from her successes. It took Amber about a year to regain her positive attitude and a willingness to do her best, no matter what the outcome. She stills likes to see an A at the top of a paper, but she has realized that she is motivated intrinsically more by what she learns than by what grade she earns.

How would you describe how Amber's mindset changed? How would you describe your own? What can you learn about your mindset by walking through the exercise in Table 2.1?

Table 2.1 ❯ Mindsets: Which Sounds More like You?

For each pair of statements, select the one that sounds more like you.

a. You believe that your efforts won't change your grades.
b. You believe that with effort you can improve your grades.

a. You believe that a good grade means you have learned everything you need to know.
b. You believe that you can always learn more, even if you have received an A.

a. You tend to blame the world around you when things go wrong.
b. You try to solve the problems when things go wrong.

a. You are often afraid to try new things because you fear you will fail.
b. You believe that failure is an opportunity to learn more.

a. You believe that some jobs are for "women only" or for "men only."
b. You are open to exploring all job opportunities.

a. You believe that leaders are born, not made.
b. You believe that leadership can be developed.

a. You tend to believe negative things that others say about you.
b. You don't allow others to define who you are.

If you selected mostly "a" statements, you likely have a fixed mindset; if you selected mostly "b" statements, you have a growth mindset. As mentioned above, your mindset can change depending on the task. Which tasks do you approach with more of a growth mindset? Which tasks do you approach with more of a fixed mindset? Remember that a mindset that is fixed today might not be fixed tomorrow—with some motivation you can challenge yourself, take some risks, and develop a positive attitude about your ability to grow and change.

Whether you're in your college classes, your job setting, or your home, your mindset—similar to your attitude—can influence how you think about yourself and others, your opportunities, and your relationships. A fixed mindset will cause you to limit the things you do, the people you meet, and even the classes you take in college. A growth mindset will help you be more willing to explore classes and activities out of your comfort zone. It will help you stay motivated because you will see disappointments or failures as opportunities to learn.

2.2

RESILIENCE

Motivation requires a clear vision, courage, and persistence. And it takes **resilience**—not giving up or quitting when faced with difficulties and challenges. A resilient person maintains a positive attitude even when faced with difficult situations. Students who are resilient—who bounce back quickly from difficult situations—will be more successful in college and in life. They stay focused on achieving their purpose. Learning to keep going when things are hard is one of the most important lessons you'll learn in this class.

There are many other terms that are used to describe resilience and determination. One of these terms is **grit**, a combination of perseverance, passion, and resilience. Psychologist Angela Duckworth has studied grit and has found that people who are "gritty" are more likely to be both academically and personally successful.[2] Another term that encompasses

---

[2]See apa.org/monitor/nov07/grit.aspx.

resilience comes from Finland: **Sisu** is a word that dates back hundreds of years and is described as being central to understanding Finnish culture. It means going beyond one's mental or physical ability, taking action even when things are difficult, and displaying courage and determination in the face of challenge and repeated failures.

Resilience is such an important concept in psychological health that the American Psychological Association has developed a list of resilience strategies: "10 Ways to Build Resilience."[3] These are as follows:

1. **Make connections.** Good relationships with close family members, friends, or others are important. Accepting help and support from those who care about you and will listen to you helps you to become more resilient. Some people find that being active in civic groups, religious organizations, or other community groups gives them support and encouragement. Assisting others in their time of need also can benefit the helper.

2. **Avoid seeing crises as problems that can't be overcome.** You can't change the fact that highly stressful events happen, but you can change how you view and respond to these events. Try looking beyond the present and think about how things will be better in the future.

3. **Accept that change is a part of living.** Obstacles might keep you from achieving certain goals. Accepting situations that cannot be changed can help you focus on those that you can change.

4. **Move toward your goals.** Develop some realistic goals. Do something regularly—even if it seems like a small accomplishment—that enables you to move toward your goals. Instead of focusing on tasks that seem impossible, ask yourself, "What's one thing I know I can accomplish today that helps me move in the direction I want to go?"

5. **Take decisive actions.** Don't wait for problems to disappear on their own. Take decisive actions, rather than staying away completely from problems and stresses and wishing they would just go away.

6. **Look for opportunities for self-discovery.** Struggles often make people stronger and teach them what they're made of. Consider what you have learned about yourself from going through tough times.

7. **Develop a positive view of yourself.** Developing confidence in your ability to solve problems and trusting your instincts helps build resilience.

8. **Keep things in perspective.** Even when facing very painful events, try to consider the big picture and keep a long-term perspective. Avoid blowing the event out of proportion.

9. **Maintain a hopeful outlook.** An optimistic outlook enables you to expect that good things will happen in your life. Try visualizing what you want, rather than worrying about what you fear.

10. **Take care of yourself.** Pay attention to your own needs and feelings. Engage in activities that you enjoy and find relaxing. Exercise regularly. Taking care of yourself helps to keep your mind and body ready to deal with situations that require resilience.

---

[3]See **apa.org/helpcenter/road-resilience.aspx**. Accessed September 4, 2015.

Show your grit. Have sisu. Be resilient. If your goal is to graduate, overcome the obstacles that get in your way, no matter what they are.

Lucian3D/Shutterstock.com

There are other ways to deal with challenges and stressful situations. For example, some people write about their deepest thoughts and feelings related to trauma or other stressful events in their life. Meditation and spiritual practices help some people to build connections and restore hope.

Think about your own reactions to frustration and stress. Do you often give up because something is just too hard or because you can't figure it out? Do you take responsibility for what you do, or do you blame others if you fail? For example, how have you reacted to receiving a D or F on a paper, losing a student government election, or getting rejected for a work-study job? Do you have trouble making connections with others in class?

Negative experiences might cause you to question whether you should be in college at all. Resilient students, though, look past negative experiences, learn from them, and try again. For instance, what could you do to improve your grade on your next paper? Perhaps you didn't allow yourself enough time to do the necessary research. Why did someone else get the work-study job that you wanted? It's possible that you need to work on your interview skills. How can you feel more comfortable in your classes? Maybe it would help to join a study group or go to the learning center. You were born with the ability to be resilient.

Many well-known and successful people overcame tough circumstances and failure. For instance, J. K. Rowling, the author of all the Harry Potter books, was divorced and penniless when she wrote the first Harry Potter book. That book was rejected by twelve publishers before it was finally accepted. Walt Disney's first animation company went bankrupt, and he was fired by a news agency because he "lacked imagination." Michael Jordan was cut by his high school basketball team. Jordan has been quoted as reporting that he missed 9,000 shots in his career. These people and many others did not let failure get in the way of their ultimate success.

So far in this chapter we have asked you to consider how thoughts and feelings affect behavior. We've discussed motivation, attitude, and resilience and have asked you to explore what motivates you, to think about your own attitude and how it helps or hurts you sometimes, and to reflect on whether you are able to bounce back from difficulty. These topics are part of a broader discussion of emotions, which we turn to next.

YOUR TURN > DISCUSS IT

Think about a challenge you faced in the past. How did you feel and respond to this challenge? Be prepared to discuss your strategies in dealing with this challenge in class.

UNDERSTANDING EMOTIONAL INTELLIGENCE

2.3

Emotional intelligence (EI) is the ability to recognize, understand, use, and manage emotions—moods, feelings, and attitudes. It should come as no surprise that your emotional intelligence is related to how resilient you are, and it affects your ability to stay motivated and committed to your goals. As we said earlier in the chapter, how you think and feel will make all the difference in whether you succeed or give up. Developing an awareness of emotions allows you to use your feelings to improve your thinking. If you are feeling sad, for instance, you might view the world in a negative way, while if you feel happy, you are likely to view the same events differently. Once you start paying attention to emotions, you can learn not only how to cope with life's pressures and demands but also how to use your knowledge of the way you feel for more effective problem solving, decision making, and creativity. This is all part of developing your emotional intelligence, and as your ability to deal with life's challenges is based on your emotional intelligence, it's critical to understand this concept.

Particularly in the first year of college, many students have difficulty establishing positive relationships with others, dealing with pressure, or making wise decisions. Other students are optimistic and happy and seem to adapt to their new environment without any trouble. Being optimistic doesn't mean that you ignore your problems or pretend that they will go away, but optimistic people believe in their own abilities to address problems successfully as they arise. You'll recall the discussion earlier in this chapter of the impact that attitude has on college success and success in life.

Emotions are a big part of who you are; you should not ignore them. Being aware of your own and others' feelings helps you gather correct information about the world around you and allows you to respond in appropriate ways. If you are a returning student, you probably have a great deal of life experience in dealing with tough times, and you can draw on this experience in college.

As you read this section and the next, think about the behaviors that help people, including yourself, do well and the behaviors that interfere with success. Get to know yourself better, and take the time to examine your feelings and the impact they have on the way you act. You can't always control the challenges of life, but with practice you *can* control how you respond to them. Remember that emotions are real, can be changed for the better, and significantly affect whether a person is successful.

Perceiving and Managing Emotions

Perceiving emotions involves the ability to monitor and identify feelings correctly (nervous, happy, angry, relieved, and so forth) and to determine why you feel the way you do. It also involves predicting how others might feel in a given situation. Emotions contain information, and the ability to understand and think about that information plays an important role in behavior.

Managing emotions is based on the belief that feelings can be modified, even improved. At times, you need to stay open to your feelings, learn from them, and use them to take appropriate actions. Other times, it is better to disengage from an emotion and return to it later. Anger, for example, can blind you and lead you to act in negative or antisocial ways; used positively, however, anger can help you take a stand against bias or injustice. Learning how to put yourself in the right mood to handle different situations is important.

♥ Don't Roll the Dice

As you learn to identify and manage your emotions, you won't be rolling the dice when it comes to responding to the challenges of everyday life and establishing positive relationships with others.
Kostasgr/Shutterstock.com

The Role of Emotional Intelligence in Everyday Life

Emotional intelligence may be a new term for you, but your emotions have guided your behavior throughout your life, even if you did not realize it. For example, whether you just graduated from high school or have worked for several years, you have now decided to pursue higher education. This decision might have been based on your family's encouragement, your career goals, or changes in your current job. Maybe you wanted to go to a different college but found out that you and your family could not afford to do that now. In that case, how do you think your emotions affected your final decision about college?

Naming and labeling emotions, in addition to focusing on related experiences, improves emotional intelligence. For example, new college students often fear social rejection. Did you think that you would see lots of people from your neighborhood but have found that you don't know anyone? If you are an older student, are your classes filled with younger students with whom you have nothing

in common? When you acknowledge and name your feelings, they are less likely to control you. You will be in a better place to confront certain fears by walking up to other students, even those of a different age, introducing yourself, and perhaps asking to join their discussions. As you work to develop your emotional intelligence, consider how to use logic rather than your own emotional reactions to evaluate a situation and help yourself and others.

Your daily life gives you many opportunities to take a hard look at how you handle emotions. Here are some questions that can help you begin thinking about your own EI.

EMOTIONAL INTELLIGENCE QUESTIONNAIRE

1. What do you do when you are under stress?
- ☐ a. I tend to deal with it calmly and rationally.
- ☐ b. I get upset, but it usually blows over quickly.
- ☐ c. I get upset but keep it to myself.

2. My friends would say that:
- ☐ a. I play, but only after I get my work done.
- ☐ b. I am ready for fun anytime.
- ☐ c. I hardly ever go out.

3. When something changes at the last minute:
- ☐ a. I easily adapt.
- ☐ b. I get frustrated.
- ☐ c. I don't care, since I don't really expect things to happen according to plan.

4. My friends would say that:
- ☐ a. I am sensitive to their concerns.
- ☐ b. I spend too much time worrying about other people's needs.
- ☐ c. I don't like to deal with other people's petty problems.

5. When I have a problem to solve, such as having too many assignments due at the end of the week:
- ☐ a. I write down a list of the tasks I must complete, come up with a plan indicating specifically what I can accomplish and what I cannot, and follow my plan.
- ☐ b. I am very optimistic about getting things done and just dig right in and get to work.
- ☐ c. I get a little overwhelmed. Usually I get a number of things done and then push aside the things I can't do.

Review your responses. a responses indicate that you probably have a good basis for strong EI. **b** responses indicate that you may have some strengths and some challenges in your EI. **c** responses indicate that your success in life and in school could be negatively affected by your EI.

Anger Management. Humans experience a wide range of emotions and moods. On the one hand, we can be very generous and positive, and on the other hand, we can lash out in anger. Anger management is an EI skill that is important to develop. Anger can hurt others and can harm your mental and physical health. You may even know someone who uses his or her anger to manipulate and control others.

In spite of the problems it creates, anger does not always lead to negative results. Psychologists see anger as a primary and natural emotion that has value for human survival because it can help us to stand up for what is right.

Managing Priorities. Using healthy emotional intelligence to prioritize involves deciding what's most important to you and then allocating your time and energy according to these priorities. For example, if exercise, a healthy diet, friends, and studying are most important to you, then you must make time for them all. When you successfully make time in your days and weeks for what is most important to you, your emotional health benefits. You feel more confident, more in control, and more capable of handling your life with a positive attitude and others with patience. On the other hand, if you cannot keep what is most important to you at the top of your list of priorities, your attitude becomes more negative, you feel stressed out, and you have less patience for other people. Part of developing a strong emotional intelligence involves paying attention to your priorities and making adjustments when needed.

Improving Emotional Intelligence

As you reflect more on your own attitudes and behavior and learn why you have the emotions that you do, you'll improve your emotional intelligence. Studying unfamiliar subjects and interacting with new and diverse people will challenge your EI skills and force you to step outside of your comfort zone. Your first year of college is especially critical and gives you a significant opportunity to grow as a person.

Emotional intelligence includes many capabilities and skills that influence a person's ability to cope with life's pressures and demands. Researcher Reuven Bar-On[4] developed the model that is adapted in Table 2.2. This model shows how categories of emotional intelligence directly affect general mood and lead to effective performance.

Identifying Your EI Skills and Competencies

Table 2.2, which is based on Bar-On's work, lists skills that influence a person's ability to cope with life's pressures and demands. Which skills do you think you already have? Which ones do you need to improve? Which ones

---

[4]"What Is Emotional Intelligence?" from *Bar-On EQ-i Technical Manual.* Copyright © 1997, 1999, 2000 Multi-Health Systems, Inc., Toronto, Canada. Used by permission of Multi-Health Systems, Inc.

do you lack? Consider the emotional intelligence skills and competencies listed below and rank them accordingly:

A = Skills I already have   B = Skills I need to improve   C = Skills I lack

Then go back and rank each one in terms of the priority you assign it right now to your challenges of being a successful college student.

Table 2.2 ❯ Emotional Skills and Competencies

Skills	Competencies	Rank
Intrapersonal	**Emotional self-awareness.** Knowing how and why you feel the way you do.	
	Assertiveness. Standing up for yourself when you need to without being too aggressive.	
	Independence. Making important decisions on your own without having to get everyone's opinion.	
	Self-regard. Liking yourself in spite of your flaws (and we all have them).	
	Self-actualization. Being satisfied and comfortable with what you have achieved in school, work, and your personal life.	
Interpersonal	**Empathy.** Making an effort to understand another person's situation or point of view.	
	Social responsibility. Establishing a personal link with a group or community and cooperating with other members in working toward shared goals.	
	Interpersonal relationships. Seeking out healthy and mutually beneficial relationships —such as friendships, professional networks, family connections, mentoring, and romantic partnerships—and making a persistent effort to maintain them.	
Stress Management	**Stress tolerance.** Recognizing the causes of stress, responding in appropriate ways, and staying strong under pressure.	
	Impulse control. Thinking carefully about potential consequences before you act and delaying gratification for the sake of achieving long-term goals.	
Adaptability	**Reality testing.** Ensuring that your feelings are appropriate by checking them against external, objective criteria.	
	Flexibility. Adapting and adjusting your emotions, viewpoints, and actions as situations change.	
	Problem solving. Approaching challenges step-by-step and not giving up in the face of obstacles.	
	Resilience. The ability to bounce back after a setback.	
General Mood	**Optimism.** Looking for the bright side of any problem or difficulty and being confident that things will work out for the best.	
	Happiness. Being satisfied with yourself, with others, and with your situation in general.	

HOW EMOTIONS INFLUENCE SUCCESS AND WELL-BEING

Emotions are strongly tied to physical and psychological well-being. For example, some studies have suggested that cancer patients who have strong EI live longer than those with weak EI. People who are aware of the needs of others tend to be happier than people who are not. An extensive study done at the University of Pennsylvania found that the best athletes succeed in part because they're extremely optimistic. A number of studies link strong EI skills to college success in particular. These studies indicate that emotionally intelligent students get higher grades. Researchers looked at students' GPAs at the end of their first year of college. Students who had tested high for intrapersonal skills, stress tolerance, and adaptability when they entered college did better academically than those who had lower overall EI test scores. Strong EI also affects students' willingness to persist in college. Persistent students keep moving forward through challenging situations, even if progress is slow. And finally students who can delay gratification tend to do better overall. This means that many times while you are in college you are going to have to delay certain fun activities so that you will have more time to succeed in your academic work.

Healthy EI contributes to overall academic success, positive professional and personal relationships, including romantic ones, and career development and satisfaction. EI skills can be enhanced in a college

❯ EI Is in Demand

More and more, employers are looking for strong interpersonal skills in job applicants.

Randy Glasbergen

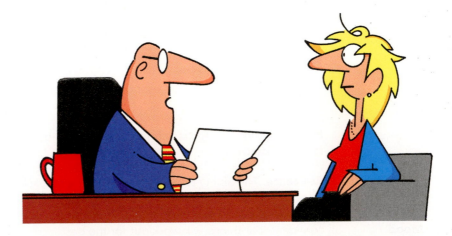

GLASBERGEN
© Randy Glasbergen
www.glasbergen.com

"Any other people skills, besides 400 Facebook friends?"

success course. Studies show that because these skills can be learned, infusing them in a college success course can improve first-year students' emotional intelligence, and thus their ultimate success.[5] Here are a few other highlights of these studies:

- Students with intrapersonal skills (emotional self-awareness, assertiveness, independence, self-regard, and self-actualization), stress tolerance, adaptability skills (reality testing, flexibility, and problem solving), and stress management skills (stress tolerance and impulse control) do better academically than those who lack these skills.

- Students who can't manage their emotions struggle academically. Some students experience panic attacks before tests, and far too many students turn to risky behaviors (such as drug and alcohol abuse) in an effort to cope.

- Even students who manage to succeed academically in spite of emotional difficulties can be at risk if unhealthy behavior patterns follow them after college.

If you think you need help developing some of these skills, especially if you feel that you are not happy or optimistic, do something about it. You can get by in college without strong EI, but you might miss out on the full range and depth of competencies and skills that can help you succeed in your chosen field and have a fulfilling and meaningful life. Although you can look online for tips about being an optimistic person, there is nothing like getting some in-person help from a professional. Consider visiting your academic adviser or a wellness or counseling center on campus. Look for any related workshops that are offered on campus or nearby.

---

[5]N.S. Schutte and J.M. Malouff, "Incorporating emotional skills in a college transition course enhances student retention," *Journal of the First-Year Experience and Students in Transition* 14 (2002): 7–21.

BUILDING A DIGITAL PERSONA

THE PROBLEM *You're open and honest with just about everyone online and when you use mobile apps.*

THE FIX *Carefully manage your online image to ensure it sends the appropriate message to the world.*

HOW TO DO IT

1. **Honesty is the best policy, but oversharing is not, especially in the digital age.** This goes double for students. Colleges and employers—present *and* future—can look you up online.

2. **The best way to manage your image online is to be proactive and aware.** Make sure your privacy settings on Facebook are up to par. For instance, allow only your friends to see your page, and if you list your birthday, don't put the year. Be careful about expressing controversial opinions online that could work against you. Encourage your friends to put mobile devices away during activities that shouldn't be recorded and not to share photos or videos that might be harmful to your or someone else's reputation. If you do find yourself tagged in a picture that makes you look reckless or irresponsible, ask that the photo be removed immediately.

   It's not that you can't be yourself, but your online presence should be something you can be proud of. Remember, once you put something online, it is public forever, regardless of your privacy settings. You have very little control over what happens to material after you make it public. This is also the case with mobile apps. For instance, Snapchat allows users to capture videos and pictures that supposedly self-destruct after a few seconds, but there is evidence that such material can indeed be restored. The guiding rule should be never to assume that something that's vanished is truly gone.

3. **Delete old accounts.** If you have MySpace, LiveJournal, Blogger, or any other account that is still open to the public but not being updated, delete it. Not only do old accounts include out-of-date information and possibly tales of your high school crushes, but since you rarely if ever check those sites, you may not notice if your account has been hacked. You don't want a potential employer to find your name associated with spam and questionable promotional links.

4. **Stay one step ahead.** Google yourself regularly, especially when applying for jobs. Make sure you know what potential employers can see. Look into free services like kgb people (**kgbpeople.com**), which can dig up every mention of you online, drawing from regular search engines, social networks, and other video and photo sites. For more information on protecting your virtual reputation, visit **blog.kgbpeople.com**.

THINK

Emotional intelligence might be a term that you were not familiar with before reading this chapter. What did you find to be the most interesting information in this chapter? Make a note of any information that was hard to understand or apply to your own life. What kinds of questions do you still have for your instructor?

WRITE

Write a description of yourself as a successful person ten years after you complete your current certificate or degree program. What kinds of skills will you have? What do you think you will have done to develop those skills? Don't just focus on your degree or a job description; include the competencies that help explain why you will be successful.

APPLY

1. Working with one or two other students, agree to watch at least one show or a movie during the coming week. All group members should watch the same show or movie. Take brief notes on how the fictional or nonfictional characters handle their emotions, especially in stressful situations. How many of the emotional intelligence competencies were represented—either positively or negatively—in the show or the movie you watched? During next week's class, discuss what you saw and what you learned.

2. No one has the same mindset in all situations. You may be willing to challenge yourself on the playing field but not in the classroom. In what areas are you the most "fixed" in your self-assessment, and where do you welcome opportunities for challenge and growth?

3. Your emotional reactions, whether positive or negative, affect your interactions with other people. Pretend that you are your own therapist. In what kinds of situations have you reacted with defensiveness, anger, sadness, annoyance, resentment, or humiliation? Take a step back and "process" these reactions. Think about what you said or did in response to your feelings, and why. Then talk with a trusted friend or classmate about how you reacted and whether you could have chosen to act differently. What can you do to take control and make good choices the next time you are faced with a potentially volatile situation?

USE YOUR RESOURCES

Below are suggestions for resources that are available at many colleges and the online resources that are available to everyone.

AT YOUR COLLEGE

VISIT . . .	IF YOU NEED HELP . . .
Counseling Center	thinking and talking about problems you are having with motivation or managing your emotions. It is normal to seek such assistance. This kind of counseling is strictly confidential (unless you are a threat to yourself or others) and usually is provided at no charge, which is a great benefit.
Library	finding books and articles about motivation, resilience, or emotional intelligence.

ONLINE

GO TO . . .	IF YOU NEED HELP . . .
TED: ted.com/talks	getting motivated. Search TED talks for topics like motivation, failure, and resilience for inspiring talks such as this one: **ted.com/talks/dan_pink_on_motivation**.
Mindtools.com: mindtools.com/pages/article /ei-quiz.htm	testing your emotional intelligence skills.
Sivers.org: sivers.org/mindset	finding additional perspectives on mindsets.
About.com: psychology.about.com/od /psychologytopics/tp /theories-of-motivation.htm	exploring theories of motivation.

MY COLLEGE'S RESOURCES

_____

_____

_____

_____

LaunchPad for _Understanding Your College Experience_ is a great resource. Go online to master concepts using the LearningCurve study tool and much more. **macmillanhighered.com/gardnerunderstanding**

3 Managing Time, Energy, and Money

PRE-READING ACTIVITY: This chapter is about managing your most valuable resources: time, energy, and money. Managing each of these is challenging for almost all college students. List two challenges you have in managing your time, energy, and money. Do you have control over how you spend your time and money? How about how you manage your energy?

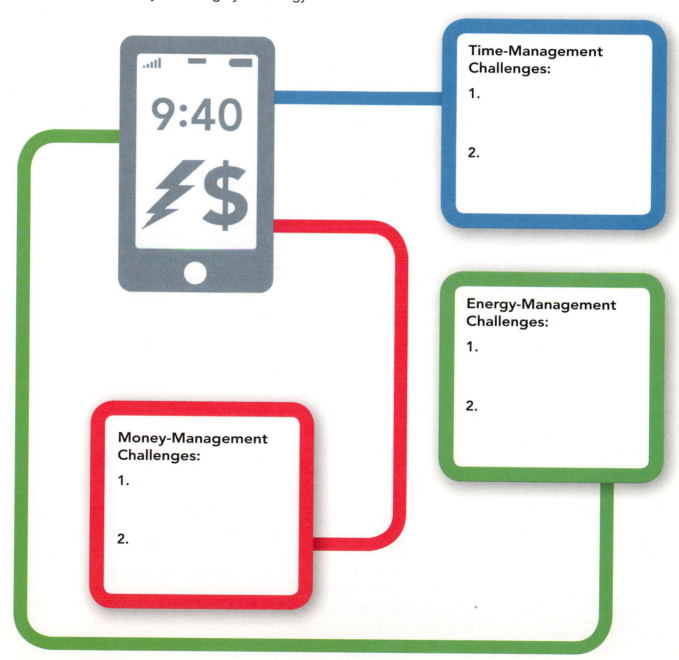

Time-Management Challenges:

1.

2.

Energy-Management Challenges:

1.

2.

Money-Management Challenges:

1.

2.

📁 **PROFILE**

Jasmine Williams, 25
Business Major, *Broward College–South Campus, Florida*

Tyler Olson/Shutterstock.com

When Jasmine Williams started college, she knew that she would have many competing obligations: work, family, and studying for her courses. Holding a job as a nursing assistant and taking care of her family were already demanding, and Jasmine was determined to pursue her educational goal of becoming a registered nurse. In the middle of her first term, she felt pressure from her job responsibilities, family members who needed her time and attention, and school assignments that were getting more complex, particularly a couple of the courses she was taking online that required more discipline. She did not have enough energy to do it all. "Sometimes I just got overwhelmed with school and just wanted to work or take care of my family and would put my schoolwork on the back burner. This happened more often with my online courses as there were no scheduled class meetings, and unless I logged into the system, they were pushed to the side. This had some bad side effects," she explains. "Once I saw the drop in my grades in the online courses, I knew that I had to reprioritize and get back on track."

> **"It's like each part of my life is a puzzle piece. If I don't make sure that each piece fits, or if any piece is missing, the puzzle doesn't work and breaks apart."**

Jasmine needed to work, but she realized if she put herself and her family on a strict budget, she could cut back on her work hours. Then she prioritized her time to maintain her busy schedule and her sanity; she made a calendar with all the exam and assignment dates, and highlighted the ones that she needed to submit online. "My main priorities are family, school, and work," she says. "I find places in my schedule to fit them in every week and also find time to reenergize myself a little bit, too. All of these things are important and essential for me to be successful and happy. It's like each part of my life is a puzzle piece. If I don't keep making sure that each piece fits, or if any piece is missing, the puzzle doesn't work and breaks apart."

LaunchPad
macmillan learning

To access the Learning-Curve study tool, Video Tools, and more, go to LaunchPad for *Understanding Your College Experience.* macmillanhighered.com /gardnerunderstanding

One of the keys to Jasmine's success is organization across the three main aspects of her life—family, work, and college. Because there is only so much time in a day, Jasmine focused on prioritizing and scheduling to make room for everything, including time to relax and enjoy life. She prioritized her family and college over her work, and she was able to cut back on her work hours and stick to a budget. Getting organized involves learning how to use your resources—time, energy, and money—in the most effective ways possible.

MANAGING YOUR TIME

Different people approach time differently based on their personality and background. Some people are always on time while others are almost always late. In every class, some students enter all due dates for assignments on a calendar as soon as they receive each syllabus, and this is probably a predictor of greater success for these students. Other students take a more laid-back approach and prefer to go with the flow rather than follow a daily or weekly schedule. These students might deal well with the unexpected, but they also might leave everything to the last minute and not be as successful as they could be if they managed their time differently. Improving your organizational skills can help you do better at school, work, and life. Many college students have a lot of responsibilities in addition to attending classes and studying; they often work and have families to take care of. For these students in particular, more organization almost always leads to more success, so the time and energy they spend to get organized will pay off. In our interviews with highly successful college students, they report that their number one success strategy is time management. Think of it this way: If *you* were hiring someone for a job, wouldn't you select an organized person who gets things done on time?

Taking Control of Your Time and Making Choices

The first step to effective time management is recognizing that you can be in control. The next time you find yourself saying, "I don't have time," stop and ask yourself whether this is actually true. Do you *really* not have time, or have you made a choice not to make time for a particular task or activity?

When we say we don't have time, we imply that we don't have a choice, but we actually do. We have control over how we use our time and how many commitments we make. We have control over what time we get up in the morning, how much sleep we get, and how much time we spend studying, working, and exercising. While these might seem like small decisions, they have a big cumulative impact on our success in college and in life.

How you manage your time reflects what you value and what consequences you are willing to accept when you make certain choices. If you value time with friends above all, your academic work likely takes a backseat to social activities. How you manage your time corresponds to how successful you will be in college and life. Almost all successful people use some sort of calendar or planner, either digitally or on paper, to help them keep up with their appointments, assignments, tasks, and other important activities. It would be very difficult to find a successful person—no matter what they are successful at doing—who does not use a calendar. Using your head as your only planner, trying to remember everything you have to do without recording it anywhere, means that you will probably forget important events and deadlines.

Planning the Academic Term

Getting a bird's-eye view—or big picture—of each academic term will allow you to plan effectively. In preparing your calendar, first refer to your college **academic calendar**, which shows important dates that are specific to your campus: financial aid, registration, and add/drop deadlines; midterm and final exam dates; holidays; and graduation deadlines. Add important dates and deadlines to your calendar, such as when the registration starts and ends, when you need to pay for your courses, or when you should file your application for financial aid or scholarships. You may have received an academic calendar when you registered for classes; you can also find the academic calendar posted on your college website.

After adding these important dates, you should add deadlines for specific assignments, papers, and exams to your calendar. Remember that you have to keep track of important dates not only in your own life but also in the lives of those close to you—birthdays, doctors' appointments, work schedules that may keep changing, travel, your children's activities, visits from out-of-town guests, and so on. Different aspects of your life have different sorts of time requirements, and the goal is to stay on top of all of them.

You might prefer to use a digital calendar on your phone, tablet, laptop, or other devices. (See the Tech Tip at the end of this chapter for different options.) Regardless of the format you prefer, it's a good idea to begin the academic term by reviewing your syllabus for each course and then completing a preview (Figure 3.1), recording all of your commitments for each day, and using different colors for each category:

- Classes, tests, quizzes, and major assignment due dates (pink)
- Homework and study time for each class you're taking (green)
- Work (blue)
- Personal obligations, social activities, and other events (yellow)

Recording your daily commitments allows you to examine your toughest weeks each month and during the term. If research paper deadlines and test dates fall during the same week, find time to finish some assignments early to free up study time. If you use an electronic calendar, set reminders for these important deadlines and dates. If you are taking online courses, it is very important to understand that online course management systems do not allow late submissions. You must record the deadlines for submitting assignments and meet them all.

Overall, you should have monthly (Figure 3.1), weekly (Figure 3.2), and daily (Figure 3.3) views of your calendar. All three views are available when you use your digital devices to create them, but if you are using paper calendars, you can create monthly, weekly, and daily ones, too.

Once you complete your monthly templates, you can put them together to preview your entire academic term. Remember to provide details such as the number of hours you anticipate spending on each assignment or task.

FIGURE 3.1 > Monthly Calendar

Using the course syllabi provided by your instructors, create your own monthly calendars for your entire term. Provide details such as the number of hours you anticipate spending on each assignment or task.

Calendar ⌄		◀ **September** 2016 ▶				
● Work ● Classes ● Homework ● Events						
Sunday	**Monday**	**Tuesday**	**Wednesday**	**Thursday**	**Friday**	**Saturday**
			1	**2**	**3**	
4	**5**	**6** First Day of Classes 9-12 Psychology 2-5 Work 8-9 Psychology: Read Ch. 1	**7** 9-12 Work 1-4 Math 8-10 Math HW 1	**8** 10-1 English 2-5 Work 8-10 English: Read Ch. 1	**9** 10-12 Work 2-4 Mom's doctor's appointment 9-10 Psychology: Review Notes	**10** 10-4 Work 8-9 Math HW 1 9-10 English: Read Ch. 1
11 2-4 Review Math Notes 6-10 Party at Susan's [555-523-6898]	**12** 9-12 Work 1-5 Biology 6-8 Nina's Parent-Teacher Conference	**13** 9-12 Psychology 2-5 Work 8-10 Biology: Read Ch. 1	**14** 9-12 Work 1-4 Math 8-10 Psychology: Read Ch. 2	**15** 10-1 English 2-5 Work 7-8 Math HW 2 9-11 Biology: Read Ch. 1	**16** 10-12 Work 1-3 Lunch with Mary 6-7 Start English Summary Paper	**17** 10-4 Work 4-6 Shopping 9-10 Finish English Summary Paper
18 10-1 Study for Psychology Test 6-8 Review Math notes for Quiz 1	**19** 9-12 Work 1-5 Biology 7-10 Study for Psychology Test	**20** 9-12 Psychology Psychology Test 1 2-5 Work 8-9 Review Math Notes for Quiz 1(1 hr)	**21** Work 9-12 Math 1-4 Math Quiz 1 8-9 Revise English Summary Paper	**22** 10-1 English English Summary Paper due 2-5 Work 8-10 Biology: Read Ch. 2	**23** 10-12 Work 1-2 Attend Student Club Meeting 6-9 Math HW 3	**24** 10-4 Work 5-7 Psychology: Read Ch. 3 9-10 English: Read Ch. 2
25 10-12 Biology: Read Ch. 2 9-10 Biology: Lab Report 1	**26** 9-12 Work 1-5 Biology 6-8 Math Tutoring 10-11 Math HW 3	**27** 9-12 Psychology 2-5 Work 8-10 Biology: Read Ch. 3 10-11 Math HW 3	**28** 9-12 Work 1-4 Math 8-9 Psychology: Read Ch. 4 9-10 Prepare English Paper Outline	**29** 10-1 English 2-5 Work 7-9 Math HW 9-10 Review Biology Notes	**30** 10-12 Work 1-3 Meet with Biology Study Group 8-9 Biology: Lab Report 2 9-11 English: Read Ch. 3	**1** 10-4 Work 4-6 Nina's Birthday Party Preparation 8-9 English: Read Ch. 3

FIGURE 3.2 > Weekly Timetable

Using your term calendar, create your own weekly timetable using a conventional template or one that uses an app such as iCal or LifeTopix. At the beginning of your term, track all of your activities for a full week by entering into your schedule everything you do and how much time each task requires. Use this record to help you estimate the time you will need for similar activities in the future.

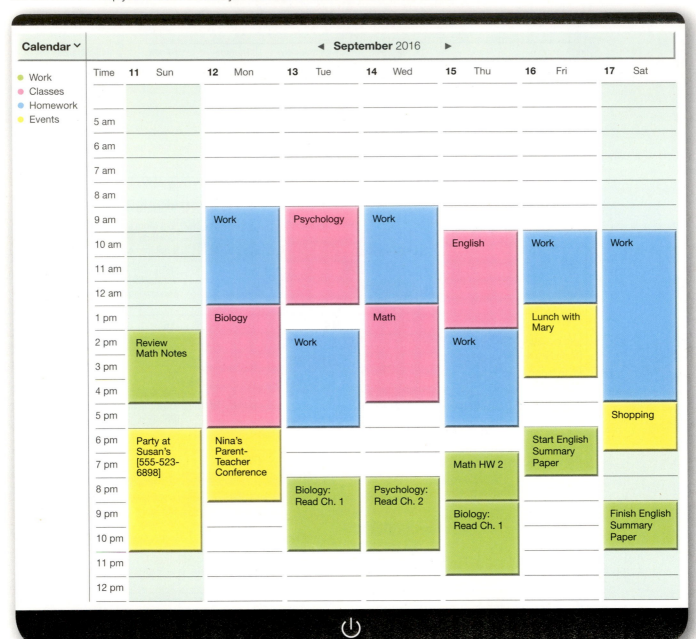

As you create your schedule, try to reserve study time for each class and for each assignment. Not all assignments are equal. Estimate how much time you will need for each one, and begin your work well before the assignment is due. Considering that these are estimates, you may have to revise them as you get more familiar with the demands of each course and better understand the actual time required to complete readings and assignments.

A good time manager frequently finishes assignments before actual due dates to allow for emergencies. If you are also working on or off campus, reconsider how many hours per week it will be reasonable for you to work above and beyond this commitment and whether you need to reduce your credit load or other obligations. Although you might have to work to pay your tuition or cover living expenses, many college students work too many hours just to support a certain lifestyle. Remember that managing your time effectively requires practice. You may have to rearrange your schedule a few times, rethink some priorities, and try to use your time differently. The more you apply time-management skills, the more time you can save. This time becomes available for other activities you might rather pursue. In this sense, time management makes time.

Being a good student does not necessarily mean studying day and night and doing little else. Scheduling time for work and pleasure is important, too. After all, most students have to juggle a *lot* of responsibilities. You might have to work to help pay for school, and you probably want to spend time with family or friends to recharge your battery—you might even need to take care of loved ones. And you will need time for yourself to relax and unwind; that time should include getting some exercise, and maybe reading a book for pleasure, or seeing a movie. Notice that the daily planner (Figure 3.3) includes time for other activities as well as time for classes and studying.

FIGURE 3.3 ❭ Daily Planner

Notice how college, work, and personal activities are noted on this daily planner.

Friday, September 30, 2016	
8 am	
9 am	
10 am	Work
11 am	
12 pm	
1 pm	Meet with Biology Study Group
2 pm	
3 pm	
4 pm	
5 pm	
6 pm	
7 pm	
8 pm	Biology: Lab Report 2
9 pm	
10 pm	English: Read Ch. 3
11 pm	

When using a digital calendar, it's a good idea to back up the calendar on iCloud or another online storage platform in case you lose your phone, experience a computer crash, or leave your charger at home. Carry your calendar with you in a place where you're not likely to lose it. Checking your calendar regularly helps you keep track of commitments and maintain control of your schedule. This practice will become invaluable to you in your career. Check your calendar daily for the current week as well as the coming week. It takes just a moment to be certain that you aren't forgetting something important, and it helps relieve stress. Consider setting regular times to check your calendar every day, perhaps right after eating breakfast or in the evening to see what's coming in the days and weeks ahead.

Keep the following points in mind as you organize your day:

- **Set realistic goals for your study time.** Assess how long it takes to read a chapter in different types of textbooks and how long it takes you to review your notes from different courses.

- **Use waiting, commuting, and travel time to review.** Allow time to review your notes after each class and as soon as you can. You can review your notes if you have a break between classes or while you're waiting for the bus or riding the train. If you have a long bus or train ride, consider formally budgeting this time in your planner, and use it wisely to study and review notes or listen to recorded notes. Make a habit of using waiting time, and soon you'll do it without even thinking—it becomes bonus study time to help compensate for unexpected events that might pop up in your day and throw off your schedule.

- **Limit distracting and time-consuming communications.** Check your phone, tablet, or computer for messages or updates at a set time, not whenever you think of it. Constant texting, browsing, or posting can keep you from achieving your academic goals. Particularly if you are taking online courses and need to be connected when studying, turn off all the notifications on your device to avoid being distracted. The notifications may tempt you to check messages or posts and waste valuable study time. Remember that when time has passed, you cannot get it back.

- **Avoid multitasking.** Multitasking, or doing more than one thing at a time, requires that you divide your attention among the tasks. You might think that you are good at multitasking. Most college students assume that multitasking is a skill. However, the reality is (and research shows) that you can get tasks done faster and more accurately if you concentrate on one at a time.[1] But don't take our word for it: Try setting aside time in your schedule to focus on one important task at a time; you'll probably find you do a better job on your assignment, test, or project and will remember more about the experience.

---

[1] E. Ophir, C. Nass, and A. Wagner, "Cognitive Control in Media Multitaskers," *Proceedings of The National Academy of Sciences* 106, no. 37 (2009): 15583–15587. Accessed November 24, 2015. http://www.pnas.org /content/106/37/15583.full.

- **Be flexible.** You cannot anticipate every disruption to your plans. Build extra time into your schedule so that unexpected events do not prevent you from meeting your goals. You need breaks in your schedule for relaxation, catching up with friends and family, or spending time in the cafeteria or campus center.

YOUR TURN > TRY IT

Use the following to map your schedule; include the most important tasks, exams, and assignment due dates for the current month. Later in the chapter you'll be asked to prioritize what you write here.

Month:

Sunday	Monday	Tuesday	Wednesday	Thursday	Friday	Saturday

Completing Large Assignments

Many students think they can start and finish a large assignment, such as a major paper, in the two or three days just before the due date. Even if you set aside a couple of days to only work on a large project, you can hardly use the time efficiently to finish it without any preparation and planning. For instance, if you have to write a ten-page paper, you will find it almost impossible to choose a topic, research it to find relevant information, take notes, create an outline, write a first draft, proofread, and revise your paper all in two or three days. The processes of gathering information and writing about a topic not only take time but also require thinking about and understanding the information for proper use in the paper.

Break large assignments such as major papers into smaller steps with deadlines. For example, you can establish a deadline for yourself to choose a topic. Then you can spend time over the next few weeks to research your topic, take notes, and begin drafting your paper. Breaking a large project into smaller steps is something you will probably have to do for yourself. Most instructors won't provide this level of detailed assistance for writing assignments during class time, but you can still meet with your instructors before or after class, during office hours, or online or seek help from the writing center tutors or your college librarians. Taking a step-by-step approach to your first few papers and projects will give you experience you can apply to your future coursework. It will also give you more control over how you are spending your time and energy and reduce your stress. Finally, talk to other successful students about how they have managed large projects.

Overcoming Procrastination

Procrastination is the habit of delaying something that needs your immediate attention. Putting things off can become a serious problem for college students. Students procrastinate for many reasons:

- Lack of motivation. Some students who are uncertain about the value of college may not be willing to do assigned work, even if a failing grade is the result.

- Fear of failure is common even among students who are highly motivated. Some students do not want to start a task because they feel they may not be successful at completing it and disappoint themselves, their parents, teachers, or peers.

- Some assigned work may seem boring or irrelevant. Students who have been given busywork in the past may assume that completing assignments is useless.

Taking the Procrastination Self-Assessment on the next page will help give you a sense of whether or not procrastination is a problem for you. If procrastination is indeed a problem for you, use the following strategies for beating it:

- Remind yourself of the possible consequences if you do not get down to work, and then get started. Also, remind yourself that simply not enjoying an assignment is not a good reason to put it off; it's an *excuse*, not a valid *reason*.

- Create a to-do list. Check off items as you get them done—this simple act can be gratifying and motivating in and of itself as you can visually track how much you accomplish. Use the list to focus on the things that aren't getting done. Move them to the top of the next day's list, and make up your mind to do them. Working from a list will also give you a feeling of accomplishment and the sense that you have taken control over the activity.

- Break big jobs into smaller steps. Tackle short, easy-to-accomplish tasks first.

PROCRASTINATION SELF-ASSESSMENT

Rate each statement about your work and study habits using the following scale:

1 = Strongly Disagree
2 = Disagree
3 = Mildly Disagree
4 = Agree
5 = Strongly Agree

_____ I have a habit of putting off important tasks that I don't enjoy doing.

_____ My standards are so high that I'm not usually satisfied enough with my work to turn it in on time.

_____ I spend more time planning what I'm going to do than actually doing it.

_____ The chaos in my study space makes it hard for me to get started.

_____ The people I live with distract me from doing my class work.

_____ I have more energy for a task if I wait until the last minute to do it.

_____ I enjoy the excitement of living on the edge.

_____ I have trouble prioritizing all my responsibilities.

_____ Having to meet a deadline makes me really nervous.

_____ My biggest problem is that I just don't know how to get started.

Now, count up how many statements you rated as 4 ("agree") or 5 ("strongly agree"):

If you responded that you "agree" or "strongly agree" with two questions or fewer, then you may procrastinate from time to time, but it may not be a major problem for you. Reading this chapter will help you continue to stay focused and avoid procrastination in the future.

If you responded that you "agree" or "strongly agree" with three to five questions, then you may be having difficulties with procrastination. Revisit the questions to which you answered "agree" or "strongly agree" and look in this chapter for strategies that specifically address these issues to help you overcome obstacles. You _can_ get a handle on your procrastination!

If you responded that you "agree" or "strongly agree" with six or more questions, then you may be having a significant problem with procrastination, and it could interfere with your success in college if you do not make a change. Revisit the questions to which you answered "agree" or "strongly agree" and look in this chapter for strategies that specifically address these issues. Also, if you are concerned about your pattern of procrastination and you aren't having success in dealing with it yourself, consider talking to a professional counselor in your campus counseling center. It's free and confidential, and counselors have extensive experience working with students who have problems with procrastination.

- Avoid doing other things that might seem more fun, and promise yourself a reward for finishing the task, such as watching your favorite TV show or going out with friends. For completing larger tasks and assignments, give yourself bigger and better rewards.

- Find a place to study that's comfortable and doesn't allow for distractions and interruptions.

- Say "no" to friends and family members who want your attention; agree to spend time with them later, and schedule that time.

- Shut off and put away all electronic devices during planned study sessions. If you *need* to use an electronic device for studying, turn off all social media and any other applications not part of your studying—and *keep* them off.

- Be aware that it might be more difficult to stay on track in your online courses as there are few or no weekly meetings with the online instructors and classmates. Connecting with another student in your online course can help both of you stay focused and organized as many online courses have several deadlines for submitting assignments, projects, and posting comments.

- Consider asking those living with you to help keep you on track. If they see that you are not studying when you should be, ask them to remind you to get back to the books. If you study in your room, close your door.

If you find that the above ideas and strategies to overcome procrastination don't motivate you to get to work, consider re-examining your purpose and priorities in terms of college. If you are not willing or able to stop procrastinating, maybe you are not ready to commit to academic priorities at this point in your life. Only you can decide, but an academic adviser or a counselor can help you sort it out. And remember that succeeding in your academic pursuits is one of the surest paths to increased success in life.

YOUR TURN › WORK TOGETHER

With two or three other students, discuss ways to avoid procrastination. What works for you? Share examples from your experiences.

Setting Priorities

To stop procrastinating, think about how to **prioritize,** which means putting your tasks, goals, and values in order of importance (in the section on Managing Your Energy later in this chapter, we'll discuss strategies to avoid becoming overextended. This goes hand in hand with setting priorities). Ask yourself which goals are most important but also which ones are most urgent. For example, studying in order to get a good grade on tomorrow's test may have to take priority over attending a job fair today, or completing an assignment that is due tomorrow may have to take priority over driving your friend somewhere.

However, don't ignore long-term goals in order to meet short-term goals. With good time management, you can study during the week prior to the test so that you can attend the job fair the day before. Skilled time managers often establish priorities by maintaining a to-do list on which they rank the items to determine schedules and deadlines for each task.

Once you have entered your future commitments in a term planner and decided how your time will be spent each week, create your to-do list, which is especially handy for last-minute reminders. A to-do list helps you keep track of errands to run, appointments to make, and anything else you might forget. You can keep this list on your cell phone or tablet, in a notebook, or on your bulletin board. Use your to-do list to keep track of *all* the tasks you need to remember, not just academics. Consider developing a system for prioritizing the items on your list: using different colors for different groups of tasks; highlighting the most important assignments; marking items with one, two, or three stars; or adding letters A, B, C, and so on to indicate what is most important (see Figure 3.4). Cross each task off your list as you complete it. You might be surprised by how much you can accomplish and how good you feel about it.

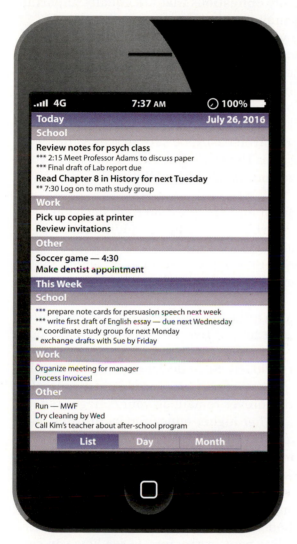

FIGURE 3.4 > To-Do List

A to-do list can help you keep track of the tasks you need to complete, appointments you need to make, and anything else you might forget. You can keep this list on your cell phone or tablet, in your notebook, or on your bulletin board. Use your to-do list to keep track of all the tasks you need to remember, not just academics. Consider prioritizing items with colors, stars, or letters.

YOUR TURN > DISCUSS IT

Review the calendar for this month that you mapped out on page 55, and use letters, numbers, or colors to prioritize your tasks. What are your most important obligations, other than your studies, that will have to fit into your time-management plan? Are any of them more important to you than doing well in college? Why or why not? Discuss your thoughts on these questions in a small group.

Finding a Balance. Another aspect of setting priorities while in college is finding a way to balance your academic schedule with the rest of your life. Social and extracurricular activities (e.g., participating in a club, writing for the college newspaper, attending lectures) are important parts of the college experience. Time spent alone and time spent thinking are also essential to your overall well-being.

For many students, the greatest challenge of prioritizing will be balancing college with work and family obligations that are equally important and are not optional. Advance planning will help you meet these challenges. You should also talk with your family members and your employer to make sure that they understand your academic responsibilities. For example, you may be able to take a day off from work to prepare yourself for the final exam for a challenging course. But keep in mind that your employer may not give you flexibility in your work schedule, so you should plan ahead. Most instructors will work with you when conflicts arise, but if you have problems that can't be resolved easily, be sure to seek support from your college's counseling center. The counselors will understand your challenges and help you prioritize your many responsibilities.

Staying Focused. Many students of all ages question their decision to attend college and sometimes feel overwhelmed by the additional responsibilities it brings. Some first-year students, especially recent high school graduates, might temporarily forget their main purposes for coming to college and spend their first term engaging in a wide array of new experiences.

Allowing yourself a little time to adjust to college is OK within limits, but you don't want to spend the next four or five years trying to make up for poor decisions made early in your college career, such as skipping class and not taking your assignments seriously. Such decisions can lead to a low GPA and the threat of academic probation or, worse, academic dismissal. Keep in mind that your grades will forever remain on your college transcript. If you plan to transfer to another higher education institution, you must send your transcript with your transfer application, and some employers might ask for a copy when you apply for a job.

A great way to focus (and to keep your priorities on track) is to finish what *needs* to be done before you move from work to pleasure. From time to time, you might have competing responsibilities; for example, you might have to work additional hours when you have an exam. In cases like these, talk to the people involved, including your instructors, to see how you can manage the conflict.

Appreciating the Value of Time

Think of the last time you made an appointment with someone who either forgot the appointment entirely or was very late. How did you feel? Were you upset or disappointed because the person wasted your time? Most of us have experienced the frustration of having someone else disrespect our time. In college, if you repeatedly arrive late for class or leave early, you are breaking the basic rules of politeness and showing a lack of respect for your instructors and your classmates.

> **Getting from Here to There**

College students have the responsibility to get themselves to class on time and must plan transportation carefully, whether walking, driving, bicycling, ride-sharing, taking public transportation, or using another method of getting from place to place. If you have an emergency situation that causes you to run late, talk to your instructor. He or she will understand a real emergency and help you make up work you missed.

Forestpath/Shutterstock.com

Punctuality, or being on time, is expected in college, at work, and elsewhere in our society. Being strictly on time may be a difficult adjustment for you if you grew up in a home or culture that is more flexible in its approach to time, but it is important to recognize the value of punctuality. Although you should not have to alter your cultural identity to succeed in college, you must be aware of and meet the expectations that instructors typically have for students.

Here are a few basic guidelines for respectful behavior in class and in other interactions with instructors:

- Be in class on time. This means getting enough sleep at night and waking up at a time that allows you to arrive in class early enough to take off your coat, shuffle through your backpack, and have your completed assignments and notebooks ready to go. Make transportation plans in advance (and have a backup plan). There might be consequences for being late to class. Some professors may penalize you and not accept any excuses. Check the syllabus for the instructor's attendance policy.

- Be on time for all scheduled appointments.

- Avoid behaviors that show a lack of respect for both the instructor and other students, such as answering your cell phone during class, unless it is a legitimate emergency. Similarly, texting, doing homework for another class, falling asleep, talking (even whispering) during a lecture, or even wearing caps or hats in class are all considered rude by some instructors.

Not only is time management important for you, but it is also a way in which you show respect for your coworkers, friends, family, and college instructors—and yourself.

List your current priorities in order of importance. What does your list say about you and your values? Why do you consider some things more important? Less important? As you review your list, think about whether you have put any items in the wrong place. What should you change, and why?

More Important	Important	Less Important	Not Important
1.	1.	1.	1.
2.	2.	2.	2.
3.	3.	3.	3.
4.	4.	4.	4.
5.	5.	5.	5.

3.2

MANAGING YOUR ENERGY

Your best plans will not work if you do not have the energy to make them happen. You may plan to spend a couple of hours on your math homework before you go to bed in the evening after a busy day. However, you may find that you are too tired to concentrate and solve the math problems. While learning to manage your time effectively, you must also learn to manage your energy so that you have more control over your life and can achieve success in college.

Along with time, energy is an essential resource, and we have a choice in how we use it. Although energy is renewable, each one of us has a limited amount of it in the 24-hour day. Each person has a daily pattern of physical, emotional, and mental activity. For instance, some people are early risers and have a lot of energy in the morning to get things done; others feel the least energetic and productive in the morning and can accomplish tasks at the end of the day more effectively, especially those tasks that require mental energy and concentration. You can better manage your energy by recognizing your daily pattern and establishing a routine around it. Use Table 3.1 to record your high, average, and low energy level every day for one week. Use **H** for high, **A** for average, and **L** for low to identify which times of day you feel more or less energetic.

TABLE 3.1 ❯ Monitoring Your Energy Level

Time	Sun	Mon	Tues	Wed	Thurs	Fri	Sat
	Energy Level						
Early morning							
Late morning							
Early afternoon							
Late afternoon							
Evening							
Late evening							
Late night							

What did you learn about yourself by completing Table 3.1? What are the best and worst times for you to study? Considering your daily energy level, obligations, and potential distractions, decide whether you study more effectively in the morning, afternoon, evening, or some combination. Determine whether you are capable of getting up very early in the morning to study or how late you can stay up at night and still get to morning classes on time.

Your energy level also depends on your diet and other habits such as exercise or lack of it. If you are juggling many responsibilities across several locations, you can use some very simple strategies to take care of yourself:

- Carry healthy snacks with you, such as fruit, nuts, or yogurt. You'll save time and money by avoiding trips to snack bars and convenience stores, and you'll keep your energy up by eating better.
- Drink plenty of water.
- Take brief naps when possible. Research shows that naps are more effective than caffeine.[2]

Establishing a Routine

Consider what you have learned about yourself by completing Table 3.1. Now that you have a sense of the best and worst times for you to study, establish a study routine that is based on your daily energy pattern. The more firmly you set a specific time to study, the more effective you will be

---

[2] S. Medrick, D. Cai, S. Kanady, and S. Drummond, "Comparing the Benefits of Caffeine, Naps and Placebo on Verbal, Motor and Perceptual Memory," *Behavioural Brain Research* 193, no. 1 (2008): 79–86.

> **Stay Awake**
Like this student, you probably have a lot of demands on your time. Make sure to effectively manage your energy by getting enough rest, eating properly, and pacing yourself, or you might find yourself falling asleep while studying.
© 237/Sam Edwards/Ocean/Corbis

at keeping up with your schedule. If you have more energy on the weekend, for example, take advantage of that time to review or catch up on major projects, such as term papers, that can't be completed effectively in short blocks of time. Break down large tasks and focus on one thing at a time to make progress toward your academic goals.

Schedule some down-time for yourself to regain your energy. Different activities help different people relax and get energized. For example, you may watch TV for an hour or take a nap before you start doing your homework. Just make sure that you do not go over the amount of time you set aside as your down-time.

YOUR TURN ❯ STAY MOTIVATED

Are you trying to do too much, and is your crazy schedule reducing your motivation for college? Are you working too many hours? Are you feeling really stressed out? In a small group, discuss strategies for reducing your stress level and maintaining your motivation for being successful in your academic work.

Being Overextended

Being **overextended,** or having too much to do given your available resources, is a primary source of stress for college students. Determine what a realistic workload is for you, but note that this can vary significantly from one person to another, and only you can determine what is realistic. Although being involved in social and family life is very important, try not to allow your academic work to take a backseat to other time commitments. Take on only what you can handle. Learn to say "no," as this is an effective time-management strategy! Say "no" to requests that will prevent you from meeting your academic goals. Remember that even if you can find the time for extra tasks, you may not be able to find the energy. If you are feeling stressed, reassess your time commitments and let go of one or more. If you choose to drop a course, make sure you do so before the drop deadline so that you won't have a low grade on your permanent record. If you receive financial aid, keep in mind that you must be registered for a minimum number of credit hours to be considered a full-time student to receive your current level of financial aid (you will read more about financial aid in the next section of this chapter).

YOUR TURN > WORK TOGETHER

Energy management often requires the use of the word *no*. Discuss with another student how saying "no" relates to the way you can manage your energy.

MANAGING YOUR MONEY

3.3

Lack of money—just like lack of time—can lead to stress, which will use up energy you need for studying and other commitments. Because college is expensive, and most students have limited financial resources, a budget for college is a must. As with time and energy, you have control over how you spend money. By using the tools and strategies in this section, your level of control over money will increase.

Let's begin by learning how to budget. A **budget** is a spending plan that tracks all sources of income (financial aid, wages, money from parents, etc.) and expenses (rent, tuition, books, etc.) during a set period of time (weekly, monthly, etc.). Creating and following a budget will allow you to pay bills on time, cut costs, put some money away for emergencies, and finish college with as little debt as possible.

Budgeting

A budget will help you to live within your means, put money into savings, and possibly invest down the road. Here are a few tips to help you get started:

- **Gather basic information.** First, determine how much money is coming in (from a job, your savings, gifts from relatives, student loans, scholarship dollars, or grants) and when. List all your income sources, making note of how often you receive each type of income (weekly paychecks, quarterly loan payments, one-time gifts) and how much money you can expect each time.

- **Determine where your money is going and when.** Track your spending for a week or two (or, even better, a full month) by recording every bill you pay and every purchase you make. The kinds of expenses you should consider, like rent/mortgage, utilities, gas, food, or child care, will vary depending on your situation. If you are a returning student with a job and a family of your own to support, you will calculate your expenses differently than if you are a full-time college student fresh out of high school. Whatever your situation, keeping track of your expenses and learning about your spending behaviors are important habits to develop.

- **Build a plan.** Knowing when your money is coming in will help you decide how to structure your budget. For example, if most of your income comes in monthly, you'll want to create a monthly budget. If you are paid every other week, a biweekly budget might work better. Several tools are available online to help you create a budget, such as easy-to-use spreadsheets or budget wizards that you can download for free. To sample what's available, visit CashCourse (**cashcourse.org**). You can also use apps such as Pocket Expense Personal Finance, Goodbudget Budget Planner, Best Budget, or Money Monitor.

- **Identify fixed and variable expenses.** A **fixed expense** is one that will cost you the same amount every time you pay it (like your rent). A **variable expense** is one that may change (like textbooks, because the number and cost of them will be different each term). Although you will know, more or less, how much your fixed expenses will be during each budget period, you might need to estimate your variable expenses with expected costs. Use past bills, credit card statements, and previous receipts to make informed guesses. When you are in doubt, it is always better to overestimate your expenses to avoid shortfalls at the end of your budget period.

- **Do a test run and make adjustments.** Use your budget plan for a few weeks and see how things go, recording your actual costs as you pay them. Whatever you do, don't give up if your bottom line is less than you expected. Budgeting is a lot like dieting; you might slip up and eat a pizza (or spend too much buying one), but all is not lost. If you stay focused and flexible, your budget can lead you to financial stability and independence.

Cutting Costs

Once you have put together a working budget, tried it out, and adjusted it, you're likely to discover that your expenses may be more than your income. Don't panic. Simply begin to look for ways to reduce those expenses. Here are some tips for saving money in college:

- **Recognize the difference between your needs and your wants.** A *need* is something you must have (like tuition and textbooks). On the other hand, your *wants* are goods and services that you wish to purchase but

Use the following chart to begin planning your budget. Add additional rows for other expense categories that apply to you. Then find a good online budget calculator, plug in your numbers, and build your budget from there.

Monthly Budget Worksheet			
Cost Category	Fixed or Variable Expense	Expected Cost	Actual Cost
Rent/Mortgage			
Electricity			
Heat			
Water			
Cable/Internet			
Cell phone			
Transportation (bus/train fare)			
Car payment			
Auto insurance			
Medical expenses			
Food (groceries, meals at school, snacks, eating out)			
Tuition			
Books			
Child care			
Miscellaneous			
Total expenses			
Income			
– Total expenses			
= Amount of Savings			

could live without (like concert tickets and $8 lattes). Your budget should always provide for your needs before your wants.

- **Use low-cost transportation.** If owning a car takes up too much of your budget, consider lower-cost options such as taking public transportation, biking to college, carpooling with other students, or participating in a ride-sharing program.

- **Seek out discount entertainment options.** Take advantage of discounted or free tickets to concerts, movie theaters, sporting events, or other special events through your college.

- **Buy secondhand goods.** Use online resources such as Craigslist or thrift stores such as Goodwill to save a lot of money.

- **Avoid unnecessary fees.** Making late payments on your bills can lead to expensive fees and can lower your credit score (which in turn will raise your interest rates). You might want to set up automatic online payments to avoid making this costly mistake. Two of the most common and unnecessary fees many college students end up with are parking and library fines. You need to be aware that if you owe these, many colleges will not issue your transcripts or your degree or even let you register for the next term.

Understanding Financial Aid

Very few students can pay the costs of attending college without some kind of help. Luckily, several sources of **financial aid**—sources of money that support your education—are available, such as the following:

- **Student loans** are a form of financial aid that must be paid back with interest.
- **Grants** are funds provided by the government or private organizations to help students pay for college. Grants do not need to be repaid, but most of them are given to students based on their financial needs. Some grants are specific to certain areas of study.
- **Scholarships** are funds that are given to students based on their academic performance but may also be based on need.
- **Work-study** means that students who are enrolled in college and are receiving financial aid can also have part-time jobs to help cover their education expenses not covered by their aid amount.

Many students manage to enroll and succeed in college with little or no financial support from their families or employers because of the financial aid they receive. Most financial assistance requires some form of application. To receive federal aid, students must complete the U.S. Department of Education's Free Application for Federal Student Aid (FAFSA) every year. The financial aid staff at your college can help you find the way to get the largest amount of grant and scholarship money, the lowest interest rate on loans, and work-study possibilities that fit your academic program.

‹ Show Me the Money

Don't let the paperwork scare you away. If you're not already receiving financial aid, be sure to consider all the available options. And remember that your college may also offer scholarships or grants, which you don't have to repay. Talk to an adviser in your college's financial aid office to find out if you qualify for any type of aid.

While scholarships and grants are the best forms of aid because they do not have to be repaid, the federal government, states, and colleges offer many other forms of assistance, such as loans and work-study opportunities. You might also be able to obtain funds from your employer, a local or national organization, or a private foundation. In your search for support, however, beware of scams; there may be people in your area or online who use false advertising and do not tell you about the high interest rates you may be charged when you borrow money from them. Your college's financial aid office is the best place to explore sources of college funding.

Keeping Your Funding

Once you receive financial aid, make sure that you remain qualified. If you earn at least average grades, complete your courses each term, and finish your program or degree on time, you should have no trouble maintaining your financial aid. Make the grade to save your aid.

Dropping or failing a class might put all or part of your financial aid at risk. Talk with a financial aid counselor before dropping a course to be sure you meet the minimum requirements for credit hours with your other courses. If you do decide to drop a course, do so officially. Some students think that if they just stop attending a class, they have dropped it. Without the proper paperwork, however, you are still enrolled in the course and will receive a failing grade and a bill even if you have not been attending.

Achieving a Balance between Working and Borrowing

After developing your budget, deciding what you can pay from savings (if anything), and taking scholarships and grants into consideration, you might still need more income. Each academic term or year, you should decide how much you can work while maintaining good grades and how much you should borrow in the form of student loans.

Paid employment while you are in college can be important for reasons other than money. Having a job in a field related to your major can help make you more employable later because it shows you have the capability to manage several priorities at the same time.

Understanding and Managing Credit Wisely

Your **credit score** is a single number that comes from a report that has information about accounts in your name such as credit cards, student loans, utility bills, cell phones, car loans, and so on. This score can determine whether or not you will qualify for a loan (car, home, student, etc.), what interest rates you will pay, how much your car insurance will cost, and your chances of being hired by some organizations as some employers may check your credit information before they decide to offer you a job.

While using credit cards responsibly is a good way to build credit, acquiring a credit card has become much more difficult for college students. Since May 2009, college students under the age of 21 cannot get a credit card unless they can prove they are able to make the payments or unless the credit card application is cosigned by a parent or guardian.

Even if you prove you can repay credit card debt, it is important for you to fully understand how credit cards work and how they can both help and hurt you. (Table 3.2 on page 71 lists credit card dos and don'ts). A credit card allows you to buy something now and pay for it later. Each month you will receive a statement listing all purchases you made using your credit card during the previous 30 days. The statement will request a payment toward your balance and will set a payment due date. Your payment options will vary: You can pay your entire balance, pay a specified amount of the balance, or pay only a minimum payment, which may be as low as $10.

Be careful. If you make only a minimum payment, the remaining balance on your card will be charged a finance fee, or interest charge, causing your balance to increase before your next bill arrives even if you don't make any more purchases. Paying the minimum payment is almost never a good strategy and can add years to your repayment time. In fact, if you have a 13 percent interest rate and you continue to pay only $10 per month toward a $500 credit card balance, it will take you more than five years to pay it off! You'll pay more than $200 in interest—increasing the amount you'll pay for your original purchase by nearly 50 percent.

If you decide to apply for a credit card while you're in college, remember that credit cards should be used to build credit and to handle emergencies. They should not be used to buy things that you want but do not need. However, if you use your credit card just once a month and pay the balance as soon as the bill arrives, you will be on your way to a strong credit score in just a few years.

YOUR TURN > DISCUSS IT

Do you have your own credit card or one that you own jointly with your parents or spouse? If not, what are your reasons for not getting one? If you do have a card, do you feel you're in control of the way you use it? Why or why not? If you don't have a card, do you think you are ready for one? Why or why not?

Managing Debit Cards

Although you might wish to use a credit card for emergencies and to establish a good credit rating, you might also look into the possibility of applying for a debit card. The big advantage of a debit card is that you don't always have to carry cash and thus don't run the risk of losing it or having it stolen. A disadvantage is that a debit card provides direct access to your checking account, so it's important that you keep your card in a safe place and away from your personal identification number (PIN). The safest way to protect your account is to commit your PIN to memory. If you lose your debit card or credit card, notify your bank immediately.

Another advantage of a debit card is that if you choose not to participate in your bank's overdraft protection program, the amount of

‹ Debit or Credit?

Credit card use is hugely tempting. And credit card debt has now become a major cause of college students dropping out. Don't fall into this trap.

Image Source/Getty Images

your purchases will be limited to the funds in your bank account. (Overdraft protection links your checking account to a savings account, credit card, or line of credit and uses that account to pay transactions that would have otherwise triggered an overdraft fee or been declined for insufficient funds available.) In this case, using a debit card versus a credit card can help you limit your spending. Although the term *overdraft protection* may sound appealing, keep in mind that if you choose to enroll in such a program, your bank may charge a hefty fee if you spend even just a little more than what you have in your account. And speaking of fees, be aware that if you use your debit card to withdraw cash from an ATM outside your bank's network, you will likely be charged a transaction fee.

TABLE 3.2 › Credit Card Dos and Don'ts

Dos	Don'ts
Do have a credit card for emergencies if possible, even if a family member cosigns for it. And remember: Spring break is not an emergency!	**Don't** use your credit card to bridge the gap between the lifestyle you would like to have and the one you can actually afford.
Do use your credit card to build credit by making small charges and paying them off each month.	**Don't** use your credit card to make unnecessary purchases.
Do set up automatic online payments to avoid expensive late fees. Remember that the payment due date is the date the payment should be received by the credit card lender, not the date you send it.	**Don't** make late payments. Paying your bill even one day late can result in a finance charge and raise the interest rate on that card and your other credit accounts.
Do keep an eye on your credit report by visiting a free website such as **AnnualCreditReport.com** or **creditkarma.com** at least once a year.	**Don't** share your credit card number and information with anyone.

Avoiding Identity Theft

If you have a credit or debit card, you should protect your personal information against **identity theft,** which is a crime that occurs when someone uses another person's personal information. Carefully guard your social security number, credit or debit card numbers and PINs, bank account numbers, passwords, and any other identifying information that might enable someone to pretend to be you.

Identity theft can result in financial loss, ruined credit, or a harmful reputation. In some cases, the person who takes over the victim's identity may use funds in his or her accounts, apply for a credit card and use it, get loans, and even commit a crime. It is very costly for a victim to get the money back and rebuild his or her reputation. Here are a few tips to avoid identity theft:

- Shred documents that contain personal information when discarding them.
- Change your passwords frequently, and do not use your date of birth, mother's maiden name, or the last four digits of your social security number as a password.
- Review your bank, debit, and credit card statements closely, and immediately report any charges you do not recognize to your bank or your credit card company.
- When viewing personal information online, make sure your Internet connection is secure. When checking your bank account, paying bills, or shopping online with a credit card, avoid open networks such as those often available at airports and coffee shops. Only secure networks are appropriate for tasks such as these.
- You should only enter your personal and financial information on secure websites. Before doing that, you need to check the URL of the website to make sure that it starts with "https://" which indicates that there is a layer of security added.
- Use a computer virus protection software program, and update it regularly.

GET ORGANIZED—DIGITALLY

Mapping out your schedule is easy. Think of your calendar as a compass. It's a guide for navigating your current term that will also keep you pointed toward your long-term goals.

THE PROBLEM *You keep forgetting assignments and can't find your paper calendar.*

THE FIX *Replace the paper calendar with a free electronic calendar or phone app.*

HOW TO DO IT

Pick one of the following:

Google calendar (google.com/calendar)
It's free, it syncs with every type of device, and it is connected with a free Gmail account that includes document creation and storage software. With this Web application, you can input assignment deadlines and reminders, sync with group members' calendars during group projects, and even manage your social life by loading Facebook events.

iStudiez Pro app for Mac, iPhone, and iPad (istudentpro.com)
Rated the Best College Student App for 2011, iStudiez allows you to sync the following information across devices: a daily schedule, your calendar by term, assignments, grades, and instructor information.

Studious for Android (play.google .com/store/apps/details?id=com .young.studious)
If you own an Android device and want to ditch your paper planner, try out Studious. It is an all-in-one app for tracking your schedule, including upcoming homework deadlines, and can also be used for taking and managing notes. Best of all, it's free.

Then, take these steps:

- Find out if your college sells a special planner in the campus bookstore with important dates or deadlines already marked, or get the academic calendar from your school's website. If neither of the first two suggestions works for you, then grab a sheet of paper or download a blank calendar template from the Internet.

- Draw up a plan for the term, entering your commitments for each week: classes, work hours, assignment deadlines, study groups (including contact numbers), and exam and dates when school is not in session. Enter this information into an electronic calendar, or write it onto a blank calendar.

- Transfer all the information into Outlook, iCal, or a similar Share-Ware program. When you open Outlook or iCal, you can view by day, week, or month. Simply click on a date or time slot, follow instructions on the toolbar to create a new entry, and start typing.

- Highlight the most important deadlines and activities. As you type in each new entry, you'll have the option to color-code items by category (e.g., school, work, family). Set reminder alarms to keep yourself on track.

- Use the to-do list on the side of the screen to jot down and prioritize tasks. Start a new to-do list every day or once a week. Every time you complete a task, delete it from the list. You can attach due dates to each task, and set up reminders.

- Back up everything by syncing your calendar and to-do list with other electronic devices. If you need help, visit your college's computer lab or information technology (IT) department. Alternately, turn to an organized friend for advice, or click to an Outlook tutorial on the Internet. As backup, file your original paper calendar away in case you experience technical difficulties down the road.

3

THINK
WRITE
APPLY

This chapter provided several strategies to manage your time, energy, and money. Which one is the hardest for you to manage? Why? What did you learn in this chapter that you think can help you in dealing with the challenges?

WRITE

It can be frustrating to realize that you have to spend time organizing your-self in order to manage your time effectively. Write down a summary of the time-management tips in this chapter that appealed to you and explain why.

_____

_____

_____

_____

_____

_____

APPLY

1. Take control of distractions you know are difficult for you. When you allow distractions to take control of your life, you may feel anxiety about the areas of your life you have ignored. On the next page are some possible dis-tractions. Choose Yes (a problem) or No (not a problem) for each one. Are the problems you identify controllable? If so, what solutions might help you take control of your time? Use this worksheet to increase your aware-ness of what distractions are tripping you up and how to overcome them.

2. Money is a difficult subject to talk about, and sometimes it seems easier not to worry about it. Ask yourself hard questions. Do you spend money without much thought? Do you have a lot of debt? Click around the resources available at **cashcourse.org**. What did you find that can help you? Go to the notebook or file where you have taken notes on this chap-ter, and reflect and write about your thoughts on these questions.

3. Devote more time building and refining the budget that you began in the Your Turn: Try It on page 67. In the notebook or file where you have been taking notes on this chapter, write down some observations about what you have learned about your spending habits.

4. Using the templates for calendars provided in this chapter, set up a monthly calendar for all the months in this academic term. Include all of your classes. Set up a weekly calendar for the next two full weeks that are approaching, and include the due dates for all assignments during this time. Then create specific to-do lists for your first three assignments.

Possible Distractions	Yes (Y) No (N)	Controllable (C) Uncontrollable (U)	Solutions?
Cell phone			
Internet (e.g., Twitter/ Instagram)			
Gaming/videos/music			
Sports/hobbies			
Television/online videos			
Lack of sleep			
Relationship problems			
Meals/snacks			
Daydreaming			
Perfectionism			
Errands/shopping			
Lost items			
Worries/stress			
Socializing/friends			
Multitasking			
Illness (yours or someone else's)			
Work schedule			
Pleasure reading			
Family members			

USE YOUR RESOURCES

Below are suggestions for resources that are available at many colleges and the online resources that are available to everyone.

AT YOUR COLLEGE

VISIT . . .	IF YOU NEED HELP . . .
Learning Center	reading textbooks, taking notes, and studying for exams.
Counseling Center	dealing with time management, stress management, or money problems related to compulsive shopping or gambling.
Financial Aid and Scholarship Office	applying for scholarships, grants, and loans.
Career Center	finding a job, preparing résumés, or developing interview skills.
Fitness Center	keeping up an exercise routine.

ONLINE

GO TO . . .	IF YOU NEED HELP . . .
TedEd: Lessons Worth Sharing: ed.ted.com/on/7iFzKKiq	making effective to-do lists.
Budget Wizard: cashcourse.org	creating and managing your budget. The National Endowment for Financial Education (NEFE) offers this free, secure, budgeting tool.
Free Application for Federal Student Aid: fafsa.ed.gov	applying for financial aid. The online form allows you to set up an account, complete the application electronically, save your work, and monitor the progress of your application.
FastWeb: FastWeb.com	looking for free scholarships and discovering sources of educational funding you never knew existed.
Bankrate: bankrate.com	understanding credit card interest rates, fees, and penalties. This free website provides unbiased information about the interest rates, fees, and penalties associated with major credit cards and private loans. It also provides calculators that let you determine the long-term costs of different kinds of borrowing.

MY COLLEGE'S RESOURCES

_____

_____

_____

LaunchPad for *Understanding Your College Experience* is a great resource. Go online to master concepts using the LearningCurve study tool and much more. **macmillanhighered.com/gardnerunderstanding**

4 Discovering How You Learn

PRE-READING ACTIVITY: Think about something new you have learned recently in college, and in the spaces provided, specify what you learned, who helped you learn it, and how you learned it.

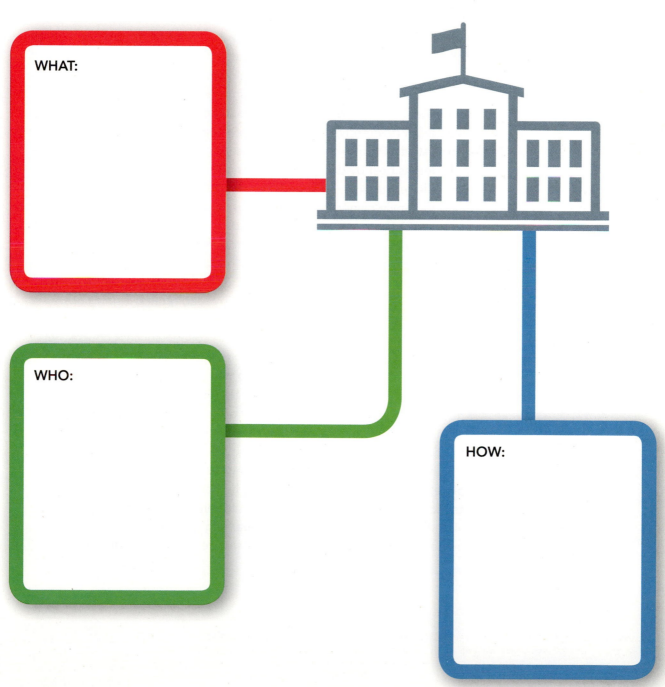

WHAT:

WHO:

HOW:

PROFILE

Daniel Graham, 24

Computer Science Major, *Harold Washington College,* *City Colleges of Chicago*

Eurobanks/Shutterstock.com

Daniel Graham from Harold Washington College, a two-year college in the City Colleges of Chicago system, didn't have much knowledge of how he learned before he started college. During high school, he struggled with some courses so much that he decided not to attend college right after graduation. A few years later, having heard from some of his high school friends about Harold Washington College and how it helped them with opportunities to be successful in receiving degrees, Daniel decided to give it a try. In his first term at the college, he enrolled in a college success course and discovered that people learn differently, and these ways of learning are referred to as learning styles. He also took a learning styles inventory and discovered that he learns best by doing. Daniel was not surprised because, like many other college students, he spends ten to fifteen hours a week working. "I work for a family-owned landscaping business." he says. "I like being able to use my hands and express myself, and I like being able to figure things out just by playing with them for a bit." He adds that he uses this hands-on approach in college by doing things like taking practice exams until he feels ready for the real exam.

Daniel realized that by reading and writing down material from class and successfully using several strategies that he learned in the college success course, he can learn more effectively. For example, he rewrites terms and concepts in his own words so that he better understands what they mean, and he uses note cards to help him memorize. Daniel says, "Knowing how I learn has improved my performance. When I take notes, I read them silently on note cards and continue to return to them, so I can memorize the meaning."

In the future, Daniel plans to finish his associate's degree and then explore job opportunities. In ten years, he hopes to be working in computer science, and he plans to continue to rely on his learning styles. He advises fellow students: "Apply your learning style to your everyday life. Eventually, you will learn in a different, smarter, and more efficient way."

> "Knowing how I learn has improved my performance."

macmillan learning

To access the Learning-Curve study tool, Video Tools, and more, go to LaunchPad for *Understanding Your College Experience.* macmillanhighered.com /gardnerunderstanding

To do well in college, understanding how you learn is important. Maybe you have trouble paying attention to a long lecture, or maybe listening is the way you learn best. You might like classroom discussion, or you might consider hearing what other students have to say in class a big waste of time. In almost all courses, you'll learn by reading printed or electronic textbooks or online and digital content.

College instructors have their own ways of teaching and communicating. You might notice these differences in the ways that courses are organized and taught. Many instructors lecture; others use lots of visual aids. In science courses, instructors will help you conduct experiments or lead field trips where you can observe or touch what you are studying. In dance, theater, or physical education courses, learning takes place in both your body and your mind. You've read about the importance of building relationships with your instructors, and in order to do this you'll have to navigate differences in how your instructors communicate. You might find that some instructors are friendly and warm, while others seem to want little interaction with students.

This chapter begins with an exploration of learning theory—that is, how and in what environments the brain works to produce learning. We will then introduce you to three ways to think about your personal approach to learning: the VARK Learning Styles Inventory, the Myers–Briggs Type Indicator (MBTI), and the Theory of Multiple Intelligences. The VARK will help you explore your learning preferences, the MBTI will introduce you to how basic personality characteristics affect learning, and the theory of Multiple Intelligences will help you realize how different abilities link to learning. These learning frameworks will help you think of ways to meet the expectations of each course and instructor. This chapter will also explore learning disabilities, which are common among college students.

4.1

HOW PEOPLE LEARN

People learn differently, and understanding how the brain functions helps explain why. An entire field of study called neuroscience focuses on the brain. Neuroscientists and psychologists have developed many theories about how and why people learn differently. Some of the many theories about learning are relevant for college students, especially first-year students.

Learning Theories

One of the most well-known learning theories comes from Abraham Maslow, a psychologist.[1] Using Maslow's "hierarchy of needs," one might logically argue that in order for students to learn, their needs must be

---

[1] A. H. Maslow, *Motivation and Personality* (New York: Harper & Row, 1970).

FIGURE 4.1 › The Hierarchy of Needs Pyramid

This figure illustrates Maslow's theory. IQoncept/Shutterstock.com

- SELF-ACTUALIZATION
- SELF-ESTEEM
- LOVE & BELONGING
- SAFETY & SECURITY
- PHYSIOLOGICAL NEEDS

met—basic needs such as food, water, and shelter; safety and security needs such as employment and property; needs for love and belonging; needs for self-esteem that comes from achievement, and self-actualization that can be reached through having a purpose and meeting your potential. You probably have found that when you're hungry, fearful, or lonely, it is very hard—nearly impossible—to learn effectively. If your basic needs are met, you develop friendships, and you experience success, it becomes easier to focus on your courses and continue to learn.

Albert Bandura, a psychological researcher, developed a theory of social learning, which suggests that people learn from each other by observing others' actions and the results of those actions.[2] These observations help them repeat or avoid certain attitudes and behaviors. If you had older brothers and sisters, you probably observed their interactions in the family and learned how to stay out of trouble with your parents. In college you will observe other students—those who are successful and those who are not. If you pay attention, you can figure out what behaviors actually lead to success. It's not just about "being smart." Successful students come to class, spend time studying, interact with instructors, and take advantage of the academic support available on campus.

In her work on how adult students learn, Nancy Schlossberg, a counseling psychologist, developed a theory of transition.[3] She found that adults learn new roles when they go through change or transition in their lives. As adults, we constantly change our roles; for example, we change from being a high school student to a college student, from a college student to an employee, or from an employee to a college student. Often we juggle multiple roles at the same time. We also experience changes in our personal roles when we get married or divorced or have children. The transition theory states that change actually helps adults grow and learn new ways of thinking and behaving. During the transition process, the more help and support we receive from people around us, the more easily we will adapt to change. For example, college students who ask for help from their instructors, classmates, tutors, advisers, and even their families and friends can make a more successful transition to college life and deal with the challenges of a new environment more effectively than students who do not seek such assistance.

---

[2]A. Bandura, *Social Learning Theory* (Englewood Cliffs, NJ: Prentice Hall, 1977).

[3]M. Anderson, J. Goodman, and N. Schlossberg, *Counseling Adults in Transition: Linking Theory with Practice in a Diverse* World (New York: Springer, 2011).

Learning Styles

In addition to looking at theories about learning, we can think about how people learn by focusing on personal learning styles. Simply put, learning styles are ways of learning. Through work and other prior experience, you may have some sense of how you like or don't like to learn. At the start of the chapter, we asked you to consider how you learn best: listening in lectures, reading your textbooks, doing experiments in science labs, working in groups, and so on. These "preferences" that you have relate to your learning style. Researchers have developed formal methods and tools—some are simple, and some are complex—to identify, describe, and understand the different learning preferences. These tools help students learn to adapt their learning styles to different classroom situations. Remember, it is your responsibility to take charge of your learning in order to be successful in college.

In this chapter, we introduce three of the most commonly used tools and theories for understanding learning styles. They all can help you to begin discovering your *own* learning style and strategies for improving your learning. These are the VARK Learning Styles Inventory, the Myers–Briggs Type Indicator, and Multiple Intelligences. As you are making these discoveries, keep in mind that your learning style cannot be boiled down to one or two defining characteristics, especially given that learning styles are complex and can vary based on content and context. But the knowledge you will gain about yourself from working through this chapter is a significant step in taking responsibility for your learning.

THE VARK LEARNING STYLES INVENTORY

4.2

The **VARK Inventory** includes a sixteen-item questionnaire that focuses on how learners prefer to use their senses (hearing, seeing, writing and reading, or experiencing) to learn. The letters in VARK stand for *visual, aural, read/write,* and *kinesthetic.*

- **Visual learners** prefer to learn information through charts, graphs, symbols, and other visual means.
- **Aural learners** prefer to hear information.
- **Read/write learners** prefer to learn information that is displayed as words.
- **Kinesthetic learners** prefer to learn through experience and practice, whether simulated or real.

To determine your learning style according to the VARK Inventory, respond to the following questionnaire (you can also take the VARK online at **vark-learn.com/the-vark-questionnaire**).

This questionnaire is designed to tell you about your preferences in working with information. Choose answers that explain your preference(s). Select *as many boxes as apply to you.* If none of the options applies to you, leave the question blank.

1. You are helping someone who wants to go to the airport, town center, or railway station. You would:
   - ☐ A. go with her.
   - ☐ B. tell her the directions.
   - ☐ C. write down the directions.
   - ☐ D. draw, or show her a map, or give her a map.

2. You are planning a vacation for a group. You want some feedback from them about the plan. You would:
   - ☐ A. describe some of the highlights they will experience.
   - ☐ B. use a map to show them the places.
   - ☐ C. give them a copy of the printed itinerary.
   - ☐ D. phone, text, or e-mail them.

3. A website has a video showing how to make a special graph. There is a person speaking, some lists and words describing what to do, and some diagrams. You would learn most from:
   - ☐ A. reading the words.
   - ☐ B. listening.
   - ☐ C. watching the actions.
   - ☐ D. seeing the diagrams.

4. You are going to cook something as a special treat for your family. You would:
   - ☐ A. cook something you know without the need for instructions.
   - ☐ B. ask friends for suggestions.
   - ☐ C. look on the Internet or in some cookbooks for ideas from the pictures.
   - ☐ D. use a cookbook where you know there is a good recipe.

5. A group of tourists want to learn about the parks or wildlife reserves in your area. You would:
   - ☐ A. talk about, or arrange a talk for them, about parks or wildlife reserves.
   - ☐ B. show them maps and Internet pictures.
   - ☐ C. take them to a park or wildlife reserve and walk with them.
   - ☐ D. give them a book or pamphlets about the parks or wildlife reserves.

6. You are about to purchase a digital camera or mobile phone. Other than price, what would most influence your decision?
   - ☐ A. Trying or testing it.
   - ☐ B. Reading the details or checking its features online.
   - ☐ C. It is a modern design and looks good.
   - ☐ D. The salesperson telling me about its features.

7. Remember a time when you learned how to do something new. Avoid choosing a physical skill (e.g., riding a bike). You learned best by:
   - ☐ A. watching a demonstration.
   - ☐ B. listening to somebody explaining it and asking questions.
   - ☐ C. diagrams, maps, and charts—visual clues.
   - ☐ D. written instructions—e.g., a manual or book.

8. You have a problem with your heart. You would prefer that the doctor:
   - ☐ A. gave you something to read to explain what was wrong.
   - ☐ B. used a plastic model to show what was wrong.
   - ☐ C. described what was wrong.
   - ☐ D. showed you a diagram of what was wrong.

9. You want to learn a new program, skill, or game on a computer. You would:

☐ A. read the written instructions that came with the program.

☐ B. talk with people who know about the program.

☐ C. use the controls or keyboard.

☐ D. follow the diagrams in the book that came with it.

10. I like websites that have:

☐ A. things I can click on, shift, or try.

☐ B. interesting design and visual features.

☐ C. interesting written descriptions, lists, and explanations.

☐ D. audio channels where I can hear music, radio programs, or interviews.

11. Other than price, what would most influence your decision to buy a new nonfiction book?

☐ A. The way it looks is appealing.

☐ B. Quickly reading parts of it.

☐ C. A friend talks about it and recommends it.

☐ D. It has real-life stories, experiences, and examples.

12. You are using a book, CD, or website to learn how to take photos with your new digital camera. You would like to have:

☐ A. a chance to ask questions and talk about the camera and its features.

☐ B. clear written instructions with lists and bullet points about what to do.

☐ C. diagrams showing the camera and what each part does.

☐ D. many examples of good and poor photos and how to improve them.

13. You prefer a teacher or a presenter who uses:

☐ A. demonstrations, models, or practical sessions.

☐ B. question and answer, talk, group discussion, or guest speakers.

☐ C. handouts, books, or readings.

☐ D. diagrams, charts, or graphs.

14. You have finished a competition or test and would like some feedback. You would like to have feedback:

☐ A. using examples from what you have done.

☐ B. using a written description of your results.

☐ C. from somebody who talks it through with you.

☐ D. using graphs showing what you had achieved.

15. You are going to choose food at a restaurant or café. You would:

☐ A. choose something that you have had there before.

☐ B. listen to the waiter or ask friends to recommend choices.

☐ C. choose from the descriptions in the menu.

☐ D. look at what others are eating or look at pictures of each dish.

16. You have to make an important speech at a conference or special occasion. You would:

☐ A. make diagrams or get graphs to help explain things.

☐ B. write a few key words and practice saying your speech over and over.

☐ C. write out your speech and learn from reading it over several times.

☐ D. gather many examples and stories to make the talk real and practical.

Scoring the VARK

Now you will match up each one of the boxes you selected with a category from the VARK Questionnaire using the following scoring chart (if you opted to take the questionnaire online, the scoring was done for you). Circle the letter (V, A, R, or K) that corresponds to each one of your responses (A, B, C, or D). For example, if you marked both B and C for question 3, circle both the V and R in the third row.

Responses to Question 3:	A	B	C	D
VARK letter	K	(V)	(R)	A

Count the number of each of the VARK letters you have circled to get your score for each VARK.

Scoring Chart

Question	A Category	B Category	C Category	D Category
1	K	A	R	V
2	V	A	R	K
3	K	V	R	A
4	K	A	V	R
5	A	V	K	R
6	K	R	V	A
7	K	A	V	R
8	R	K	A	V
9	R	A	K	V
10	K	V	R	A
11	V	R	A	K
12	A	R	V	K
13	K	A	R	V
14	K	R	A	V
15	K	A	R	V
16	V	A	R	K

Total number of Vs circled = _____   Total number of As circled = _____

Total number of Rs circled = _____   Total number of Ks circled = _____

Because you could choose more than one answer for each question, the scoring is not just a simple matter of counting. It is like four stepping stones across some water. Enter your scores from highest to lowest on the stones in the figure below, with their V, A, R, and K labels.

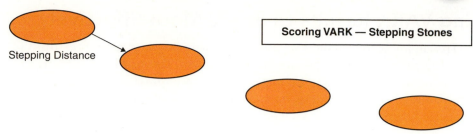

Stepping Distance

Scoring VARK — Stepping Stones

Your stepping distance comes from this table:

The total of my four VARK scores is	My stepping distance is
16–21	1
22–27	2
28–32	3
More than 32	4

Follow these steps to establish your preferences:

1. Your first preference is always your highest score. Check that first stone as one of your preferences.

2. Subtract your second-highest score from your first. If that figure is larger than your stepping distance, you have a single preference. Otherwise, check this stone as another preference and continue with Step 3.

3. Subtract your third score from your second one. If that figure is larger than your stepping distance, you have a strong preference for two learning styles (bimodal). If not, check your third stone as a preference and continue with Step 4.

4. Subtract your fourth score from your third one. If that figure is larger than your stepping distance, you have a strong preference for three learning styles (trimodal). You may also find that you prefer the four learning styles equally. Otherwise, check your fourth stone as a preference, and you have all four modes as your preferences!

Note: If you are bimodal or trimodal or you have checked all four modes as your preferences, you can be described as multimodal in your VARK preferences.

YOUR TURN > DISCUSS IT

Did your VARK score surprise you at all? Did you know what type of learner you were before using this tool? If so, when did you discover this? How do you use your learning style to your benefit? Be prepared to discuss your results and reflections with the class.

Using VARK Results to Study More Effectively

Meet Trevor, an accomplished soccer player who has just been recruited to play on his college's soccer team. After two years, Trevor plans to transfer to a nearby university, where he hopes to continue playing soccer. In Trevor's college success course, he took the VARK and learned that he is a kinesthetic learner. This was welcome news. Trevor had always thought he was just a slow learner, but he found that he struggled mainly when the material he listened to or read didn't seem related to the real world. He began asking instructors to give real-world examples as part of their lectures, and when he studied he worked hard to apply course content to his personal experiences to make it relevant. This was easier for some courses than for others, but Trevor began making a habit of connecting academic material to his world—both present and past. Trevor's experience and his improved grades convinced several of his instructors to make real-world application part of their courses to meet the needs of students who, like Trevor, are kinesthetic learners.

Considering how taking the VARK benefited Trevor, how can knowing *your* VARK score help *you* do better in your college classes? Table 4.1 offers suggestions for using learning styles to develop your own study strategies. To succeed in college, you need to develop various study habits that may not be in line with your preferred learning style. A successful student is one who can adapt to various teaching styles. It would be a good idea to consider each of the courses you are currently taking. Which of the learning styles we discuss above might best describe how each instructor is presenting the course material and what she/he expects you to master? Given the learning style preferences that you have identified by taking the VARK, what adjustments might you have to make? For example, if your instructor in U.S. history only lectures (no video, no discussion, no interactive activities), you could reasonably conclude that the ideal fit between this instructor and you as a learner would be if your preferred learning style was "aural," meaning you process best what you hear. But if instead you are a kinesthetic learner, you need to actively take notes while you are listening to the lecture. Go through this kind of analysis for each course you are taking.

Table 4.1 ❯ Study Strategies by VARK Learning Style

Visual	Aural	Read/Write	Kinesthetic
Underline or highlight your notes.	Talk with others to make sure your lecture notes are accurate.	Write and rewrite your notes.	Use all your senses in learning: sight, touch, taste, smell, and hearing.
Use symbols, charts, or graphs to display your notes.	Record lectures (with permission) or record yourself reading your notes aloud and listen to either or both.	Read your notes silently.	Add to your notes with real-world examples.

‹ Bodies in Motion
The theater arts have strong appeal for kinesthetic learners who prefer to learn through experience and practice.
Hill Street Studios/Blend Images/Getty Images

4.3

THE MYERS–BRIGGS TYPE INDICATOR

One of the best-known and most widely used personality inventories that can also be used to describe learning styles is the **Myers–Briggs Type Indicator (MBTI)**.[4] While the VARK Inventory measures your preferences for using your senses to learn, the MBTI examines basic personality characteristics and how those relate to human interaction and learning. The MBTI was created by Isabel Briggs Myers and her mother, Katharine Cook Briggs. The inventory identifies and measures psychological types and is given to several million people around the world each year. Employers often give this inventory to employees to get a better understanding of how they perceive the world, make decisions, and get along with other people. You might have taken the MBTI in school or in the workplace, but if not, your college career center can give you more information about taking the inventory and determining your own Myers–Briggs type. You can also visit **myersbriggs.org/my-mbti-personality-type/take-the-mbti-instrument/**.

All the psychological types described by the MBTI are normal and healthy. There is no good or bad or right or wrong; people are simply different. When you complete the MBTI, your score represents your "psychological type" or the combination of your preferences on four different scales. These scales measure how you take in information and how you then make

---

[4] Isabel Briggs Myers, *Introduction to Type*, 6th ed. (Palo Alto: CPP, 1998).

decisions or come to conclusions about that information. Based on these scales, you can be one of the types shown in Table 4.2.

Table 4.2 › MBTI Types

Extravert	OR	Introvert
directing your energy and attention toward the outer world of people, events, and things		directing your energy and attention toward the inner world of thoughts, feelings, and reflections
Sensing Type	**OR**	**Intuitive Type**
perceiving the world and taking in information directly, through your five senses		perceiving the world and taking in information indirectly, by using your intuition
Thinking Type	**OR**	**Feeling Type**
making your decisions through logical, rational analysis		making your decisions through your personal values, likes, and dislikes
Judging Type	**OR**	**Perceiving Type**
approaching the outside world by making decisions and judgments		approaching the outside world by observing and perceiving

Because each of the four different preferences has two possible choices, sixteen psychological types are possible. No matter what your Myers–Briggs type is, all components of personality have value in the learning process. The key to success, therefore, is to use all the attitudes and functions in their most positive sense.

As you go about your studies, use Table 4.3 for recommended strategies that can be helpful to you based on your characteristics and strengths.[5] To be successful, take full advantage of the strategies that match your characteristics, but remember that you should also learn to use some study strategies that may not come to you naturally because doing so will lead to more success in college, career, and life in general.

What you can learn about yourself from taking the MBTI has the power to improve your learning and how you relate to others. Consider Tricia, who is a returning student at her college. Tricia has two small children and describes herself as a person who likes to "get right to the point." Recently in her psychology class, Tricia's instructor assigned her to a group that is supposed to do a group project on important psychologists. Tricia has been very frustrated by the experience of working with other students. She is doing more than her fair share of the work, and even worse, others in the group come up with "stupid" ideas. Tricia is losing patience, and she's quite blunt when she speaks during group meetings—she's much more interested in saying exactly what she thinks than in worrying about how her comments might make others feel. Other group members told her that she's "mean" and "insensitive," but Tricia wasn't buying it.

---

[5]Ibid.

Table 4.3 ❯ MBTI Types and Study Strategies

Characteristics	Actions	Study Strategies
Extraversion	• Act on your plan. • Do whatever it takes.	• Create note cards and outlines. • Form or join study groups. • If you are working on a paper, start writing now.
Introversion	• Think it through. • Before you take any action, carefully review everything.	• Create mind maps. • Study independently. • Find a quiet study space.
Sensing	• Get the facts. • Use sensing to find and learn the facts. • Look for the evidence for what is being said.	• Use diagrams and outlines. • Take notes and create flash cards.
Intuition	• Get the ideas. • Identify the reasons for facts being presented. • Use intuition to consider what those facts mean. • Determine what concepts and ideas are being supported by those facts. • Think about the implications.	• Study in blocks of time. • Use your creativity. • Consider the big picture.
Thinking	• Critically analyze. • Use thinking to analyze the pros and cons of what is being presented. • Identify the gaps in the evidence.	• Focus on the logic of the presented information. • Determine if the facts really support the conclusions. • Think of alternative explanations.
Feeling	• Make informed value judgments. • Determine the importance of the material. • Form your personal opinion.	• Find connections in the material. • Study with strong and motivated students.
Judging	• Organize and plan. • Don't just plan in your head, either; write your plan down, in detail.	• Study in an organized environment. • Try different study strategies. • Keep your notes organized.
Perceiving	• Change your plan as needed. • Be flexible. • Expect the unexpected. • Figure out what's wrong, then come up with another plan and start following that.	• Keep a calendar and mark it with deadlines. • Complete tasks. • Don't give up easily. • Don't procrastinate.

Only after taking the Myers–Briggs Type Inventory did Tricia discover that she's a high "T" (a thinking type) and a low "P" (a perceiving type). That means she tends to be very logical and rational but lacks sensitivity to the feelings of others. What she learned about herself explained a great deal about her relationships not only with her classmates but also with others in her immediate family. In the end, she decided that even when she feels impatient, she needs to find a way to get her point across without hurting others' feelings.

> **Take a Time-out**

Do you find that you need some occasional time by yourself? Although introverts are more likely to enjoy time alone, even extraverts can benefit from private time to relax or escape from the hustle and bustle of daily life.

India Picture/Shutterstock.com

4.4

MULTIPLE INTELLIGENCES

Another way of looking at how we learn is the theory of **multiple intelligences,** which suggests that all human beings have at least eight different types of intelligence. This theory was developed in 1983 by Howard Gardner. Gardner's theory is based on the idea that the traditional definition of human intelligence is very limited. Gardner argues that students should be encouraged to develop the abilities they have and that evaluation should measure all forms of intelligence.

Gardner's work is controversial because it questions our traditional definitions of intelligence. According to Gardner's theory, all human beings have at least eight different types of intelligence, described here as follows:

1. A person with **verbal/linguistic** intelligence likes to read, write, and tell stories and is good at memorizing information.

2. A person with **logical/mathematical** intelligence likes to work with numbers and is good at problem solving and logical processes.

3. A person with **visual/spatial** intelligence likes to draw and play with machines and is good at puzzles and reading maps and charts.

4. A person with **bodily/kinesthetic** intelligence likes to move around and is good at sports, dance, and acting.

5. A person with **musical/rhythmic** intelligence likes to sing and play an instrument and is good at remembering melodies and noticing pitches and rhythms.

6. A person with **interpersonal** intelligence likes to have many friends and is good at understanding people, leading others, and mediating conflicts.

7. A person with **intrapersonal** intelligence likes to work alone, understands himself or herself well, and is an original thinker.

8. A person with **naturalistic** intelligence likes to be outside and is good at preservation, conservation, and organizing a living area.

To get a better sense of your multiple intelligences, complete the inventory below.

MULTIPLE INTELLIGENCES INVENTORY[6]

Put a check mark next to all the items within each intelligence that apply to you.

Verbal/Linguistic Intelligence

___ I enjoy telling stories and jokes.

___ I enjoy word games (for example, Scrabble and puzzles).

___ I am a good speller (most of the time).

___ I like talking and writing about my ideas.

___ If something breaks and won't work, I read the instruction book before I try to fix it.

___ When I work with others in a group presentation, I prefer to do the writing and library research.

Logical/Mathematical Intelligence

___ I really enjoy my math class.

___ I like to find out how things work.

___ I enjoy computer and math games.

___ I love playing chess, checkers, or Monopoly.

___ If something breaks and won't work, I look at the pieces and try to figure out how it works.

Visual/Spatial Intelligence

___ I prefer a map to written directions.

___ I enjoy hobbies such as photography.

___ I like to doodle on paper whenever I can.

___ In a magazine, I prefer looking at the pictures rather than reading the text.

___ If something breaks and won't work, I tend to study the diagram of how it works.

Bodily/Kinesthetic Intelligence

___ My favorite class is gym because I like sports.

___ When looking at things, I like touching them.

___ I use a lot of body movements when talking.

___ I tend to tap my fingers or play with my pencil during class.

___ If something breaks and won't work, I tend to play with the pieces to try to fit them together.

Musical/Rhythmic Intelligence

___ I enjoy listening to CDs and the radio.

___ I like to sing.

___ I like to have music playing when doing homework or studying.

___ I can remember the melodies of many songs.

___ If something breaks and won't work, I tend to tap my fingers to a beat while I figure it out.

Interpersonal Intelligence

___ I get along well with others.

___ I have several very close friends.

___ I like working with others in groups.

___ Friends ask my advice because I seem to be a natural leader.

___ If something breaks and won't work, I try to find someone who can help me.

(continued)

---

[6]Greg Gay and Gary Harms, "The Multiple Intelligences Inventory." From **atsp.atutorspaces.com**. Reprinted by permission of Greg Gay.

Intrapersonal Intelligence

___ I like to work alone without anyone bothering me.

___ I don't like crowds.

___ I know my own strengths and weaknesses.

___ I find that I am strong-willed, independent, and don't follow the crowd.

___ If something breaks and won't work, I wonder whether it's worth fixing.

Naturalist Intelligence

___ I am keenly aware of my surroundings and of what goes on around me.

___ I like to collect things like rocks, sports cards, and stamps.

___ I like to get away from the city and enjoy nature.

___ I enjoy learning the names of living things in the environment, such as flowers and trees.

___ If something breaks down, I look around me to try and see what I can find to fix the problem.

Now, count up the check marks for each intelligence, and write the total for each here. Your score for each intelligence will be a number between 1 and 6.

Total Score

___ Verbal/Linguistic   ___ Musical/Rhythmic

___ Logical/Mathematical   ___ Interpersonal

___ Visual/Spatial   ___ Intrapersonal

___ Bodily/Kinesthetic   ___ Naturalist

Your high scores of 3 or more will help you to get a sense of your own multiple intelligences. Depending on your background and age, some intelligences are likely to be more developed than others.

Now that you know what your intelligences are, you can work to strengthen the other intelligences that you do not use as often. How do your college courses measure ways in which you are intelligent? Where do they fall short? Looking to the future, you can use your intelligences to help you make decisions about a major, choose activities, and explore career options. It is important for you to be aware of your intelligences and share them with your academic adviser, who can help you make sound future educational and career plans. This information will also help you appreciate your own unique abilities and also those of others.

YOUR TURN > TRY IT

Pick a challenge you are facing right now. How many of the eight intelligences could help you deal with this challenge?

WHEN LEARNING STYLES AND TEACHING STYLES CONFLICT

This may not be surprising, but instructors tend to teach in ways that fit their *own* particular styles of learning. So instructors who learn best in a read/write mode or aural mode will probably just lecture and give the class little opportunity for either interaction or visual and kinesthetic learning. Instructors who prefer a more interactive, hands-on environment will likely involve students in discussion and learning through experience.

Which learning situations work best for you? Think about the following questions:

- Do you enjoy listening to lectures, or do you find yourself bored?
- When your instructor assigns a group discussion, what is your immediate reaction?
- Do you dislike talking with other students, or is that the way you learn best?
- How do you react to lab sessions when you have to conduct an actual experiment? Is this an activity you look forward to or one that you do not like?

Each of these learning situations is more interesting for some students than for others, but all are certainly going to be part of your college experience. Your college has intentionally designed courses that give you opportunities to listen to instructors who are well educated and trained in their fields, to interact with other students in structured groups, and to learn by doing. Because these are all essential components of your college education, it's important for you to make the most of each situation, learn the content of each course, and in general learn how to learn better.

When you recognize a mismatch between how you best learn and how you are being taught, you need to take control of your learning process and develop some strategies to learn the material the way you prefer. For instance, if you don't like listening to a lecture, you will want to sit close to the front of the classroom to reduce distractions. With the instructor's permission, you might also want to record the lecture, using apps such as QuickVoice or Voice Recorder, so that you can listen to it again. Don't depend on the instructor or the classroom environment to give you everything you need to make the most of your learning. Use your own preferences, talents, and abilities to develop many different ways to study and retain information. If you are comfortable doing so, visit your instructor during office hours to discuss the challenges you are having and ask for suggestions for strategies you can try. Also, visit your college's learning center, where staff members can help you adapt your learning style to the realities of any classroom.

> **Learn to Adapt**

In college you will find that some instructors may have teaching styles that are challenging for you. Seek out the kinds of classes that conform to the way you like to learn, but also develop your adaptive strategies to make the most of any classroom setting.

William G. Brown

"As we start a new school year, Mr. Smith, I just want you to know that I'm an Abstract-Sequential learner and trust that you'll conduct yourself accordingly!"

Look back through this chapter to remind yourself of the ways that you can use your own learning style to be more successful in any class you take. If you are interested in reading more about learning styles, the library and your college learning center will have many resources.

YOUR TURN > TRY IT

List your favorite and least favorite courses you are taking this term. Then add the instructor's teaching style for each class on your list. Do your preferences have something to do with the way the classes are taught? Why or why not?

4.6

LEARNING WITH A LEARNING DISABILITY

While everyone has a learning style, some people have a **learning disability**, a general term that covers a wide variety of specific learning problems resulting from neurological disorders that can make it difficult to acquire certain academic and social skills. A learning disability is a very common challenge to learning for students of any age. Learning disabilities are usually recognized and diagnosed in grade school, but some students can enter college without having been properly diagnosed or assisted.

Learning disabilities can show up as specific difficulties with spoken and written language, coordination, self-control, or attention. Such difficulties can impede learning to read, write, or do math. The term *learning disability* covers a broad range of symptoms and outcomes. Because of this, it is sometimes difficult to diagnose a learning disability or pinpoint the causes. The types of learning disabilities that most commonly affect college students are **attention disorders**, which affect the ability to focus and concentrate, and **cognitive disorders**, which affect the development of academic skills, including reading, writing, and mathematics.

You might know someone who has been diagnosed with a learning disability, such as dyslexia, a reading disability that occurs when the brain does not properly recognize and process certain symbols, or an attention deficit disorder that affects concentration and focus. It is also possible that you have a special learning need and are not aware of it. This section seeks to increase your self-awareness and your knowledge about such challenges to learning. The earlier in life—and college—you address any learning challenges you might have, the better you will perform.

Attention Disorders

Attention disorders are common in children, adolescents, and even adults. Some students who have attention disorders appear to daydream a lot; even if you do get their attention, they can be easily distracted. Individuals with attention deficit disorder (ADD) or attention deficit/hyperactivity disorder (ADHD) often have trouble organizing tasks or completing their work. They don't seem to listen to or follow directions, and their work might be messy or appear careless. Although in legal and medical terms they are not strictly classified as learning disabilities, ADD and ADHD can seriously interfere with academic performance, leading some educators to classify them along with other learning disabilities.[7]

If you have trouble paying attention or getting organized, you won't really know whether you have ADD or ADHD until you are evaluated. It may be that you simply have too much to do or that you're trying unsuccessfully to multitask. Do not assume that you have a learning disability until you consult with an expert in your learning center or in the community. After you have been evaluated, follow the professional advice you get, which may or may not mean taking medication. If you do receive a prescription for medication, be sure to take it according to the doctor's directions. In the meantime, if you're having trouble getting and staying organized, whether or not you have an attention disorder, you can improve your focus through your own behavioral choices. The world-famous Mayo

---

[7]Adapted and reprinted from the public domain source by Sharyn Neuwirth, *Learning Disabilities* (Darby, PA: National Institute of Mental Health, 1993), 9–10.

Clinic website offers the following suggestions for adults with ADD or ADHD.[8]

- Make a list of tasks to be accomplished each day. Make sure you're not trying to do too much.
- Break down tasks into smaller, more manageable steps.
- Use sticky pads to write notes to yourself. Put them on the fridge, on the bathroom mirror, in the car, or in other places where you'll benefit from having a reminder.
- Keep an electronic calendar to track appointments and deadlines.
- Carry a notebook or electronic device with you so that you can note ideas or things you'll need to remember.
- Take time to set up systems to file and organize information, both on your electronic devices and for paper documents. Get in the habit of using these systems consistently.
- Follow a routine that's consistent from day to day and keep items, like keys and your wallet, in the same place.
- Ask for help from family members or friends.

Cognitive Learning Disabilities

Cognitive learning disabilities are related to mental tasks and processing. Dyslexia, for example, is a developmental reading disorder classified as a cognitive learning disability. A person can have problems with any of the tasks involved in reading. However, scientists have found that a significant number of people with dyslexia are not able to distinguish or separate the sounds in spoken words. For instance, dyslexic individuals sometimes have difficulty assigning the right sounds to letters, either individually or when letters combine to form words.

There is, of course, more to reading than recognizing words. If the brain is unable to form images or relate new ideas to those stored in memory, the reader can't understand or remember the new concepts. So other types of reading disabilities can appear when the focus of reading shifts from identifying words to comprehending a written passage.[9]

Writing, too, involves several brain areas and functions. The networks of the brain that control vocabulary, grammar, hand movement, and memory must all be in good working order. So a developmental writing disorder might result from problems in any of these areas. Someone who can't distinguish the sequence of sounds in a word will often have problems with spelling. People with writing disabilities, particularly expressive language disorders (the inability to express oneself using accurate language or sentence structure), are often unable to write complete, grammatical sentences.[10]

---

[8]See mayoclinic.org/diseases-conditions/adult-adhd/basics/lifestyle-home-remedies/con-20034552.

[9]See ldaamerica.org/types-of-learning-disabilities/dyslexia/.

[10]Ibid.

A student with a developmental arithmetic disorder will have difficulty recognizing numbers and symbols, memorizing facts such as the multiplication table, and understanding abstract concepts such as place value and fractions.[11]

Exploring Resources

If you have a documented learning disability, make sure to notify the office of disabled student services at your college to receive reasonable accommodations as required by law. Reasonable accommodations might include use of a computer during some exams, readers for tests, in-class note-takers, extra time for assignments and tests, and use of audio textbooks, depending on need and the type of disability.

If you don't yet have a "documented" learning disability but think you might, the disabled student services office would be a good place to start. You could also discuss this issue with your academic adviser, a learning center professional, or an adviser or counselor in your college counseling center. All of them can get you to the right source for evaluation and assistance.

Anyone who is diagnosed with a learning disability is in good company. Actors Keanu Reeves, Keira Knightley, and Daniel Radcliffe, filmmaker Steven Spielberg, celebrity chef Jamie Oliver, and former football star Tim Tebow are just a few of the famous and successful people who have diagnosed learning disabilities. Here is a final important message: A learning disability is a learning difference but is in no way related to intelligence. Having a learning disability is not a sign that you are stupid. In fact, some of the most intelligent individuals in human history have had a learning disability.

---

[11]See ldaamerica.org/types-of-learning-disabilities/dyscalculia/.

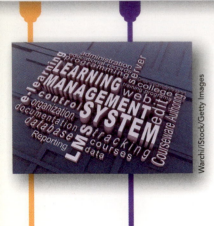

Warchi/iStock/Getty Images

MANAGE ONLINE LEARNING WITH YOUR LEARNING STYLE

Do you like the idea of being able to take a class online? Maybe that would be a good fit for your work or family schedule. Maybe it would be easier than looking for a parking space on your campus. But would you still learn, even if you didn't go to a class meeting?

Many colleges and universities use an online learning management system (LMS) for online learning. An LMS is a website that helps you connect with the material you're studying—as well as with your instructors and classmates. There is something for every learning style in the LMS environment.

THE PROBLEM *You have some idea about how you learn best, but you don't really understand what an LMS is or how to use one.*

THE FIX *Understand your learning style and what kind of learning environment will work best for you.*

HOW TO DO IT

Explore your school's LMS.

Be open-minded and patient with yourself. Find out if there is an orientation seminar or video you can watch; you can ask your instructors or visit the student learning center. Take online surveys to understand your learning style. Here are two sites to try: **edutopia.org/multiple-intelligences-learning-styles-quiz** and **vark-learn.com/**.

An LMS offers lots of ways to connect with your instructors, classmates, and material. It lets you keep track of your grades and assignments and offers a digital drop box where you can submit your work. It can also offer a lot of fun things, such as online discussion forums and interactive group projects where you can sketch ideas on whiteboards that other students can view, or even collaborate on written assignments in real time. Some platforms have videos, recorded lectures, or even your instructor's lecture notes.

1. If you're an **auditory learner**, you'll love audio recordings. Read your notes and textbook aloud as you study (you can even record them

to play back to yourself). Consider listening to audio-books and joining a study group for discussions. Another tip: View videos once and then play them back with your eyes closed.

2. If you're a **visual learner**, you'll love videos, pictures, maps, and graphs. Whenever you take notes, illustrate them, playing up key points with colored highlighters, pictures, or symbols. You can also create your own graphs or charts.

3. If you're a **hands-on learner**, you'll love labs, group projects, and fieldwork. Be sure to take notes and read things aloud as you study. Build models or spreadsheets.

IS IT FOR YOU?

Now that you know what kind of learner you are and something about your college's LMS:

- Are you disciplined enough to work independently?
- Would you miss interacting with your instructor or classmates if you didn't attend classes?

You need to know yourself because learning is up to you.

THINK

Recognizing that people learn in different ways can be a relief. After reading this chapter, do you have a better understanding of your own learning style? What did you find to be the most interesting point in this chapter? What would you like to learn more about? What changes might you want to make?

_____

_____

_____

_____

_____

_____

WRITE

Now that you know more about your learning style and how you prefer to learn, what do you consider your strengths to be? How do you learn best and easily, and how can you apply these positive experiences to other learning situations? What are some of your weaknesses, and how can you address them?

_____

_____

_____

_____

_____

_____

APPLY

1. It is important to understand various learning styles for education purposes, but it is also important to understand how learning preferences affect career choices. Considering your preferred learning style, what might be the best careers for you? Why?
2. Use the table on the following page to list all the classes you are taking this term. Based on the VARK Inventory, try to figure out the instructor's teaching style in each class. Then add your learning style. Does the teaching style in each class match your learning style? If not, list a strategy you can use to adapt. Remember, you must take responsibility for your learning in order to be successful in college.

My Classes	Instructor's Teaching Style	My Learning Style	Match: Yes or No?	Strategy to Adapt
Psychology	PowerPoint slides with lecture: Visual and Auditory	Read/Write	No	Read the chapter before the lecture, take notes during the lecture, and review notes after class.

Below are suggestions for resources that are available at many colleges and the online resources that are available to everyone.

AT YOUR COLLEGE

VISIT . . .	IF YOU NEED HELP . . .
Counseling Center	understanding learning styles.
Career Center	learning how the Myers–Briggs Type Indicator can be used in career planning or how to align your Myers–Briggs type with your interests and career development options on campus.
Disabled Student Services/ Counselor	getting advice on learning disability testing and diagnosis and on receiving accommodations if you have a learning disability.

ONLINE

GO TO . . .	IF YOU NEED HELP . . .
Myers & Briggs Foundation: myersbriggs.org/my-mbti-personality-type/take-the-mbti-instrument/	learning more about these personality types and accessing a questionnaire to find out more about your type.
LD Pride: ldpride.net/learningstyles.MI.htm	obtaining general information about learning styles and learning disabilities and using an interactive diagnostic tool to determine your learning style.
National Center for Learning Disabilities: ncld.org	locating resources to diagnose and understand learning disabilities.
Assistive Technology Solutions: atsolutions.biz/learning_disabilities.htm	learning about assistive technology programs for students with disabilities.
Facebook: facebook.com	finding groups on Facebook created by students who have learning disabilities or ADHD. These groups are a great way to connect with other students with learning disabilities at your college or other colleges. If you have been diagnosed with a disability, the members of these groups can offer support and help you seek out appropriate resources in order to be successful in college.
National Institute of Mental Health: nimh.nih.gov/health/publications /attention-deficit-hyperactivity-disorder /can-adults-have-adhd.shtml	getting information about how adults who have ADD or ADHD can get diagnosed and treated.

LaunchPad for *Understanding Your College Experience* is a great resource. Go online to master concepts using the LearningCurve study tool and much more. **macmillanhighered.com/gardnerunderstanding**

PART TWO
SUCCEEDING IN COLLEGE

5 GETTING THE MOST OUT OF CLASS

STUDENT GOALS

6 READING TO LEARN FROM COLLEGE TEXTBOOKS

STUDENT GOALS

7 STUDYING, UNDERSTANDING, AND REMEMBERING

STUDENT GOALS

8 TAKING TESTS SUCCESSFULLY

STUDENT GOALS

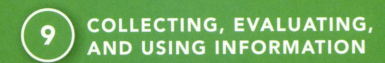

9 COLLECTING, EVALUATING, AND USING INFORMATION

STUDENT GOALS

5 Getting the Most Out of Class

PRE-READING ACTIVITY: In this chapter, you will learn different ways to be engaged in class to get the most out of being there. What do you think you can do before, during, and after class to be fully engaged in learning?

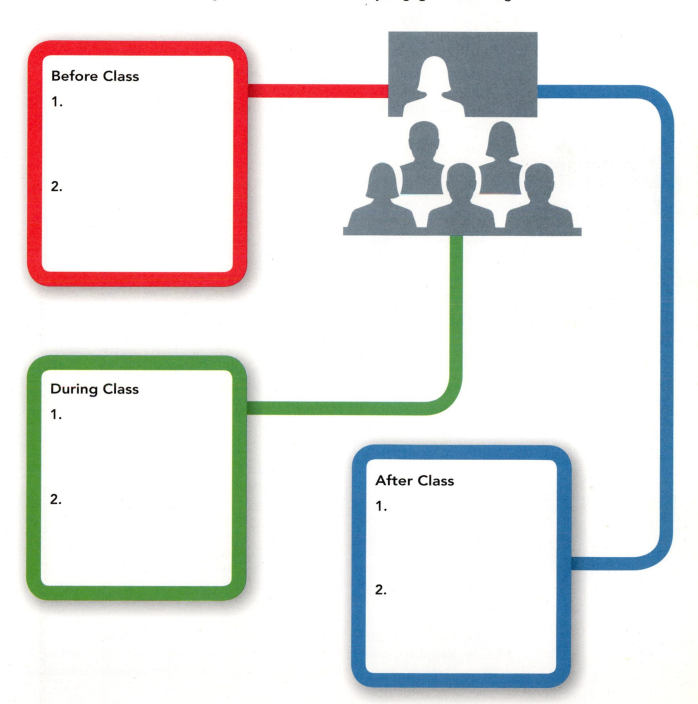

Before Class

1.

2.

During Class

1.

2.

After Class

1.

2.

PROFILE

Dillon Watts, 19
History Major, *San Bernardino Valley College, California*

Monkey Business Images/ Shutterstock.com

Dillon Watts grew up in San Bernardino, California. He left high school after his junior year and obtained his GED. The benefits of participating in class and being engaged in learning are obvious to Dillon. "Most of the time the questions you have are questions that will help the whole class," Dillon says. "Everyone in the class benefits from an instructor's answer." He points out, however, that no one appreciates a student asking questions just to earn participation points or to show off. "I try to be direct and simple when asking questions, so the class can get direct and simple answers," Dillon says.

> "I try to be direct and simple when asking questions, so the class can get direct and simple answers."

This same attitude is also present in the way Dillon prepares for class. He explains: "I just make sure to be there on time, every time, and to try to stay until the class is over. I'm not a great note-taker. I find myself distracted as much as the next guy. But as long as I make an effort to pay attention, write down key points, read the chapter sections in books I'm supposed to read, and study regularly, I find it pretty easy to maintain good grades." Dillon has learned to use multiple note-taking techniques and formats in different classes and found that this strategy helps improve his grades.

Dillon plans to transfer to Sacramento State University, or another four-year California school. In ten years he hopes to be a journalist or history teacher. He also hopes to put his class participation skills to good use. "It is my dream to take part in debates and public speeches," he says. His advice to other first-year students: "Try to get as much as you can out of your classes, and try to do your best, whether or not you feel like it. It always pays off in the end."

These challenges are not unique to Dillon. If you want to earn high grades in college, you'll need to play an active role in your classes by listening carefully, taking notes, asking questions, contributing to discussions, and providing answers. These active learning behaviors will improve your ability to understand complex ideas, find new possibilities, organize those ideas, and remember more of the material once the class is over.

Many of the questions on college exams will be drawn from class lectures and discussions. Therefore, you need to attend each class and be actively involved. In addition to taking notes, you might consider recording the lecture and discussion, if you have the instructor's permission. If you don't understand some points, take the time to meet with the instructor after class or during office hours. Another strategy to increase your learning is to meet with a study group to compare your understanding of course material with that of your classmates.

This chapter reviews several note-taking methods. Try out each one and choose the one that works best for you. Because writing down everything the instructor says is probably not possible, and you might not be sure what is most important, ask questions in class. Asking questions will ensure that you understand your notes. Reviewing your notes with a friend from class or with a tutor in your campus learning center can also help you clarify your understanding of the most important points.

Most of all, be sure to speak up. When you have a question to ask or a comment to share, don't let embarrassment or shyness stop you. You will be more likely to remember what happens in class if you are an active participant.

YOUR TURN ❯ TRY IT

If you have saved any of your high school notebooks, look at the way you took notes and think about whether this method works for you now. If you can't locate your old notes, try taking notes while watching the news on TV or reading news online and see how you do.

BECOME ENGAGED IN LEARNING

5.1

Engaged students are those who are fully involved with the college experience and spend the time and the energy necessary to learn, both in and out of class. Engaged learners who have good listening and note-taking skills get the most out of college.

You can learn by listening to a lecture, and you can think about and better understand that information by considering what the information means to you. Practice the techniques of **active learning,** which means learning through engagement and participation in activities such as talking with others, participating in online or in-class discussions, asking questions in class, studying in groups, solving problems, and going beyond the lecture material and required reading. Explore other information sources in the library or on the Internet. Think about how the material relates to your own life or experience. For instance, a psychology class might help you recognize patterns of behavior in your own family, or a sociology class may shed light on a team or group to which you belong. When you are actively engaged in learning, you will not only learn the material in your notes and textbooks, but will also be practicing valuable skills that you can apply to college, work, and your personal life such as the following:

- **Working with others.** Learning to do professional work with others is one of the most important skills you can develop for success in college and in your career. To do so, you can become active in a co-curricular organization where you acquire leadership opportunities; and you can join study groups that meet online or face-to-face to discuss the material and exchange study notes.

- **Improving your thinking, listening, writing, and speaking skills.** These are the primary skills that define a college-educated person.

- **Functioning independently and teaching yourself.** Your first year of college will help you become an independent learner. Such learners do not wait for an instructor to point them in the right direction.

- **Managing your time.** Time management sounds easy, but it is a challenge for almost all students, regardless of their academic ability. And it is the number one college success strategy reported by many successful students.

- **Gaining sensitivity to cultural differences.** The world we live in requires all of us to develop our own knowledge about, and respect for, cultures that are different from our own.

Engagement in learning requires your full and active participation in the learning process. Your instructors will set the stage and provide valuable information, but it's up to you to do the rest. For instance, if you disagree with what your instructor says, politely share your opinion. Most instructors will listen. They might still disagree with you, but they might also appreciate your independent thinking efforts.

Not all instructors teach in a way that encourages active learning. Ask your friends for recommendations for instructors who encourage students to participate in class, work in groups, explore materials independently, and otherwise engage fully in learning.

> **Stay Engaged**

Students of all kinds will benefit from active learning strategies, whether in arts and science courses or professional training situations, requiring students to apply what they learn in their courses.

Hero Images/Getty Images

STAY ENGAGED BEFORE CLASS AND BETWEEN CLASS MEETINGS

Have you ever noticed how easy it is to learn the words of a song? It's easier to remember song lyrics than other kinds of information because songs follow a tune, have a beat, and often relate to things in our personal lives. It is easier to remember new information if you can connect it to what you already know.

In your first-year classes, you'll be listening to and reading material that might seem hard to understand. Beginning on the first day of class, you will be more likely to remember what you hear and read if you try to link it to something you have already learned or experienced.

A very important first step toward success is to prepare before you attend each class session by listening, learning, and remembering the material. Here are some strategies that are simple, yet very important to your success:

1. **Do the assigned reading.** Doing the assigned reading before class will help you understand new terms, listen better, and pick out the most important information when taking notes in class. Some instructors assign readings during class; others expect you to follow the **syllabus** (course outline) to keep up with the assigned readings. As you read, take good notes (more on note taking later in this chapter). In books you have purchased, **annotate** (add explanatory notes in the margins), highlight, or underline key points. In books you do not own, such as library books, paraphrase the content and then annotate or highlight what you have written.

2. **Pay careful attention to your course syllabus.** The syllabus you receive at the start of each course will include the course requirements, your instructor's expectations, and the course grading breakdown. Instructors expect students to understand and follow the syllabus with few or no reminders. You might find that this is a key difference between college and high school.

3. **Make use of additional materials provided by the instructors.** Many instructors post lecture outlines or notes in the course or learning management system (CMS or LMS) before class. Download and print these materials for easy use during class. CMS materials often provide hints about the topics that the instructor considers most important; they also can create an organizational structure for taking notes.

4. **Warm up for class.** Review chapter introductions and summaries that refer to related sections in your text, and quickly review your notes from the previous class period. This prepares you to pay attention, understand, and remember.

5. **Get organized.** Decide how you want to take notes. If you handwrite your notes, using three-ring binders can help you organize them; punch holes in syllabi and other course handouts, and keep them with class notes. You might want to buy notebook paper with a large

left-hand margin so that you can annotate your lecture notes (more on this later in the chapter). You can also download and print blank notebook paper from several free websites or download note-taking apps such as OneNote, Evernote, or Simplenote that can provide you with tools to take or organize your notes on your mobile device.

If you take notes on a laptop or tablet, keep your files organized in separate folders for each of your classes, and make sure that the file name of each document includes the date and topic of the class. See the Tech Tip at the end of this chapter for more information on using your computer or mobile device to take effective notes.

5.3

PARTICIPATE IN CLASS

To learn how to play a sport—and not just watch it—you have to participate. Participation is the heart of active learning. To really learn, you must listen carefully, talk about what you are learning, write about it, and connect it to past experiences. Talking and writing about what you are supposed to be learning deepens the imprinting of these ideas in your brain's storage capacity and increases the probability of recalling the material when you are asked to do so on exams. When you say something in class, whether in answering a question or as part of a question you are asking, you are more likely to remember it than when you just listen to someone else saying it.

Listen Actively and with an Open Mind

Listening in class is different from watching and listening to a TV show, listening to a friend, or even listening during a meeting. In such everyday activities, you might not be required to remember later or use the information you hear. Knowing how to listen in class can help you get more out of what you hear, understand better what you have heard, and save time. Here are some suggestions:

1. **Be ready for the message.** Prepare yourself to hear, to listen, and to receive the message. If you have done the assigned reading, you will already know details from the text, so you can focus your notes on key concepts during the lecture. You will also notice information that the text does not cover and will be prepared to pay closer attention when the instructor presents new material in class or online.

2. **Focus on the main concepts and central ideas, not just on facts and figures.** Although facts are important, they will be easier to remember and will make more sense when you can place them within concepts, themes, and ideas. These main ideas are usually identifiable from headings and from what is repeated most often.

3. **Listen or read for new ideas.** Even if you are an expert on a topic, you can still learn something new. Do not assume that college instructors and textbooks will present the same information you learned in a similar course in high school. Even if you're listening to a similar lecture or reading about the same topic, you will pick out and learn new information. As an engaged student, make a note of questions in your mind as you listen and read, but save the judgments for later.

4. **Repeat mentally.** Words can go in one ear and out the other unless you make an effort to remember them. Think about what you hear, and say it silently in your own words. If you cannot translate the information into your own words, ask the instructor for more explanation.

5. **Decide whether what you have heard is not important, somewhat important, or very important.** While most of what your instructors say and do in class is important, occasionally they may make comments or tell stories that are only somewhat related to the class material or may not be related at all. If an instructor's comment is really unrelated to the focus of the class, you don't need to write it down. If it's very important, make it a major point in your notes by highlighting or underlining it, or use it as a major topic in your outline if that's the method you use for taking notes. If it's somewhat important, try to relate it to a very important topic by writing it down as a part of that topic.

6. **Keep an open mind.** Every class holds the promise of letting you discover new ideas and uncover different opinions. Some instructors might present information that challenges your ideas and values on purpose. College is supposed to teach you to think in new ways and train you to provide support for your own beliefs. Instructors want you to think for yourself; they don't necessarily expect you to agree with everything they or your classmates say. However, if you want people to respect your values and ideas, you must show respect for theirs as well by listening to what they have to say with an open mind. Some of your instructors may actually say things in an attempt to provoke you to react. All they are trying to do is to get you to think in new ways and to become a more critical thinker.

7. **Ask questions.** Early in the term, determine whether your instructor wants you to ask questions during the lecture. Some instructors prefer that students ask their questions after the lecture, during separate discussion sections, labs, or office hours. If your instructor answers questions when students ask them, speak up if you did not hear or understand what was said. Ask for explanations immediately, if possible; other students are likely to have the same questions. If you can't hear another student's question or response, ask him or her to repeat the question. Asking questions is particularly important in online courses; do not hesitate to e-mail your professor or other classmates to find answers to the questions that you have. And if you feel reluctant to ask a question yourself, conspire with a fellow student to ask the question for you. It doesn't matter who asks the question just so long as it gets asked. Most faculty really do like students to ask them questions, which means they welcome what might appear to you to be an "interruption."

8. **Sort, organize, and categorize.** When you listen and read, try to match what you are hearing and reading with what you already know. Take an active role in deciding how best to remember what you are learning. If you find yourself daydreaming during a lecture or reading your textbook, quickly refocus your thoughts on the topic and actively take notes. If your daydreaming produces an idea that you want to remember, write it down so you don't have to worry about forgetting it and then you can come back to it after class. After class or during your instructor's next office hours, ask him or her to help you fill in any gaps in your notes, or get together with another student—preferably one who is doing well in the course—and share and compare notes.

Speak Up

Naturally, you will be more likely to participate in a class in which the instructor emphasizes class discussion, calls on students by name, shows signs of approval and interest, and avoids criticizing students for an incorrect answer. Often, answers you and other students offer may not be quite correct, but they can lead to new perspectives on a topic. In certain types of courses there are fewer "correct" answers, and what matters is how well you can interpret what is being read and discussed and support your views with evidence and arguments.

Whether you are in a large, small, or online class, you might be nervous about asking a question, fearing you will make a fool of yourself. However, it is likely that other students have the same question but were too nervous to ask it. If so, they may thank you silently or even aloud! Many instructors set time aside to answer questions in class, so to take full advantage of these opportunities, try using the following techniques:

1. **Take a seat as close to the front as possible and keep your eyes on the instructor.** Sitting close to the front can help you concentrate better and not get distracted by other students. It will also make it easier to maintain eye contact with your instructors.

2. **Focus on the lecture and class discussions.** Avoid distractions. Sit away from friends who can distract you, do not engage in side conversations, and turn off all digital devices that you are not using for class.

3. **Raise your hand when you don't understand something.** If you don't understand something, you have the right to ask for an explanation. Never worry that you're asking a stupid question. The instructor might answer you immediately, ask you to wait until later in the class, or throw your question to the rest of the class. In each case, you benefit in several ways. The instructor will get to know you, other students will get to know you, and you will learn from both the instructor and your classmates. But don't overdo it, or you'll

❤ Hands Up!

Participating in class not only helps you learn but also shows your instructor that you're interested and engaged. Like anything else, you may be anxious the first time you raise your hand. But after that first time, you'll probably find that participating in class raises your interest and enjoyment.

PeopleImages/DigitalVision/ Getty Images

risk disrupting class. Office hours provide the perfect opportunity for following up. If you are taking an online course, you can e-mail your questions to your instructor.

4. **Speak up in class.** Ask a question, volunteer to answer a question, or make a comment. This becomes easier every time you do it.

5. **When the instructor calls on you to answer a question, don't bluff.** If you know the answer, give it. If you're not certain, begin with, "I think . . . , but I'm not sure I have it all correct." If you don't know, just say so.

6. **If you have recently read a book or article that is relevant to the class topic, bring it in.** Use it either to ask questions about the topic or to provide information that was not covered in class. You could also share your reading with your instructor privately either before or after class and ask what his/her opinion is of the source you have found.

YOUR TURN > TRY IT

Think about the number of times during the past week you have raised your hand in a particular class or e-mailed your online course instructor to ask a question. How many times has it been? Do you ask questions frequently, or is this something you avoid? Make a list of the reasons you either do or don't ask questions in class. Do this for each of the courses you are taking, and then compare your findings with your current grades in these courses. Do you see any link between your current grades and the extent to which you ask questions? Would asking more questions help you earn better grades? Do you feel more comfortable e-mailing your questions to your instructor?

TAKE EFFECTIVE NOTES

5.4

What are effective notes? They are notes that cover all the important points of the lecture or reading material without being too detailed or too limited. Most important, effective notes prepare you to do well on quizzes or exams. They also help you understand and remember concepts and facts. Becoming an effective note-taker requires time and practice, but this skill will help you improve your learning and your grades in the first year and beyond.

Note-Taking Formats

You can make class time more productive by using your listening skills to take effective notes, but first you have to decide on one of the following four commonly used formats: Cornell, outline, paragraph, and list formats. Any format can work as long as you use it consistently.

Cornell Format. Using the Cornell format, one of the best-known methods for organizing notes, you create a "recall" column on each page of your notebook or your Word document by drawing a vertical line about two to three inches from the left border or inserting a two-column table (see Figure 5.1). As you take notes during class—whether writing down or typing ideas, making lists, or using an outline or paragraph format—write or type only in the wider column on the right; leave the recall column on the left blank. The recall column is the place where you write down or type the main ideas and important details for tests and examinations as you go through your notes, which you should do as soon after class as possible, preferably within an hour or two. Many students have found the recall column to be an important part of note taking, one that becomes an effective study tool for tests and exams.

FIGURE 5.1 › Note Taking in the Cornell Format

Psychology 101
1/27/16
Theories of Personality

Personality trait define	Personality trait="durable disposition to behave in a particular way in a variety of situations"
Big 5: Name + describe them	Big 5–McCrae + Costa–(1)extroversion (or positive emotionality)=outgoing, sociable, friendly, upbeat, assertive; (2)neuroticism=anxious, hostile, self-conscious, insecure, vulnerable; (3)openness to experience=curiosity, flexibility, imaginative; (4)agreeableness=sympathetic, trusting, cooperative, modest; (5)conscientiousness=diligent, disciplined, well organized, punctual, dependable
Psychodynamic Theories: Who?	Psychodynamic Theories–focus on unconscious forces
3 components of personality: name and describe	Freud–psychoanalysis–3 components of personality–(1)id=primitive, instinctive, operates according to pleasure principle (immediate gratification); (2)ego=decision-making component, operates according to reality principle (delay gratification until appropriate); (3)superego=moral component, social standards, right + wrong
3 levels of awareness: name and describe	3 levels of awareness–(1)conscious=what one is aware of at a particular moment; (2)preconscious=material just below surface, easily retrieved; (3)unconscious=thoughts, memories, + desires well below surface, but have great influence on behavior

Outline Format. Some students find that an outline is the best way for them to organize their notes. In a formal outline, Roman numerals (I, II, III, etc.) mark the main ideas. Other ideas relating to each key idea are marked by uppercase letters (A, B, C, etc.), numbers (1, 2, 3, etc.), and low-ercase letters (a, b, c, etc.) in descending order of importance or detail. Using the outline format allows you to add details, definitions, examples, applications, and explanations (see Figure 5.2).

FIGURE 5.2 ‹ Note Taking in the Outline Format

Psychology 101
1/27/16
Theories of Personality

I. Personality trait = "durable disposition to behave in a particular way in a variety of situations"

II. Big 5–McCrae + Costa

   A. Extroversion (or positive emotionality)=outgoing, sociable, friendly, upbeat, assertive

   B. Neuroticism=anxious, hostile, self-conscious, insecure, vulnerable

   C. Openness to experience=curiosity, flexibility, imaginative

   D. Agreeableness=sympathetic, trusting, cooperative, modest

   E. Conscientiousness=diligent, disciplined, well organized, punctual, dependable

III. Psychodynamic Theories – focus on unconscious forces – Freud –psychoanalysis

   A. 3 components of personality

      1. Id=primitive, instinctive, operates according to pleasure principle (immediate gratification)

      2. Ego=decision-making component, operates according to reality principle (delay gratification until appropriate)

      3. Superego=moral component, social standards, right + wrong

   B. 3 levels of awareness

      1. Conscious=what one is aware of at a particular moment

      2. Preconscious=material just below surface, easily retrieved

      3. Unconscious=thoughts, memories, + desires well below surface, but have great influence on behavior

Paragraph Format. When you are taking notes on what you are reading, you might decide to write summary paragraphs—a note-taking format in which you write two or three sentences that sum up a larger section of material (see Figure 5.3). This method might not work well for class notes because it's difficult to summarize a topic until your instructor has covered it completely. By the end of the lecture, you might have forgotten critical information.

FIGURE 5.3 > Note Taking in the Paragraph Format

Psychology 101
1/27/16
Theories of Personality

A personality trait is a "durable disposition to behave in a particular way in a variety of situations"

Big 5: According to McCrae + Costa most personality traits derive from just 5 higher—order traits: extroversion (or positive emotionality), which is outgoing, sociable, friendly, upbeat, assertive; neuroticism, which means anxious, hostile, self-conscious, insecure, vulnerable; openness to experience characterized by curiosity, flexibility, imaginative; agreeableness, which is sympathetic, trusting, cooperative, modest; and conscientiousness means diligent, disciplined, well organized, punctual, dependable

Psychodynamic Theories: Focus on unconscious forces

Freud, father of psychoanalysis, believed in 3 components of personality: id, the primitive, instinctive, operates according to pleasure principle (immediate gratification); ego, the decision-making component, operates according to reality principle (delay gratification until appropriate); and superego, the moral component, social standards, right + wrong

Freud also thought there are 3 levels of awareness: conscious, what one is aware of at a particular moment; preconscious, the material just below surface, easily retrieved; and unconscious, the thoughts, memories, + desires well below surface, but have great influence on behavior

List Format. The list format can be effective in taking notes on terms and definitions, facts, or sequences such as personality types. It is easy to use lists in combination with the Cornell format.

FIGURE 5.4 › Note Taking in the List Format

Psychology 101
1/27/16
Theories of Personality

- A personality trait is a "durable disposition to behave in a particular way in a variety of situations"
- Big 5: According to McCrae + Costa most personality traits derive from just 5 higher-order traits
  - extroversion (or positive emotionality), which is outgoing, sociable, friendly, upbeat, assertive
  - neuroticism, which means anxious, hostile, self-conscious, insecure, vulnerable
  - openness to experience characterized by curiosity, flexibility, imaginative
  - agreeableness, which is sympathetic, trusting, cooperative, modest
  - conscientiousness, means diligent, disciplined, well organized, punctual, dependable
- Psychodynamic Theories: Focus on unconscious forces
- Freud, father of psychoanalysis, believed in 3 components of personality
  - id, the primitive, instinctive, operates according to pleasure principle (immediate gratification)
  - ego, the decision-making component, operates according to reality principle (delay gratification until appropriate)
  - superego, the moral component, social standards, right + wrong
- Freud also thought there are 3 levels of awareness
  - conscious, what one is aware of at a particular moment
  - preconscious, the material just below surface, easily retrieved
  - unconscious, the thoughts, memories, + desires well below surface, but have great influence on behavior

YOUR TURN › TRY IT

Using the list format, review the previous chapter and list the key ideas in your notebook or on a digital device. Add definitions, examples, and other explanations related to each key idea.

Note-Taking Techniques

Whatever note-taking format you choose, follow these important steps:

1. **Identify the main ideas.** The first principle of effective note taking is to identify and record the most important ideas in the lecture or reading. Although supporting details are important as well, focus your note taking on the main ideas. Such ideas can be buried in details, statistics, examples, or problems, but you will need to identify and record them for further study. Some instructors announce the purpose of a lecture or offer an outline of main ideas, followed by details. Other instructors develop presentation slides. If your instructor makes such materials available on a course/learning-management system (CMS/LMS) beforehand, you can print them out and take notes on the outline or next to the slides during the lecture. Some instructors change their tone of voice or repeat themselves for each key idea. Some ask questions or provide an opportunity for discussion. If an instructor says something more than once, chances are it is important. Ask yourself, "What does my instructor want me to know at the end of today's class?"

2. **Don't try to write down everything.** Some first-year students try to do just that. They stop being thinkers and become just note-takers. As you take notes, leave spaces so that you can fill in additional details that you might have missed during class but remember or read about later. Take the time to review and complete your notes as soon after class as possible. Once you have decided on a format for taking notes, you might also want to develop your own system of abbreviations. For example, you might write "inst" instead of "institution" or "eval" instead of "evaluation." Just make sure you will be able to understand your abbreviations when it's time to review.

3. **Don't be thrown by a disorganized lecturer.** When a lecture is disorganized, it's your job to try to organize what is said into general and specific points. When information is missing, you will need to indicate in your notes where the gaps are. After the lecture, review the reading material or ask your classmates to fill in these gaps, or ask your instructor. Some instructors have regular office hours for student appointments while others are willing to spend time after each class session to answer students' questions. The questions you ask might help your instructor realize which parts of the lecture need more attention or repetition. If your college offers what is known as "Supplemental Instruction" (SI), go for it—it is voluntary, and students who participate do earn better grades. In the SI session, you get the opportunity to share with the SI leader the concepts you did NOT understand in that week's class; in turn, the SI leader reports that information to the instructor, who will hopefully provide additional explanation in the next class meeting.

4. **Keep your notes and supplementary materials for each course separate.** Whether you use folders, binders, or some combination, label your materials with the course number and name. Before class, label and date the paper you will be using for taking notes; after class, organize your notes chronologically. In your folder or binder, create

separate tabbed sections for homework, lab assignments, graded and returned tests, and other materials. If you take notes on a digital device, you should create separate files and folders with specific names and dates. You can create a course folder and add subfolders for notes, assignments, and projects within each folder for that course.

5. **Download online notes, outlines or diagrams, charts, and graphs from the CMS/LMS site and bring them to class.** You might be able to save yourself a lot of time during class if you do not have to try to copy graphs and diagrams while the instructor is talking. Instead, you can focus on the ideas being presented while adding your own labels and notes.

6. **If handouts are distributed in class, label them and place them near your notes.** Add handouts to your binder or folder as you review your notes each day.

Taking Notes in Online Courses. When you are taking an online course, note taking becomes an essential activity because you need to summarize the reading material and put it in your own words, record your ideas and thoughts for online discussions, or keep track of the questions you may have to e-mail your instructor or your classmates at a later time.

Taking Notes in Nonlecture Courses. Always be ready to change your note-taking methods based on the situation. Group discussion is a popular way to teach in college because it engages students in active participation. On your campus you might also have courses with opportunities outside class to discuss the information covered in class.

How do you keep a record of what's happening in such classes? Assume you are taking notes in a problem-solving group assignment. You would begin your notes by asking yourself, "What is the problem?" and writing down the answer. As the discussion continues, you would list the solutions that are offered. These would be your main ideas. The important details might include the positive and negative aspects of each view or solution. The important thing to remember when taking notes in nonlecture courses is that you need to record the information presented by your classmates as well as by the instructor and to consider all reasonable ideas, even those that differ from your own. Make sure though that you designate in your notes what are the ideas of your instructor versus those of fellow students.

When a course has separate lecture and discussion sessions, you will need to understand how the discussion sessions relate to and add to the lectures. If the material covered in the discussion session is different from what was covered in the lecture, you might need to ask for help in organizing your notes. When similar topics are covered, you can combine your notes so that you have full coverage of each topic.

How to organize the notes you take in a class discussion depends on the purpose or form of the discussion. It usually makes good sense to begin with the list of issues or topics of the discussion. Another approach is to list the questions raised for discussion. If the discussion explores reasons for and against a particular argument, divide your notes into columns or sections for each set of reasons. When different views are presented in discussion, record all the ideas. Your instructor might ask you to compare your own opinions to those of other students and explain why and how you formed those opinions.

Taking Notes in Mathematics and Science Courses. Many mathematics and science courses build on one another from term to term and from year to year. When you take notes in one of these courses, you will likely need to go back to those notes in a future course. For example, when taking organic chemistry, you might need to review the notes you took in earlier chemistry courses. This can be particularly important if some time has passed since you completed your last related course, such as after a summer or a winter break.

Taking notes in math and science courses can be different from taking notes in other classes. The following tips can help:

- Write down any equations, formulas, diagrams, charts, graphs, and definitions that the instructor puts on the board or screen.
- Write the instructor's words as precisely as possible. Technical terms often have exact meanings and cannot be changed.
- Use standard symbols, abbreviations, and scientific notation.
- Write down all worked problems and examples step-by-step. The steps are often necessary in answering exam questions. Actively engage in solving the problem yourself as it is being solved at the front of the class. Be sure that you can follow the logic and understand the sequence of steps. If you have questions you cannot ask during lecture, write them down in your notes so that you can ask them in discussion, in the lab, or during the instructor's office hours.
- Consider taking your notes in pencil or erasable pen. You might need to make changes if you are copying long equations while also trying to pay attention to the instructor. You want to keep your notes as neat as possible. Later, you can use colored ink to add other details.
- Listen carefully to other students' questions and the instructor's answers. Take notes on the discussion and during question-and-answer periods.
- Use asterisks, exclamation points, question marks, or symbols of your own to highlight important points in your notes or questions that you need to come back to when you review.
- Refer back to the textbook after class; the text might contain better diagrams and other visual representations than you can draw while taking notes in class. If they are not provided in handouts or on the CMS, you might even want to scan or photocopy diagrams from the text and include them with your notes in your binder.
- Keep your binders for math and science courses until you graduate. They will serve as good review materials for later classes in math and science. In some cases, these notes can also be helpful in the workplace.

Using Technology to Take Notes. While some students use laptops, tablets, or other mobile devices for note taking (see the Tech Tip in this chapter), others prefer taking notes by hand so that they can easily circle important items or copy equations or diagrams while they are being presented. If you handwrite your notes, typing them after class for review purposes might be helpful, especially if you are a kinesthetic learner, preferring to learn through experience and practice. After class you can also cut and paste diagrams and other visuals into your notes and print a copy that might be easier to read than notes you wrote by hand.

Some students—especially aural learners, who prefer to hear information—find it advantageous to record lectures. Try an app like QuickVoice Recorder, Voice Recorder, or Super Notes. But if you record, don't become passive; listen actively. Students with specific types of learning disabilities might be urged to record lectures or use the services of note-takers, who type on a laptop while the student views the notes on a separate screen.

YOUR TURN ▸ DISCUSS IN CLASS

Use the following table to list the advantages and disadvantages of taking notes on a mobile device and by hand, and be prepared to discuss your ideas in class.

Typing notes on a mobile device		Handwriting notes on paper	
Advantages	Disadvantages	Advantages	Disadvantages

Review Your Notes

Unless we take steps to remember it, we forget much of the information we receive within the first 24 hours; in fact, the decline of memory over time is known as the **forgetting curve**. So if you do not review your notes almost immediately after class, it can be difficult to remember the material later. In two weeks, you will have forgotten up to 70 percent of it! Forgetting can be a serious problem when you are expected to learn and remember many different facts, figures, concepts, and relationships for a number of classes.

Immediate reviewing will help your overall understanding as well as your ability to remember important details during exams. Use the following three strategies:

1. **Write down the main ideas.** For five or ten minutes, quickly review your notes and select key words or phrases. Fill in the details you still remember but missed writing down. You might also want to ask your instructor or a classmate to quickly look at your notes to see if you have covered the major ideas.

2. **Repeat your ideas out loud.** Repeat a brief version of what you learned from the class either to yourself or to someone else. For many, the best way to learn something is to teach it to others. You will understand something better and remember it longer if you try to explain it to someone else such as your kids, your coworker, or a classmate. This helps you discover your own reactions and find the gaps in your understanding of the material. Asking and answering questions in class can also provide you with the feedback you need to make certain your understanding is accurate.

3. **Review your notes from the previous class just before the next class session.** As you sit in class the next time it meets, waiting for the instructor to begin, use the time to quickly review your notes from the previous class session. This will prepare you for the lecture that is about to begin and help you to ask questions about material from the earlier lecture that might not have been clear to you.

What if you have three classes in a row and no time for studying between them? Repeat the information as soon after class as possible. Review the most recent class first. Never delay doing this; if you do, it will take you longer to review, select main ideas, and repeat the ideas. With practice, you can complete the review of your main ideas from your notes quickly, perhaps between classes, during lunch, or while waiting for or riding the bus.

Compare Notes

Comparing notes with other students in a study group, online course, SI session, or learning community has a number of benefits. You will probably take better notes when you know that

- someone else will be looking at them,
- you will have a chance to see whether your notes are as clear and organized as those of other students, and
- you will be able to assess whether you agree on the most important points.

Take turns testing each other on what you have learned. This will help you predict exam questions and find out if you can answer them. In addition to sharing specific information from the class, you can also share with one another how you take and organize your notes. You might get new ideas that will help your overall learning.

Be aware, however, that merely copying another student's notes, no matter how good those notes are, does not benefit you as much as comparing notes does. If you had to be absent from a class because of illness or a family emergency, it's fine to ask for another student's notes to see what you missed, but just rewriting those notes might not help you learn the material. Instead, summarize the other student's notes in your own words so that you know you understand the important points.

Class Notes and Homework

Once you have reviewed your notes, you can use them to complete homework assignments. Follow these steps:

1. **Do a warm-up for your homework.** Before doing the assignment, look through your notes again. Use a separate sheet of paper to rework examples, problems, or exercises. If there is related assigned material in the textbook, review it. Go back to the examples. Cover any answers or solutions, and try to respond to the questions or complete the problems without looking. Keep in mind that it can help to go back through your course notes, reorganize them, highlight the important items, and create new notes that let you connect with the material.

‹ Many Heads Are Better Than One

Researchers have discovered that learning is enhanced by group study. Give it a try.

Clerkenwell/Getty Images

2. **Do any assigned problems and answer any assigned questions.** When you start doing your homework, read each question or problem and ask: What am I supposed to find or find out? What is most important? What is not all that important? Read each problem several times, and state it in your own words. Work the problem without referring to your notes or the text, as though you were taking a test. In this way, you will test your knowledge and know when you are prepared for exams.

3. **Don't give up too soon.** Start your homework with the hardest subject first while you are most energetic. When you face a problem or question that you cannot easily solve or answer, move on only after you have tried long enough. After you have completed the whole assignment, come back to any problems or questions that you could not solve or answer. Try once more, and then take a break. You might need to think about a particularly difficult problem for several hours or even days. Inspiration might come when you are waiting at a stoplight or just before you fall asleep. Remember, you need to be resilient and not give up when you face challenges and setbacks.

4. **Complete your work.** When you finish an assignment, talk to yourself about what you learned from it. Think about how the problems and questions were different from one another, which strategies were successful, and what form the answers took. Be sure to review any material you have not mastered. Ask for help from the instructor, a classmate, a study group, the campus learning center, or a tutor to learn how to answer questions that stumped you.

YOUR TURN ❯ STAY MOTIVATED

Now that you've read suggestions about taking notes and studying for class, and practiced using different note-taking formats, which ideas are you motivated to use in your own note taking? Come to class ready to explain which ideas appeal to you most and why.

EXPLORE NOTE-TAKING PROGRAMS AND APPS

Studies have shown that people remember only half of what they hear, which is a major reason to take notes during lectures. Solid note taking will help you better understand key concepts and make them easier to study and remember. Writing things down is important for you to start the process of creating your own way of understanding the materials.

THE PROBLEM *You don't take good notes because you aren't sure what is important. You have access to technology but aren't sure how to use it to take notes effectively.*

THE FIX *Along with making use of the note-taking formats presented in this chapter, use your smartphone, tablet, or laptop to save information and create tools that will help you study.*

HOW TO DO IT

MICROSOFT FEATURES

1. Microsoft **Word** is great for most classes. To highlight main ideas, you can bold or underline text, change the font size and color, highlight whole sections, and insert text boxes or charts. You can make bullet points or outlines and insert comments. As you review your notes, you can cut and paste to make things more coherent. You can also create a folder for each class so you can find everything you need easily.

2. Microsoft **Excel** is especially good for any class that involves calculations or financial statements. You can embed messages in the cells of a spreadsheet to explain calculations (the notes will appear as you hover your cursor over that cell).

3. Microsoft **PowerPoint** can be invaluable for visual learners. Instead of creating one giant, potentially confusing Word file, you can make a slideshow with a new slide for each key point. Some instructors also post the slides that they plan to use in class before each session. You can write notes on printouts of the slides, or download them and add your notes in PowerPoint.

APPS FOR NOTE TAKING AND REVIEWING

1. **Pocket** (iOS and Android) allows you to store and review written content from your phone.

2. **Evernote** (iOS and Android) lets you take a picture of handwritten or printed notes—or anything else you want to recall. Then you can file content and search it by keyword later.

3. **Simplenote** allows your notes to stay updated across all your devices, backs up your notes when you change them, and lets you find notes quickly with instant searching and simple tags.

4. **CamScanner** (iOS and Android) allows you to photograph, scan, share, and store notes.

5. **Tiny Scanner** (iOS) lets you scan any document and convert it into a PDF, saving time and money.

6. **TinyTap** (iOS) lets you create multiple-choice quizzes that you can take as practice and share with other students.

7. **StudyBlue** (iOS, Android, and Web Apps) allows you to make amazing-looking flash cards.

EXTRA STYLE POINTS

No matter what program or app you use, some rules always apply:

- Write down main points using phrases or key terms instead of long sentences.

- Date your notes; keep them in order and in one place; save files using file names with the course number, name, and date of the class; and back up everything.

- Keep a pen and paper handy for sketching graphs and diagrams.

- If you find it hard to keep up, practice your listening and typing skills. Consider a typing class, program, or app to learn how to type properly.

- If you prefer a spiral notebook and a ballpoint pen, that's OK; these formats are tried and true.

THINK

Reflect on what you have learned in this chapter about being engaged in learning and getting the most out of class. List some of the ways you can fully participate in your classes and increase your engagement based on what you have learned.

_____

_____

_____

_____

_____

_____

_____

_____

_____

WRITE

This chapter explores multiple strategies for being an active listener and reader and being engaged in class. What new strategies did you learn that you had never thought about or used before? What questions about effective note taking do you still have?

_____

_____

_____

_____

_____

APPLY

1. During the next week, try using the Cornell format in one class and the outline format in another class. Then compare your notes and decide which format helps you the most when you are studying and preparing for tests.
2. Create a PowerPoint or Prezi presentation on the main points of this chapter.

USE YOUR RESOURCES

Below are suggestions for resources that are available at many colleges and the online resources that are available to everyone.

AT YOUR COLLEGE

VISIT . . .	IF YOU NEED HELP . . .
Learning Center	preparing for class, taking notes, organizing your notes, and reviewing your notes with a tutor. Most centers offer note-taking tips and workshops for first-year students.
Computer Center	using Word, Excel, PowerPoint, OneNote, Simplenote, or Evernote to organize your notes.
Math Center	improving the notes you take in your math classes.
Disabled Student Services	arranging for a note-taker if you cannot take notes due to your documented disability.
Fellow college students	finding a tutor or joining a study group. Often, the best help you can get comes from those who are closest to you: fellow students. Keep an eye out in your classes for the most serious students. Those are the ones to seek out. It does not diminish you in any way to seek assistance from your peers.

ONLINE

GO TO . . .	IF YOU NEED HELP . . .
School for Champions: school-for-champions.com/grades/speaking.htm	locating guidelines for speaking in class.
Knowledge NoteBook: knowledgenotebook.com/review/best-note -taking-tips-from-10-colleges.html	finding note-taking tips.

MY COLLEGE'S RESOURCES

_____

_____

_____

6 Reading to Learn from College Textbooks

PRE-READING ACTIVITY: This chapter offers strategies for learning from college textbooks. What are some of the challenges you are facing in reading and understanding your textbooks this term?

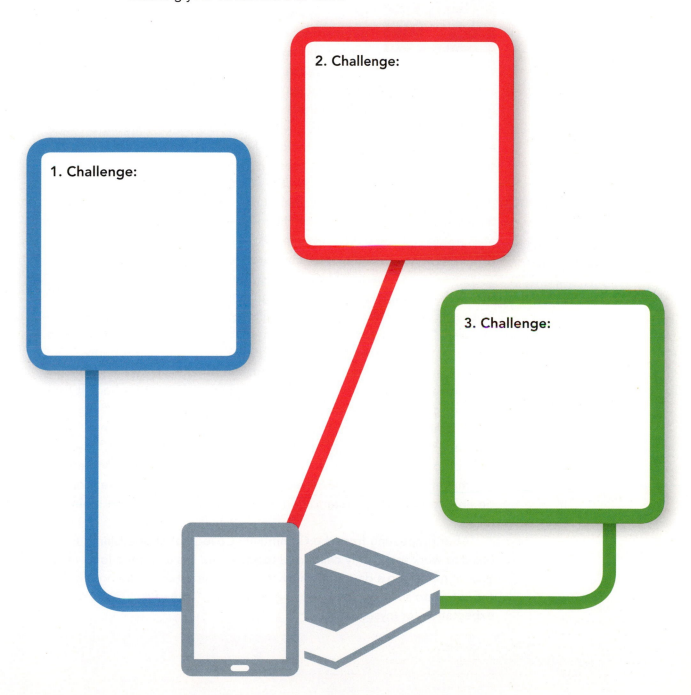

1. Challenge:

2. Challenge:

3. Challenge:

6.1 A Plan for Active Reading

6.2 Strategies for Reading Textbooks

6.3 Improving Your Reading

 PROFILE

Irene Ramirez, 25

Early Childhood Education Major, *Community College of Rhode Island*

 Irene Ramirez was born in New York City and spent most of her childhood in the Dominican Republic, where she also went to high school. After graduating, Irene returned to the United States to attend college. She first started at a community college but left at the end of her first term when she decided to get married. Recently, she decided to re-enroll in school and again chose to attend a community college because of smaller class sizes and more personal instruction, which she values highly, both as a student and as a mother raising two small children.

"It isn't easy being a mom, a wife, and also a full-time student," Irene explains. "Time is the hardest thing to find when you have toddlers, but they are my motivation." Irene uses a number of strategies to maximize her time and do the amount of reading expected in college. "I take small chunks of time and get the work done. I use my children's nap time as study time. I know nap time gives me at least two hours to go over an assignment." She uses those small blocks of time to learn. "If I don't have a lot of time, I skim over the material. When I have more time, I highlight the things that stuck in my head and identify main ideas." Irene also types her notes. "That way," she explains, "my mind focuses on the material more so than when I just read it. Even if I don't remember something after reading it, I'll probably remember it after typing it." Most important, though, Irene is careful to give herself enough time to learn the way that works best for her. "It took me a long time to figure out how it was easiest for me to learn," she says, "but I finally did, and I use the learning strategies that work for me."

> "It took me a long time to figure out how it was easiest for me to learn, but I finally did, and I use the learning strategies that work for me."

Irene's one piece of advice to other first-year students is: "Always read before you go to class, even if it's just before going in. Material will make a lot more sense when you have seen it once before. You will be able to better understand concepts, and you won't forget main ideas."

After graduating from the Community College of Rhode Island, Irene plans to work as an early childhood teacher. She has also set a long-term goal of managing a daycare facility. Irene isn't afraid of dreaming big. "If I set out to do something, I have to give it my all," she says. "That's my expectation for myself."

To access the LearningCurve study tool, Video Tools, and more, go to LaunchPad for *Understanding Your College Experience.* macmillanhighered.com /gardnerunderstanding

As Irene suggested, reading college textbooks is more challenging than reading high school texts or reading for pleasure. College-level texts are full of concepts, terms, and complex information that you are expected to learn on your own in a short period of time. To accomplish this, you will find it helpful to use the active reading strategies presented in this chapter. They can help you get the most out of your college reading.

Depending on how much reading you did before coming to college—reading for pleasure, for your classes, or for work—you might find that reading is your favorite or least favorite way to learn. Even if reading *isn't* your favorite thing to do, it is absolutely essential to doing well in college and at work—no matter what your major or profession might be.

A PLAN FOR ACTIVE READING

Active reading involves participating in reading by using strategies, such as highlighting and note taking, which help you stay focused. Active reading is different from reading novels or magazines for pleasure, which doesn't require you to do anything while you are reading. Active reading will increase your focus and concentration, help you understand what you read, and prepare you to study for tests and exams. These are the four steps in active reading designed to help you read college textbooks:

1. Previewing
2. Marking
3. Reading with concentration
4. Reviewing

YOUR TURN › WORK TOGETHER

With a group of your classmates, discuss which of these four steps you always, sometimes, or never take. Have one member of the group keep a tally and report results to the class. Which steps, if any, do your classmates think are necessary, and why?

Previewing

Previewing is the step in active reading where you develop a purpose for reading and take a first look at an assigned reading before you really tackle the content. Think of previewing as browsing in a newly remodeled store. You locate the pharmacy and grocery areas. You get a feel for the locations of the men's, women's, and children's clothing departments;

housewares; and electronics. You pinpoint the restrooms and checkout areas. You get a sense for where things are in relation to each other and compared to where they used to be. Then you focus on your purpose for coming to the store and identify where to find the items that you buy most often, whether they are diapers, milk, school supplies, or prescriptions. You get oriented.

Previewing a chapter in your textbook or other assigned reading is similar: The purpose is to get the big picture, to understand the main ideas in the reading and how those ideas connect with what you already know and to the material the instructor covers in class. Here's how you do it:

- Begin by reading the title of the chapter. Ask yourself: What do I already know about this subject?

- Next, quickly read through the learning objectives, if the chapter has them (usually stated as the chapter begins—or check the course syllabus), or the introductory paragraphs. **Learning objectives** are the main ideas or skills students are expected to learn from reading the chapter.

- Then turn to the end of the chapter and read the summary if there is one. A **summary** provides the most important ideas in the chapter.

- Finally, take a few minutes to skim the chapter, looking at the headings, subheadings, key terms, and tables and figures. Look for study exercises at the end of the chapter.

As part of your preview, note how many pages the chapter contains. It's a good idea to decide in advance how many pages you can reasonably expect to cover in your first study period. This can help build your concentration as you work toward your goal of reading a specific number of pages. Before long, you'll know how many pages are practical for you to read at one sitting whether in your book or on your screen.

If instead of a printed textbook for one or more of your courses you are accessing digital content, you should find effective ways to do each step of actively reading the material. Chapters in digital textbooks are often "scrollable" by learning objectives and sections. In addition, quizzes and interactive exercises allow you to test your understanding of the material and to practice concepts. Get familiar with the tools and navigation functions available to get the most out of digital products.

Previewing will require some time up front, but it will save you time later. As you preview the text material, look for connections between the text and the related lecture material. Remember the related terms and concepts in your notes from the lecture. Use these strategies to warm up. Ask yourself: Why am I reading this? What do I want to know?

Keep in mind that different types of textbooks can require more or less time to read. For example, depending on your interests and previous knowledge, you might be able to read a psychology text more quickly than a biology text that includes many unfamiliar scientific words. If you experience difficulty in reading any of your textbooks, ask for help from your instructor, another student, or a tutor at the learning center.

FIGURE 6.1 › Wheel and Branching Maps

Wheel Map

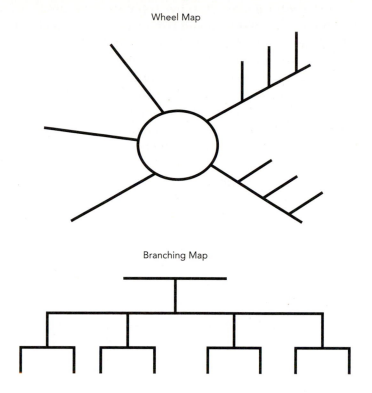

Branching Map

Mapping. Mapping is a preview strategy in which you draw a wheel or branching structure to show relationships between main ideas and secondary ideas and how different concepts and terms fit together; it also helps you make connections to what you already know about the subject (see Figure 6.1). Mapping the chapter as you preview it provides a visual guide for how different ideas in a chapter relate to each other. Because many students identify themselves as visual learners, visual mapping is an excellent learning tool not only for reading but also for test preparation.

In the wheel structure, place the central idea of the chapter in the circle. The central idea should be in the introduction to the chapter and might even be in the chapter title. Place secondary ideas on the lines connected to the circle, and place offshoots of those ideas on the lines attached to the main lines. In the branching map, the main idea goes at the top, followed by supporting ideas on the second tier, and so forth. Fill in the title first. Then, as you skim the chapter, use the headings and subheadings to fill in the key ideas.

YOUR TURN › TRY IT

Sketch either the wheel map or the branching map on a piece of notebook paper, and map this chapter.

Outlining or Listing. Perhaps you are more of a read/write learner than a visual learner and prefer a more step-by-step visual image. If so, consider making an outline of the headings and subheadings in the chapter (see Figure 6.2, which shows an outline of the first section of this chapter). You can usually identify main topics, subtopics, and specific terms under each subtopic in your text by the size of the print. Notice, also, that the different levels of headings in a textbook look different. They are designed to show relationships among topics and subtopics covered within a section. Flip through this textbook to see how the headings are designed—look at the main headings and also the subheadings.

To save time when you are outlining, don't write full sentences. Rather, include clear explanations of new technical terms and symbols. Pay special attention to topics that the instructor covered in class. If you aren't sure whether your outlines contain too much or too little detail, compare them with the outlines your classmates or members of your study

FIGURE 6.2 ❯ Sample Outline

I. Active Reading
  A. Previewing—Get lay of the land, skim
    1. Mapping
    2. Alternatives to Mapping
      a. Outlines
      b. Lists
      c. Chunking
      d. Flash cards
  B. Marking textbooks—Read and think BEFORE
    1. Underlining
    2. Highlighting
    3. Annotating (Margin notes)
  C. Reading with concentration—Use suggestions like
    1. Find proper location
    2. Turn off electronic devices
    3. Set aside blocks of time with breaks
    4. Set study goals
  D. Reviewing—Each week, review
    1. Notes
    2. Study questions
    3. Annotations
    4. Flash cards
    5. Visual maps
    6. Outlines

group have made. Check with your instructor during office hours. In preparing for a test, review your chapter outlines to see how everything fits together.

Another previewing technique is listing. A list can be effective when you are dealing with a textbook that introduces many new terms and their definitions. Set up the list with the terms in the left column, and fill in definitions, descriptions, and examples on the right as you read or reread. Divide the terms on your list into groups of five, seven, or nine, and leave white space between the clusters so that you can visualize each group in your mind. This practice is known as chunking. We learn material best when it is in chunks of five, seven, or nine.

Creating Flash Cards. Flash cards are like portable test questions—you write a question or term on the front of a small card and the answer or definition on the back. Or in a course that requires you to memorize dates, like American history, you might write a key date on one side of the card and the event on the other. To study chemistry, you would write a chemical formula on one side and the ionic compound on the other. You might use flash cards to learn vocabulary words or practice simple sentences for a language course. Creating the cards from your readings and using them to prepare for exams are great ways to retain information and are especially helpful for visual and kinesthetic learners. Some apps, such as Chegg Flashcards or StudyBlue, enable you to create flash cards on your mobile devices (see Figure 6.3). If you are using digital course materials, it is likely that each chapter offers digital flash cards that you can click through. Often digital flash cards in college course materials give students the ability to sort the cards by front or back and to make virtual piles of the terms and concepts they need to practice and those they have mastered.

FIGURE 6.3 ❯ Examples of Flash Cards

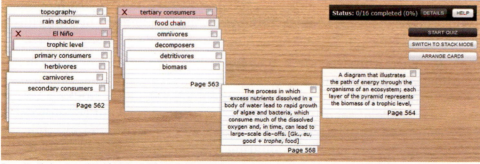

From Jay Phelan, *LaunchPad for What Is Life? A Guide to Biology*, 2nd ed. (New York: W.H. Freeman, 2013).

YOUR TURN ❯ TRY IT

Prepare flash cards for the key terms that appear in this chapter. Key terms are defined where they appear in the text.

Strategies for Reading and Marking Your Textbook

After completing your preview, you are ready to read the text actively. With your map, outline, list, or flash cards to guide you, mark the sections that are most important. To avoid marking too much or marking the wrong information, first read without using your pencil, highlighter, or any digital tools. This means you should read the text *at least* twice.

Marking is an active reading strategy that helps you focus and concentrate as you read. When you mark your textbook, you underline, highlight, or make margin notes or annotations—notes or remarks about a piece of writing—either on the book or digitally on your e-book pages. Figure 6.4 provides an example of each method. No matter what method you prefer, remember these important guidelines:

1. **Read before you mark.** Finish reading a section before you decide which are the most important ideas and concepts.

2. **Think before you mark.** When you read a text for the first time, everything can seem important. After you complete a section, reflect on it to identify the key ideas. Ask yourself: What are the most important ideas? What terms has the instructor emphasized in class? What will I see on the test? This can help you avoid marking too much material. On a practical note, if you find that you have made mistakes in how you have highlighted or that your textbooks were already highlighted by another student, select a completely different color highlighter to use. It is easier to correct highlighting mistakes on e-books by undoing them.

3. **Highlight or underline purposefully.** Highlights and underlines are intended to pull your eye only to key words and important facts. If highlighting or underlining is actually a form of procrastination for you (you are reading through the material but planning to learn it at a later date) or if you are highlighting or underlining nearly everything you read, you might be doing yourself more harm than good. You won't be able to identify important concepts quickly if they're lost in a sea of color or lines. Ask yourself whether your highlighting or underlining is helping you be more active in your learning process.

4. **Take notes while you are marking.** Rather than relying on marking alone, consider taking notes as you read. Just noting what's most important doesn't mean you learn the material, and it can give you a false sense of security. When you force yourself to put something in your own words while taking notes, you are not only predicting exam questions but also evaluating whether you can answer them. You can add your notes to the map, outline, list, or flash cards you created while you previewed the text or use the digital tools available for note taking on e-books. You can then review your notes from the reading with a friend or study group when preparing for tests and exams.

Although these active reading strategies take more time at the beginning, they save you time in the long run because they help you focus on the reading and make it easy to review.

FIGURE 6.4 ❭ Examples of Marking

Using a combination of highlighting, lines, and margin notes, the reader has made the content of this page easy to review. Without reading the text, note the highlighted words and phrases and the margin notes, and see how much information you can gather from them. Then read the text itself. Does the markup serve as a study aid? Does it cover the essential points? Would you have marked this page any differently? Why or why not?

"The Stress of Adapting to a New Culture." Adapted from D. H. Hockenbury and S. E. Hockenbury, *Discovering Psychology*, 6th ed. (New York: Worth, 2013), 534. Used with permission.

CULTURE AND HUMAN BEHAVIOR

The Stress of Adapting to a New Culture

differences affecting cultural stress

Refugees, immigrants, and even international students are often unprepared for the dramatically different values, language, food, customs, and climate that await them in their new land. The process of changing one's values and customs as a result of contact with another culture is referred to as acculturation. **Acculturative stress** is the stress that results from the pressure of adapting to a new culture (Sam & Berry, 2010).

acceptance of new culture reduces stress

also speaking new language, education, & social support

Many factors can influence the degree of acculturative stress that a person experiences. For example, when the new society accepts ethnic and cultural diversity, acculturative stress is reduced (Mana & others, 2009). The transition is also eased when the person has some familiarity with the new language and customs, advanced education, and social support from friends, family members, and cultural associations (Schwartz & others, 2010). Acculturative stress is also lower if the new culture is similar to the culture of origin.

how attitudes affect stress

Cross-cultural psychologist John Berry (2003, 2006) has found that a person's attitudes are important in determining how much acculturative stress is experienced (Sam & Berry, 2010). When people encounter a new cultural environment, they are faced with two questions: (1) Should I seek positive relations with the dominant society? (2) Is my original cultural identity of value to me, and should I try to maintain it?

4 patterns of acculturation

The answers produce one of four possible patterns of acculturation: integration, assimilation, separation, or marginalization (see the diagram). Each pattern represents a different way of coping with the stress of adapting to a new culture (Berry, 1994, 2003).

1* Integrated individuals continue to value their original cultural customs but also seek to become part of the dominant society. They embrace a *bicultural* identity (Hunyh & others, 2011). Biculturalism is associated with higher self-esteem and lower levels of depression, anxiety, and stress, suggesting that the bicultural identity may be the most adaptive acculturation pattern (Schwartz & others, 2010). The successfully integrated individual's level of acculturative stress will be low (Lee, 2010).

2* Assimilated individuals give up their old cultural identity and try to become part of the new society. They adopt the customs and social values of the new environment, and abandon their original cultural traditions.

possible rejection by both cultures

Assimilation usually involves a moderate level of stress, partly because it involves a psychological loss—one's previous cultural identity. People who follow this pattern also face the possibility of being rejected either by members of the majority culture or by members of their original culture (Schwartz & others, 2010). The

Acculturative Stress Acculturative stress can be reduced when immigrants learn the language and customs of their newly adopted home. Here, two friends, one from China, one from Cuba, help each other in an English class in Miami, Florida.

process of learning new behaviors and suppressing old behaviors can also be moderately stressful.

3* Individuals who follow the pattern of separation maintain their cultural identity and avoid contact with the new culture. They may refuse to learn the new language, live in a neighborhood that is primarily populated by others of the same ethnic background, and socialize only with members of their own ethnic group.

In some cases, separation is not voluntary, but is due to the dominant society's unwillingness to accept the new immigrants. Thus, it can be the result of discrimination. Whether voluntary or involuntary, the level of acculturative stress associated with separation tends to be high.

separation may be self-imposed or discriminating

higher stress with separation

4* Finally, the marginalized person lacks cultural and psychological contact with *both* his traditional cultural group and the culture of his new society. By taking the path of marginalization, he lost the important features of his traditional culture but has not replaced them with a new cultural identity.

Although rare, the path of marginalization is associated with the greatest degree of acculturative stress. Marginalized individuals are stuck in an unresolved conflict between their traditional culture and the new society, and may feel as if they don't really belong anywhere. Fortunately, only a small percentage of immigrants fall into this category (Schwartz & others, 2010).

marginalized = higher level of stress

	Question 1: Should I seek positive relations with the dominant society?	
	Yes	**No**
Question 2: Is my original cultural identity of value to me, and should I try to maintain it? **Yes**	Integration	Separation
No	Assimilation	Marginalization

Patterns of Adapting to a New Culture According to cross-cultural psychologist John Berry, there are four basic patterns of adapting to a new culture (Sam & Berry, 2010). Which pattern is followed depends on how the person responds to the two key questions shown.

Reading with Concentration

You might have trouble concentrating or understanding some content when you read textbooks. This is normal, and many factors contribute to this problem: the time of day, your energy level, your interest in the material, how you manage nearby distractions, the amount of sleep you have had in the past 24 hours, and your study location.

The next time you are reading a textbook, monitor your ability to concentrate. Check your watch when you begin, and check it again when your mind begins to wander. How many minutes did you concentrate on your reading? What can you do to keep your mind from wandering?

Consider these suggestions, and decide which would help you improve your reading ability:

- **Find a quiet study place.** Choose a room or location away from traffic and distracting noises such as the campus information commons. Avoid studying in your bed because your body is conditioned to go to sleep there.

- **Mute or power off your electronic devices.** Store your cell phone in your book bag or some other place where you aren't tempted to check it. If you are reading on a device like a laptop or tablet, download what you need and disconnect from WiFi, so you're not tempted to e-mail, chat, or check social media sites.

- **Read in blocks of time, with short breaks in between.** Some students can read for 50 minutes; others find that a 50-minute reading period is too long. By reading for small blocks of time throughout the day instead of cramming in all your reading at the end of the day, you should be able to process material more easily.

- **Set goals for your study period.** A realistic goal might be "I will read 20 pages of my psychology text in the next 50 minutes." Reward yourself with a 10-minute break after each 50-minute study period.

- **Engage in physical activity during breaks.** If you have trouble concentrating or staying awake, take a quick walk around the library or down the hall. Stretch or take some deep breaths, and think positively about your study goals. Then go back to studying.

- **Actively engage with the material.** Write study questions in the margins, take notes, or recite key ideas. Reread confusing parts of the text, and make a note to ask your instructor for clarification.

- **Focus on the important portions of the text.** Pay attention to the first and last sentences of paragraphs and to words in italics or bold type.

- **Understand the words.** Use the **glossary** (a list of key words and their definitions) in the text or a dictionary to find definitions of unfamiliar terms.

- **Use organizers as you read.** Keep the maps, outlines, lists, or flash cards you created during your preview as you read, and add to them as you go. For example, you can use Table 6.1 to organize information while you are reading:

TABLE 6.1 > Example of an Organizer

Date:	Course:
Textbook:	Chapter # and Title:

What is the overall idea of the reading?

What is the **main idea** of each major section of the reading?

Section 1:

Section 2:

Section 3:

What **supporting ideas** are presented in each section of the reading? Examples? Statistics? Any reference to research?

1.

2.

3.

4.

5.

What are the **key terms**, and what do they mean?

What are the **conclusions** from the reading?

What are two or three things I remember after reading?

1.

2.

3.

Reviewing

The final step in active textbook reading is reviewing. **Reviewing** means looking through your assigned reading again. Many students expect to read through their text material once and be able to remember the ideas four, six, or even twelve weeks later at test time. More realistically, you will need to include regular reviews in your study process. Here is where your class notes, study questions, margin notes and annotations, flash cards, visual maps, or outlines will be most useful. Your study goal should be to review the material from each chapter every week. Here are some strategies for using your senses to review your reading:

- Recite aloud.
- Tick off each item on a list on your fingertips.
- Post diagrams, maps, or outlines around your living space to see them often and visualize them while taking the test.

6.2 STRATEGIES FOR READING TEXTBOOKS

As you begin reading, be sure to learn more about the textbook and its author by reading sections at the beginning of the book, such as the preface, foreword, introduction, and author's biographical sketch. The **preface**, a brief overview usually at the beginning of a book, is typically written by the author (or authors) and tells you why they wrote the book and what material the book covers; it also explains the book's organization and give insight into the author's viewpoint—all of which will likely help you see the relationships among the facts presented and comprehend the ideas presented across the book. Reading the preface can come in handy if you are feeling a little lost at different points in the term. The preface often lays out the tools available in each chapter to guide you through the content, so if you find yourself struggling with the reading, be sure you are taking advantage of these tools.

The **foreword** is often an endorsement of the book written by someone other than the author. Some books have an additional **introduction** that reviews the book's overall organization and its contents, often chapter by chapter. Some textbooks include study questions at the end of each chapter. Take time to read and respond to these questions, whether or not your instructor requires you to do so.

YOUR TURN > DISCUSS IT

How do you usually read a textbook chapter? Do you just read it? Do you highlight or take notes as you go?

Textbooks Are Not Created Equal

Textbooks in the major **disciplines**—areas of academic study—are different in their organizations and styles of writing. Some may be easier to understand than others, but don't give up if the reading level is challenging.

Math and science texts are filled with graphs and figures that you will need to understand in order to grasp the content and the classroom presentations. They are also likely to have less text and more practice exercises than other textbooks do. If you have trouble reading and understanding any of your textbooks, get help from your instructor or your college's learning center.

Textbooks must try to cover a lot of material in a limited space, and they do not necessarily provide all the things you want to know about a topic. If you find yourself interested in a particular topic, go to the **primary sources**—the original research or documents on a topic. You'll find those referenced in almost all textbooks, either at the end of the chapters or in the back of the book.

You might also go to other related sources that make the text more interesting and easier to understand. Your instructors might use the textbook only to supplement the lectures. Some instructors expect you to read the textbook carefully while others are much more concerned that you can understand broad concepts that come primarily from lectures. If your instructor hasn't made it very clear how the text will be used, then you should ask the instructor for clarification. Ask your instructors what parts of the text the tests will cover and what types of questions will be used. It is also very important to ask if the tests will be cumulative, meaning going all the way back to the beginning of the course or just covering the material since the previous test.

Finally, not all textbooks are written in the same way. Some are better designed and written than others. If your textbook seems disorganized or hard to understand, let your instructor know your opinion; other students in your class may feel the same way. You could be helping future students by encouraging the instructor to change books! Your instructor might spend some class time explaining the text, its structure, and how it will be used in the course, and he or she can meet with you during office hours to help you with the material.

❮ Getting the Most Out of Your Textbooks

Math and science texts are filled with graphs and figures that you will need to understand to learn the content and the classroom presentations. If you have trouble reading and understanding any of your textbooks, get help from your instructor or your classmates.

Math Texts

While the previous suggestions about textbook reading apply across the board, mathematics textbooks present some special challenges because they usually have lots of symbols and few words. Each statement and every line in the solution of a problem needs to be considered and processed slowly. Typically, the author presents the material through definitions, theorems, and sample problems. As you read, pay special attention to definitions. Learning all the terms that relate to a new topic is the first step toward understanding.

Math texts usually include derivations of formulas and proofs of theorems. You must understand and be able to apply the formulas and theorems, but unless your course has a particularly theoretical emphasis, you are less likely to be responsible for all the proofs. So if you get lost in the proof of a theorem, go on to the next item in the section. When you come to a sample problem, it's time to get busy. Pick up pencil and paper, and work through the problem in the book. Then cover the solution and think through the problem on your own.

Of course, the exercises in each section are the most important part of any math textbook. A large portion of the time you devote to the course will be spent completing assigned exercises. It is absolutely necessary to do this homework before the next class, whether or not your instructor collects it. Success in mathematics requires regular practice, and students who keep up with math homework, either alone or in groups, perform better than students who don't, particularly when they include in their study groups other students who are more advanced in math.

After you complete the assignment, skim through the other exercises in the problem set. Reading the unassigned problems will help you understand more about the topic. Finally, talk the material through to yourself, and be sure your focus is on understanding the problem and its solution, not on memorization. Memorizing something might help you remember how to work through one problem, but it does not help you learn the steps involved so that you can use them for solving other similar problems.

YOUR TURN > DISCUSS IT

Discuss with classmates two or three of your challenges in learning from your math textbooks. Share some strategies that you use to study math.

Science Texts

Your approach to your science textbook will depend somewhat on whether you are studying a math-based science, such as physics, or a text-based science, such as biology. In either case, you need to become familiar with the overall format of the book. Review the table of contents and the glossary, and check the material in the **appendixes** (supplemental materials at the end of the book). There you will find lists of physical constants, unit conversions, and various charts and tables. Many physics and chemistry books also include a mini-review of the math you will need in science courses (see Figure 6.5).

FIGURE 6.5 ❯ Reading Science Textbooks

This page from a chemistry textbook includes abbreviations you'd need to know for practice exercises and a formula for calculating medicine dosages. If you need help with any of your textbooks, ask your instructor or classmates.

Excerpt from page 23 of *Essentials of General, Organic, and Biochemistry*, 2nd ed., by Denise Guinn. Copyright © 2012 by W. H. Freeman. Used by permission.

PRACTICE EXERCISES

23 Using the conversions on page 12, convert the following units into calories:
   a. 5.79 kcal   **b.** 48.8 J
24 How many joules are there in 2.45 cal?
25 How many joules are there in 2,720 Calories, the amount of energy the average person consumes in a day?

Dosage Calculations

For some medicines prescribed for patients, the dosage must be adjusted according to the patient's weight. This is especially true when administering medicine to children. For example, a dosage of "8.0 mg of tetracycline per kilogram body weight daily" is a dosage based on the weight of the patient. A patient's weight is often given in pounds, yet many drug handbooks give the dosage per kilogram body weight of the patient. Therefore, to calculate the correct amount of medicine to give the patient, you must first convert the patient's weight from pounds into kilograms with an English-metric conversion, using Table 1-3.

   It is important to recognize that the dosage is itself a conversion factor between the mass or volume of the medicine and the weight of the patient. Whenever you see the word *per*, it means *in every* and can be expressed as a ratio or fraction where *per* represents a division operation (divided by). For example, 60 miles *per* hour can be written as the ratio 60 mi/1 hr. Similarly, a dosage of 8.0 mg *per* kg body weight can be expressed as the fraction 8.0 mg/1 kg. Hence, dosage *is* a conversion factor:

$$\frac{8 \text{ mg}}{1 \text{ kg}} \quad \text{or} \quad \frac{1 \text{ kg}}{8 \text{ mg}}$$

Dimensional analysis is used to solve dosage calculations by multiplying the patient's weight by the appropriate English-metric conversion factor and then multiplying by the dosage conversion factor, as shown in the following worked exercise.

> 📌 Some common abbreviations indicating the frequency with which a medication should be administered include *q.d.* and *b.i.d.*, derived from the Latin meaning administered "daily" and "twice daily," respectively. If the medicine is prescribed for two times daily or four times daily, divide your final answer by two or four to determine how much to give the patient at each administration.

WORKED EXERCISE | Dosage Calculations

1-19 Tetracycline elixir, an antibiotic, is ordered at a dosage of 8.0 mg per kilogram of body weight q.d. for a child weighing 52 lb. How many milligrams of tetracycline elixir should be given to this child daily?

Solution

Step 1: Identify the conversions. Since the dosage is given based on a patient's weight in kilograms, an English-to-metric conversion must be performed. From Table 1-3 this is 1.000 kg = 2.205 lb. The dosage itself is already a conversion factor.

Step 2: Express each conversion as two possible conversion factors. The English-to-metric conversion factors for the patient's weight are

$$\frac{1 \text{ kg}}{2.205 \text{ lb}} \quad \text{or} \quad \frac{2.205 \text{ lb}}{1 \text{ kg}}$$

The dosage *is* a conversion factor between the mass of medicine in milligrams and the weight of the patient in kilograms:

$$\frac{8.0 \text{ mg}}{1 \text{ kg}} \quad \text{or} \quad \frac{1 \text{ kg}}{8.0 \text{ mg}}$$

Notice the organization of each chapter, and pay special attention to graphs, charts, and boxes. The amount of technical detail might seem overwhelming. Remember that most textbook authors take great care in presenting material in a logical format, and they include tools to guide you through the material. Learning objectives at the start and summaries at the end of each chapter can be useful to study both before and after reading the chapter. You will usually find answers to selected problems in the back of the book. Use the answer key or the student solutions manual to increase your understanding of the chapters.

As you begin an assigned section in a science text, skim the material quickly to gain a general idea of the topic and to begin becoming familiar with the new vocabulary and technical symbols. Then look over the end-of-chapter problems so that you'll know what to look for in your detailed reading of the chapter. State a specific purpose: "I'm going to learn about recent developments in plate tectonics," or "I'm going to distinguish between mitosis and meiosis," or "Tonight I'm going to focus on the topics in this chapter that were stressed in class."

Should you underline and highlight, or should you outline the material in your science textbooks? You might decide to underline or highlight for a subject such as anatomy, which involves a lot of memorization. In most sciences, however, it is best to outline the text chapters.

Social Science and Humanities Texts

Many of the suggestions that apply to science textbooks also apply to reading in the **social sciences** (academic disciplines that examine human aspects of the world, such as sociology, psychology, anthropology, economics, political science, and history). Social science textbooks are filled with terms specific to the particular field of study (see Figure 6.6). These texts also describe research and theory building and contain references to many primary sources. Your social science texts might also describe differences in opinions or perspectives. Social scientists do not all agree on any one issue, and you might be introduced to a number of ongoing debates about particular issues. In fact, your reading can become more interesting if you seek out different opinions about the same issue. You might have to go beyond your course textbook, but your library will be a good source of various viewpoints about ongoing controversies.

Textbooks in the **humanities** (branches of knowledge that investigate human beings, their culture, and their self-expression, such as philosophy, religion, literature, music, and art) provide facts, examples, opinions, and original material such as stories or essays. You will often be asked to react to your reading by identifying central themes or characters.

YOUR TURN > WORK TOGETHER

In a small group, discuss how important you think textbooks are in your courses in terms of what the instructor expects you to learn and master. What are some other ways to access the information you want and need in order to learn?

FIGURE 6.6 › Social Science Textbook Page

Strategies for reading and note taking should change depending on what kind of textbook you are reading. When reading a social science textbook, such as the economics book shown here, you can see how a section is broken into subsections. Headings help guide you through the content. A table is included with examples that illustrate what is being discussed to help you better understand the material.

From *Core Economics*, 3rd ed., by Eric Chiang. Copyright © 2014 by Eric Chiang. Used by permission of Worth Publishers.

Determinants of Elasticity

Price elasticity of demand measures how sensitive sales are to price changes. But what determines elasticity itself? The four basic determinants of a product's elasticity of demand are (1) the availability of substitute products, (2) the percentage of income or household budget spent on the product, (3) the difference between luxuries and necessities, and (4) the time period being examined.

Substitutability The more close substitutes, or possible alternatives, a product has, the easier it is for consumers to switch to a competing product and the more elastic the demand. For many people, beef and chicken are substitutes, as are competing brands of cola, such as Coke and Pepsi. All have relatively elastic demands. Conversely, if a product has few close substitutes, such as insulin for diabetics or tobacco for heavy smokers, its elasticity of demand tends to be lower.

Proportion of Income Spent on a Product A second determinant of elasticity is the proportion (percentage) of household income spent on a product. In general, the smaller the percent of household income spent on a product, the lower the elasticity of demand. For example, you probably spend little of your income on salt, or on cinnamon or other spices. As a result, a hefty increase in the price of salt, say 25%, would not affect your salt consumption because the impact on your budget would be tiny. But if a product represents a significant part of household spending, elasticity of demand tends to be greater, or more elastic. A 10% increase in your rent upon renewing your lease, for example, would put a large dent in your budget, significantly reducing your purchasing power for many other products. Such a rent increase would likely lead you to look around earnestly for a less expensive apartment.

Luxuries Versus Necessities The third determinant of elasticity is whether the good is considered a luxury or a necessity. Luxuries tend to have demands that are more elastic than those of necessities. Necessities such as food, electricity, and health care are more important to everyday living, and quantity demanded does not change significantly when prices rise. Luxuries such as trips to Hawaii, yachts, and designer watches, on the other hand, can be given up when prices rise.

Time Period The fourth determinant of elasticity is the time period under consideration. When consumers have some time to adjust their consumption patterns, the elasticity of demand becomes more elastic. When they have little time to adjust, the elasticity of demand tends to be more inelastic. Thus, as we saw earlier, when gasoline prices rise suddenly, most consumers cannot immediately change their transportation patterns, therefore gasoline sales do not drop significantly. However, as gas prices continue to remain high, we see shifts in consumer behavior, to which automakers respond by producing smaller, more fuel-efficient cars.

Table 1 provides a sampling of estimates of elasticities for specific products. As we might expect, medical prescriptions and taxi service have relatively inelastic price elasticities of demand, while foreign travel and restaurant meals have relatively elastic demands.

Selected Estimates of Price Elasticities of Demand					TABLE 1
Inelastic		**Roughly Unitary Elastic**		**Elastic**	
Salt	0.1	Movies	0.9	Shrimp	1.3
Gasoline (short run)	0.2	Shoes	0.9	Furniture	1.5
Cigarettes	0.2	Tires	1.0	Commuter rail service (long run)	1.6
Medical care	0.3	Private education	1.1	Restaurant meals	2.3
Medical prescriptions	0.3	Automobiles	1.2	Air travel	2.4
Pesticides	0.4			Fresh vegetables	2.5
Taxi service	0.6			Foreign travel	4.0

Source: Compiled from numerous studies reporting estimates for price elasticity of demand.

Supplementary Material

Whether your instructor requires you to read material in addition to the textbook, you will learn more about the topic if you go to some of the primary and supplementary sources that are referenced in each chapter of your text. These sources can be journal articles, research papers, or original essays, and they can be found online or in your library. Reading the original source material will give you more detail than most textbooks do.

Many of these sources were originally written for other instructors or researchers. Therefore, they often refer to concepts that are familiar to other scholars but not necessarily to first-year college students. If you are reading a journal article that describes a theory or research study, one technique for easier understanding is to read from the end to the beginning. That is, first read the article's conclusion and discussion sections. Then go back to see how the author performed the experiment or formed the ideas. In almost all scholarly journals, articles are introduced by an **abstract**, a paragraph-length summary of the methods and major findings. Reading the abstract is a quick way to get the main points of a research article before you start reading it. As you're reading research articles, always ask yourself: So what? Was the research important to what we know about the topic, or, in your opinion, was it unnecessary?

6.3

IMPROVING YOUR READING

With effort, you *can* improve your reading. Remember to be flexible and to adjust *how* you read depending on *what* you are reading. If you feel that you do not understand what you are reading because you are thinking about something else, you need to stop and focus on the task and read actively, marking and taking notes. Here are a few suggestions:

- Evaluate the importance and difficulty of the assigned readings, and adjust your reading style and the time you set aside to do the reading.

How you read your math textbook is different from how you read your psychology textbook. When reading your math textbook, you should have a notebook to record your solutions to the problems. When you read your psychology textbook, you should be highlighting the important ideas or making margin notes.

- Connect one important idea to another by asking yourself: Why am I reading this? Where does this fit in? Writing summaries and preparing notes and outlines can help you connect ideas across the chapters.

- When the textbook material is exactly the same as the lecture material, you can save time by concentrating mainly on one or the other.

It takes a planned approach to read and understand textbook materials and other assigned readings and to remember what you have read.

Monitoring Your Reading

You can monitor your comprehension while reading textbooks by asking yourself: Do I understand this? If not, stop and reread the material. Look up words that are not clear. Try to clarify the main points and how they relate to one another.

Another way to check that you understand what you are reading is to try to recite the material aloud, either to yourself or to your study partner(s). Using a study group to monitor your comprehension gives you immediate feedback and is highly motivating. After you have read with concentration from the first section of the chapter, proceed to each subsequent section until you have finished the chapter.

After you have completed each section and before you move on to the next section, ask again: What are the key ideas? What will I see on the test? At the end of each section, try to guess what information the author will present in the next section.

Developing Your Vocabulary

Textbooks are full of new words and terms. A **vocabulary** is a set of words in a particular language or field of knowledge. As you become familiar with the vocabulary of an academic field, reading the texts related to that field becomes easier.

If words are such a basic and essential component of our knowledge, what is the best way to learn them? The following are some basic vocabulary-building strategies:

- **Notice and write down unfamiliar terms during your preview of a text.** Consider making a flash card for each term or making a list of terms.

- **Think about the context when you come across challenging words.** See whether you can guess the meaning of an unfamiliar term by using the words around it.

- **Consider a word's parts.** If context by itself is not enough to help you guess the meaning of an unfamiliar word, try analyzing the term to discover its **root** (or base part) and any **prefixes** (parts that come before the root) or **suffixes** (parts that follow the root). For example, *transport* has the root *port*, which means "carry," and the prefix *trans*, which means "across." Together the word means "carrying across" or "carrying from one place to another." Knowing the meaning of prefixes and suffixes can be very helpful.

- **Use the glossary of the text or a dictionary.** Textbook publishers carefully compile glossaries to help students learn the vocabulary of a given discipline. And typically, the glossary is found in the back of the text (like in this textbook). If the text has no glossary, have a dictionary on hand or do a quick online search for the word's meaning. If a given word has more than one definition, search for the meaning that fits your text. The online Merriam-Webster Dictionary (**merriam-webster. com**) is especially helpful for college students.

- **Use new words in your writing and speaking.** If you use a new word a few times, you'll soon know it. In addition, flash cards can be handy at exam time for reviewing the definitions of new words.

YOUR TURN › TRY IT

Choose a chapter in this or another textbook. As you read it, list the words that are new to you or that you're not sure you understand. Look up a few of these words in a dictionary. Set a goal to add at least one new word a week to your personal vocabulary.

What to Do When You Fall Behind on Your Reading

From time to time, life might get in the way of doing your assigned readings on time. You may get sick or have to take care of a sick family member, you may have to work extra hours, or you may have a personal problem that prevents you from concentrating on your courses for a short time. Unfortunately, some students procrastinate and think they can catch up. That is a myth. The less you read and do your assignments, the harder you will have to work to make up for the lost time.

If you try to follow the schedule for your assigned readings but fall behind, do not panic. Here are some suggestions for getting back on track with your reading:

- **Add one or two hours a day to your study time to go back and read the parts that you missed.** In particular, take advantage of every spare moment to read; for example, read during your lunch hour at work or while you are waiting for public transportation or at the doctor's office.

- **Join a study group.** If everyone in the group reads a section of the assigned chapter and shares and discusses his or her notes, summaries, or outlines with the group, you can all cover the content more quickly.

- **Ask for help.** Visit your college's learning center to work with a tutor who can help you with difficult concepts in the textbook.

- **Talk to your instructor.** Ask for extra time to make up your assignments if you have fallen behind because of a valid reason such as sickness or dealing with a personal problem. Most instructors are willing to make a one-time exception to help students catch up.

- **Do not give up.** You may have to work harder for a short period of time, but you will soon get caught up.

If English Is Not Your First Language

The English language is one of the most difficult languages to learn. Words are often spelled differently from the way they sound, and the language is full of **idioms**—phrases that cannot be understood from the individual meanings of the words. If, for example, your instructor tells you to "hit the books," she does not mean for you to physically pound your texts with your fist but rather to study hard.

If you are learning English and are having trouble reading your books, don't give up. Reading slowly and reading more than once can help you improve your comprehension. Make sure that you have two good dictionaries—one in English and one that links English with your

❮ **A Marathon, Not a Sprint**

If you fall behind in your reading, you're not alone—many students do. Remember that your studies are more like a marathon than a sprint; you should take time to catch up, but do so at a steady pace. Do your assigned readings, study with others, get help, and do not give up!

© Jerome Prevost/TempSport/Corbis

primary language—and look up every key word you don't know. Be sure to practice thinking, writing, and speaking in English, and take advantage of your college's services. Your campus might have English as a second language (ESL) tutoring and workshops. Ask your adviser or your first-year seminar instructor to help you find where those services are offered on your campus.

YOUR TURN ➤ STAY MOTIVATED

Some first-year students, especially those who have trouble managing their time, believe that they can skip some of the required reading and still get good grades on tests and exams. The best students, however, will tell you that this isn't a smart strategy. Instructors assign readings because they believe they're important to your understanding, and concepts and details in the readings will be on the tests. Maintain your motivation to do well by reading all the materials assigned by your instructors. Your instructors have told you precisely what you need to do to be successful. All you have to do is to follow it.

EMBRACE THE E-BOOK

In college we have textbooks, workbooks, and notebooks. Even though textbook publishers continue to make traditional books and materials available, students may be required (or prefer) to access some or all course material digitally. For students who are used to buying or renting printed books from the college bookstore, this can be confusing.

THE PROBLEM *You have heard about electronic books that are alternatives to traditional textbooks, but you aren't sure what device to buy to read e-books. You also want to know the advantages and disadvantages that an e-book has when compared to a traditional book.*

THE FIX *Explore different platforms that deliver e-book content, and discover how reading with a digital reader differs from (and can even be better than) reading traditional books.*

HOW TO DO IT

© W2 Photography/Corbis

Go to the library. Many libraries have tablets of different kinds. Ask a librarian to download a book in a variety of formats for you, so you can try different tablets out before choosing one to buy. **Try the different media available.** E-books give you access to the pages of the text, as well as video, audio, and web content.

PROS OF E-BOOKS

- Digital reading devices are portable and can hold thousands of books.
- E-books save trees, can be bought without shipping costs, and have a low carbon footprint.
- E-readers let you buy books online from anywhere with Web access, and you can start reading within minutes.
- You can type, highlight, and copy and paste sections. You can also undo highlighting or revise notes.
- You can print out pages by hooking the device up to your printer or connecting to a printer on WiFi.
- You can access many e-books for free from the public library—even rare books.
- Some e-books come with bonus audio, video, or animation features.
- Many digital reading devices accept audio books and can read to you aloud.
- The backlit screen means that you can read with the light off, without disturbing anyone.
- You can adjust the size of the text.
- Some e-readers have a built-in dictionary. Others link to reference websites like Google or Wikipedia when a WiFi or 4G connection is available.
- E-books are searchable and even sharable.

CONS OF E-BOOKS

- Digital reading devices are expensive, breakable, and desirable to thieves.
- Looking at a screen can cause some eye fatigue.
- If you have only limited or temporary access to e-books for your college courses, your access will expire after the academic term.

GOOD TO KNOW

Some electronic readers are no-frills, basic models designed to replicate the experience of reading a paper book. Others offer browsers, video, music, and thousands of free and for-purchase apps. Most are Web-enabled, so you can use them for other purposes like listening to music or audio books, checking e-mail, creating presentations, and writing papers. This increased functionality might be distracting, but it can also make you more productive. Remember, though: if you have no Internet or WiFi connection, you may not be able to access your e-book.

EXTRA STYLE POINTS

Price your textbooks in both the print and digital formats. Factoring in the cost of the e-reader, which format is cheaper?

THINK
WRITE
APPLY

THINK

This chapter is full of strategies for effectively reading your college textbooks. What strategies did you find the most useful? What do you think is your biggest challenge in using these strategies to improve your reading habits?

Strategies I learned and will use:

1. _____

2. _____

3. _____

Challenges in using the strategies:

1. _____

2. _____

3. _____

WRITE

It is easy to say that there is not enough time in the day to get everything done, especially when you have a long reading assignment. Challenge yourself to avoid using this excuse. How can you modify your daily activities to make time for reading? What have you learned in this chapter that can help you with that?

_____

_____

_____

_____

_____

APPLY

1. Look through your course syllabi and identify a chapter that you need to read in the next couple of weeks. Preview the chapter and prepare an outline in your notebook or on a digital device, using the following format, based on the headings and subheadings:

Title:

I. _____

    A. _____

    B. _____

        1. _____

        2. _____

            a. _____

                (1) _____

                (2) _____

            b. _____

(Continue outlining.)

2. As you read a chapter of this or another textbook, organize the information in the following table:

Date:	Course:
Textbook:	Chapter # and Title:

What is the overall idea of the reading?

What is the main idea of each major section of the reading?

Section 1:

Section 2:

Section 3:

What supporting ideas are presented in each section of the reading?
Examples? Statistics? Any reference to research?

1.

2.

3.

4.

5.

What are the key terms, and what do they mean?

What are the conclusions from the reading?

What are two or three things I remember after reading?

1.

2.

3.

USE YOUR RESOURCES

Below are suggestions for resources that are available at many colleges and the online resources that are available to everyone.

AT YOUR COLLEGE

VISIT . . .	IF YOU NEED HELP . . .
Learning Center	reading textbooks, taking notes, and studying for exams. While you are here, ask about online resources available through the center or the college library.
Fellow students	joining a study group or finding a study partner. You are much more likely to be successful if you study with other students.
Disabled Student Services	arranging for accommodations because you have a reading disability or other learning disability.

ONLINE

GO TO . . .	IF YOU NEED HELP . . .
Bucks County Community College: faculty.bucks.edu/specpop/annotate.htm	finding a guide for annotating your textbooks.
Niagara University's Office for Academic Support: niagara.edu/oas-21-tips	discovering tips for better textbook reading.

MY COLLEGE'S RESOURCES

_____

_____

_____

_____

_____

LaunchPad for *Understanding Your College Experience* is a great resource. Go online to master concepts using the LearningCurve study tool and much more. **macmillanhighered.com/gardnerunderstanding**

7 Studying, Understanding, and Remembering

PRE-READING ACTIVITY: Before you start reading, take a few minutes to look through this chapter. Which topic interests you the most? Which topic do you think can be the most helpful to you?

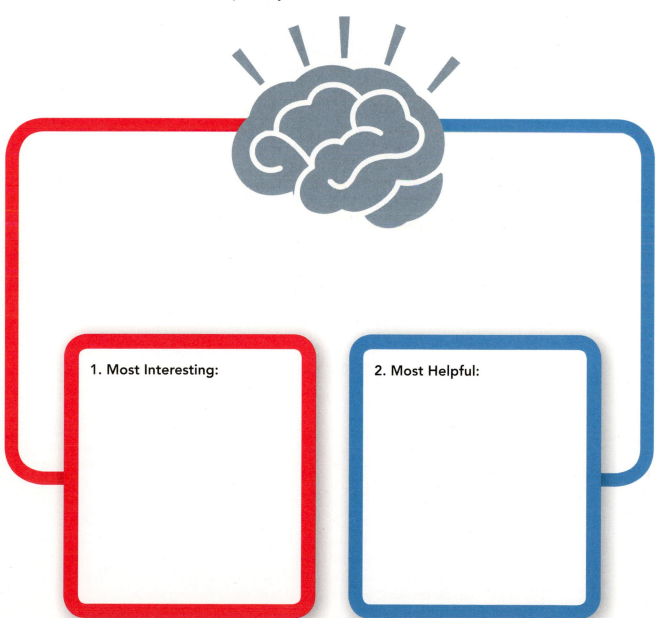

1. Most Interesting:

2. Most Helpful:

PROFILE

Joe Miranda, 19

Engineering Major, *Spokane Falls Community College, Washington*

pkchai/Shutterstock.com

Early in high school, Joe Miranda did well enough in his classes to be able to play basketball and football. He hoped to be a college athlete, but then a knee injury changed that. In his senior year of high school in Spokane, Washington, one of Joe's teachers recommended that he look into engineering as a profession. Joe had always been interested in math and science, but he hadn't done much planning for college. He researched different careers and types of engineering and found that environmental engineering excited him. Then he researched programs close to home.

Joe found an ideal pre-engineering program at Spokane Falls Community College (SFCC) that would give him all the courses he would need to be able to transfer later to Washington State University. He enrolled at SFCC, but before he could take the courses like calculus and advanced chemistry that would qualify him for transfer, Joe had to take some college-prep courses he didn't take in high school. Joe knew all his time and effort would be worth it. "I found a great tutor at the learning center on campus who is helping me keep up the good grades I am getting," he says.

> "I found a great tutor at the learning center on campus who is helping me keep up the good grades I am getting."

Joe is good at math and science, but that doesn't mean his transition to college has been easy. "In high school," he says, "my studying habits were slim to none. I was the type of high school student who was able to pass a test just from listening and from what I remembered from class."

At SFCC, Joe had to improve his study habits when he found that he wasn't able to remember everything the instructors required him to learn. "One of the biggest challenges in transitioning from high school to college was learning time management and study skills," Joe says. He notes that, compared with high school, his college classes go twice as fast and instructors expect students to do a lot more work on their own. One of the first steps Joe took to develop better study habits was to stop setting aside huge blocks of unstructured time. "I learned that studying for more than four hours straight is not the best for me. I need to study for an hour, take a half hour break, and then study another hour. I realized that after an hour I had trouble remembering things." By taking breaks to eat, exercise, or watch TV, Joe knows that he's giving his brain time to process information.

His one piece of advice to other first-year students? "The first year is going to be the hardest because it's so different," he says. "But don't give up. Before long, you'll find that it all starts making sense."

LaunchPad
macmillan learning

To access the Learning-Curve study tool, Video Tools, and more, go to LaunchPad for *Understanding Your College Experience.* macmillanhighered.com /gardnerunderstanding

You might have learned to study effectively while you were in high school or, like Joe, you might find that your high school study habits no longer work. For example, Joe quickly learned that he did have to study, rather than just listening in class, but that for him a three- to four-hour study session was too long. If you are attending college after working or raising children for a number of years, you may need to form new habits to study for college courses. You also need to find ways to structure study times that work best for you, and to set aside regular times each week to review course material, do assigned reading, and keep up with your homework. From time to time, you may also want to do additional reading not assigned by instructors and to research topics that interest you. These strategies will help you learn more.

Studying, understanding, and remembering are essential to getting the most out of your college experience. Although many students think the only reason for studying is to do well on exams, a far more important reason is to learn and understand course content. The more you understand, the better your grades will be. And if you study to increase your understanding, you are also more likely to remember and apply what you learn to future courses, to your career, and to life beyond college.

This chapter considers two related topics: concentration and memory. It will begin with the role of concentration in studying—if you cannot concentrate, you'll find it next to impossible to remember anything. Next, the chapter offers a number of tools to help you make the best use of your study time. It then concludes with a thorough discussion of what memory is, how it works, and how you can improve your own memory.

STUDYING IN COLLEGE: MAKING CHOICES AND CONCENTRATING

7.1

Learning new material takes a lot of effort on your part. You must concentrate on what you hear and read. This might sound simple, but considering all the responsibilities that college students are balancing, the opportunity to concentrate and to really focus on what you're learning and studying can be hard to come by. Start by learning to improve your ability to concentrate through what you do and where you do it.

Attending college is a huge responsibility, one you shouldn't take lightly. It is a lot of work, but it also offers you a lot of opportunities. For most people, college is a pathway to a better, more fulfilling life. As a college-level learner, you may need to change old habits and make room for new habits that will lead you to success. Tough choices are never easy, but they will have a direct, positive impact on your ability to remember and learn the information you will need in the months and years ahead.

Making a few changes in your behavior and in your environment will allow you to concentrate better and remember longer. For example, if you have small children, you need to schedule your study time when they nap. With older children, you can set aside "homework" time for all of you. Studying with others can also help you concentrate, so form or join a study group that meets regularly (e.g., every week, every weekend); the planned study time allows all the study group members to concentrate on the task at hand and keep each other focused. You can use apps such as StudyRoom or Google Hangouts for online group meetings.

With improved concentration, you'll probably need fewer hours to study because you will be using your time more efficiently. What are you willing to do to make this happen? To find out, work through the exercise in Figure 7.1.

FIGURE 7.1 > Choose to Upgrade Your Learning

Tough Choices	Your Answer: Yes or No?
Are you willing to work together with others to form study groups or partners?	
Are you willing to find a place on campus, at a public library, or elsewhere (not your home) for quiet study?	
Are you willing to be disconnected from the Internet, turn off all notifications on your mobile devices, and turn off your cell phone for reading time with no interruption?	
Are you willing to turn off distracting music or TV while you are studying?	
Are you willing to study for tests four or five days before?	
Are you willing to do assigned reading before you come to class?	
Are you willing to sit in the class where you can see and hear better?	
Are you willing to reduce stress through exercise, sleep, or meditation?	
Are you willing to go over your notes after class to clean them up or rewrite them?	
Are you willing to set aside time to review your notes every week?	
Are you willing to take a few minutes on the weekend to organize the week ahead?	

What did you learn about yourself from answering the questions in Figure 7.1? Think especially about the questions to which you answered "no." What are you unwilling to change in your life? Your job? Your study habits? Making changes in behavior now will save you a lot of headaches in the future and will show that you can change old patterns to create successful new habits. For the most part, the answers to these questions are under your control. Your success will largely depend on the choices you make.

HOW MEMORY WORKS

7.2

Learning experts describe two different processes involved in memory. The first is **short-term memory,** which involves retaining information, such as words or numbers, for about 15 to 30 seconds. After that you will forget the information stored in your short-term memory unless you take action to either keep that information in short-term memory or move it to long-term memory. Figure 7.2 shows that after nine hours, we remember less than 40 percent of the information!

FIGURE 7.2 ❯ Ebbinghaus Forgetting Curve

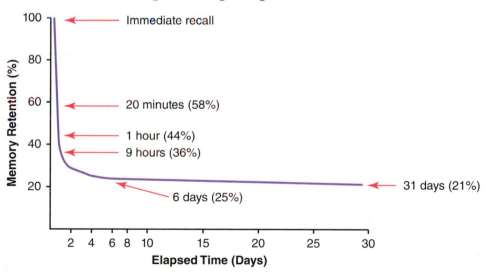

Although short-term memory is limited, it has a number of uses. It serves as an immediate holding tank for information, some of which you might not need for long. It helps you maintain your attention span so that you can keep track of topics mentioned in conversation, and it enables you to focus on the goals you have at any moment. But even these simple functions of short-term memory fail on occasion. If you're interrupted in any way, by a ringing phone or someone asking a question, you might find that your attention suffers and that you have to start over in reconstructing the contents of your short-term memory.

Long-term memory, the capacity to retain and recall information over the long term (from hours to years), is important to college success and can be divided into three categories:

- **Procedural memory** deals with knowing how to do something, such as solving a mathematical problem or driving a car. You are using your procedural memory when you ride a bicycle, even if you haven't ridden in years; when you cook a meal that you know how to prepare without using a recipe; or when you send a text.

- **Semantic memory** involves facts and meanings without regard to where and when you learned those things. Your semantic memory is used when you remember word meanings or important dates, such as your mother's birthday.

- **Episodic memory** deals with particular events, their time, and their place. You are using episodic memory when you remember events in your life—a vacation, your first day of school, the moment your child was born. Some people can recall not only the event, but also the very time and place the event happened. For others, although the event stands out, the time and place are harder to remember.

Table 7.1 recaps the differences between short- and long-term memory.

TABLE 7.1 > Short-Term and Long-Term Memory

Short-Term Memory	Long-Term Memory
Stores information for about 15 to 30 seconds	Stores information for hours to years
Can handle from five to nine chunks of information at one time	Can be described in three ways: • Procedural—remembering how to do something
Information either forgotten or moved to long-term memory	• Semantic—remembering facts and meanings
	• Episodic—remembering events, including their time and place

Connecting Memory to Deep Learning

Multitasking has become a fact of life for many of us, and many students believe that their use of multitasking makes them more efficient and productive. They even believe that multitasking is a necessity. However, this is not the case. Research summarized on the American Psychological Association website[1] shows that trying to do several tasks at once can make it harder to remember the most important things. It is difficult to focus on anything for long if your life is full of daily distractions and competing responsibilities—school, work, commuting, and family responsibilities such as caring for children or parents—or if you're not getting the sleep you

---

[1]"Multitasking: Switching Costs," American Psychological Association, accessed May 13, 2015, www.apa.org /research/action/multitask.aspx.

need. Have you ever had the experience of walking into a room with a specific task in mind and immediately forgetting what that task was? You were probably interrupted either by your own thoughts or by someone or something else. Or have you ever felt the panic that comes when your mind goes blank during a test, even though you studied hard and knew the material? If you spent all night studying or partying, lack of sleep may have raised your stress level, causing you to forget what you worked hard to learn. Such experiences happen to most people at one time or another.

To do well in college and in life, it's important that you improve your ability to remember what you read, hear, and experience. Concentration is a key element of learning and is so deeply connected to memory that you can't really have one without the other.

The benefits of having a good memory are obvious. In college, your memory will help you retain information and earn excellent grades on tests. After college, at work, and in life in general, the ability to remember important details—names, dates, appointments—will save you energy and time and will prevent a lot of embarrassment.

Most memory strategies tend to focus on helping you remember bits and pieces of knowledge: names, dates, numbers, vocabulary words, formulas, and so on. However, if you know the date the Civil War began and the name of the fort where the first shots were fired but you don't know why the Civil War was fought or how it affected history, you're missing the point of a college education. College is a time to develop **deep learning,** understanding the why and how behind the details. So while remembering specific facts is necessary to do well in college and in your career, you will need to understand major themes and ideas. You will also need to improve your ability to think deeply about what you're learning.

▲ **Avoid Multitasking**
If you want to study and learn effectively and remember the most important things in your life, multitasking is not the way to go.
Marili Forastieri/Photodisc/Getty Images

Myths about Memory

To understand how to improve your memory, let's first look at what we know about how memory works. Although scientists keep learning new things about how our brains function, author Kenneth L. Higbee[2] identifies some myths about memory (some you might have heard, and even believe). Table 7.2 lists four of these memory myths and what experts say about them:

---

[2]Kenneth L. Higbee, *Your Memory: How It Works and How to Improve It*, 2nd rev. ed. (New York: Marlowe, 2001).

TABLE 7.2 > Dispelling Myths about Memory

Myth	Reality
Some people have bad memories.	Although the memory ability you are born with is different from that of others, nearly everyone can improve his or her ability to remember and recall. Improving your concentration would certainly benefit your ability to remember!
Some people have photographic memories.	Some individuals have truly exceptional memories, but these abilities result more often from learned strategies, interest, and practice than from the natural ability to remember.
Memory benefits from long hours of practice.	Experts believe that practice often improves memory, but they argue that the way you practice is more important than how long you practice. For all practical purposes, the storage capacity of your memory is unlimited. In fact, the more you learn about a particular topic, the easier it is to learn even more.
People use only 10 percent of their brain power.	No one knows exactly how much of our brain we actually use. However, most researchers believe that we all have far more mental ability than we actively use.

7.3

IMPROVING YOUR MEMORY

Just as you can use strategies for improving your ability to concentrate, you can improve your ability to retain information—to store it in your brain for future use. It's helpful to consider how your learning preferences relate to these strategies.

Learning Style and Memory

There is a connection between your learning style and how you remember information. If you're an aural learner, you might find that when you listen to a lecture, you learn and remember better. You might find that repeating information to yourself when studying, recording yourself while doing it, and then listening to the recording work as a review strategy. Forming or joining a study group where you can listen to others reciting facts and key information can be very helpful to you.

If you're a visual learner, you might remember best by picturing the page in the book, the content on a screen, or your notes where information is presented. Creating color-coded lists, outlines, diagrams, and mind maps might help you remember. If you learn best by reading and writing, take good notes while you read and then review your notes over and over. If you're a kinesthetic learner, you may need to be active while studying. As you read course material, making and organizing flash cards—on paper cards or with an app—and reviewing them as you commute to and from campus or between errands or on a treadmill might work very well for you. If you find it hard to sit and listen to your instructors talk, you might find it useful to take notes and draw charts and diagrams to represent the key points and concepts from the lecture.

Your interest, motivation, and purpose for retaining information can also affect how you store and remember information. For instance, if the courses you are taking closely relate to your career interests, you might learn more easily because you have the desire to become familiar and knowledgeable in the field and want to be competitive in the job market. On the other hand, learning in a course that is not closely related to your program of study or your interests and career goals might be more challenging. In these cases, try to appreciate that the course still has value because it helps you make progress toward your degree and toward becoming an educated, well-rounded individual.

YOUR TURN > WORK TOGETHER

With the help of your instructor, identify other students in your class who share your learning style. With another classmate, discuss strategies for remembering material for exams using your learning style and list the most helpful ideas.

Strategies to Remember

Psychologists and learning specialists have developed a number of strategies you can use when studying to remember information. Some of these strategies may be new to you, and others may be familiar. No matter what course you are taking, you need to remember concepts and ideas in order to complete the course successfully. To store concepts and ideas in your mind, ask yourself these questions as you review your notes and course material:

1. What is the basic idea here?
2. Why does the idea make sense? What is the logic behind it?
3. How does this idea connect to other ideas in the material or experiences in my life?
4. What are some possible arguments against the idea?

To prepare for an exam that will cover large amounts of material, you need to

- Reduce your notes and text pages into manageable study units.
- Review your materials with these questions in mind:
  - Is this one of the key ideas in the chapter or unit?
  - Will I see this on the test?

- Use study tools that are effective to help you remember what you have learned: review sheets, mind maps, flash cards, summaries, and mnemonics.

Review Sheets. Use your notes to develop **review sheets**—lists of key terms and ideas that you need to remember. If you're using the Cornell format to take notes, you can make these lists in the recall column. Also be sure to use your lecture notes to test yourself or others on information presented in class.

Mind Maps. Mapping is an effective way to preview content and also a great strategy to remember content. **Mind maps** are visual review sheets that show the relationships between ideas and whose patterns provide you with clues to jog your memory. Because they are visual, mind maps help many students, particularly English-language learners, to remember the information more easily.

To create a mind map, start with a main idea and place it in the center. Then add major categories that branch out from the center. To these, add pieces of related information to form clusters. You can use different shapes or colors to show the relationships among the various pieces of information. You can find many apps for creating mind maps on your

FIGURE 7.3 › Sample Mind Map

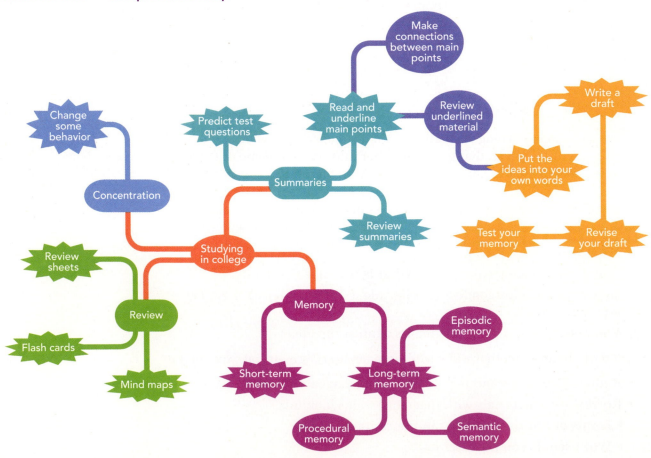

YOUR TURN > TRY IT

On a separate piece of paper or in a new document, make a mind map for another chapter of this book, and see how much more you can remember after studying your map a number of times.

computer or mobile device. Figure 7.3 includes the mind map of this chapter created by using an app called Total Recall. Other apps include Mind-Meister and SimpleMind.

Flash Cards. Just as you can create flash cards during the process of active reading, you can also use them to improve your memory. Flash cards can serve as memory aids with a question, term, or other piece of information on one side and the answer, definition, or explanation on the other. Flash cards are excellent tools for improving your vocabulary, especially if you are learning English as a second language.

One of the advantages of flash cards is that you can keep them in a pocket of your backpack, in your jacket, or on your mobile device—you can create flash cards on your mobile device using apps such as Chegg Flash-cards and StudyBlue. Review your flash cards to make good use of time that might otherwise be wasted, such as time spent on the bus or train or waiting for a friend. Review them anywhere, even when you don't have enough time to take out your notebook to study.

Summaries. An immediate benefit of writing summaries of class topics is that they can help you answer short-answer and essay questions successfully. You can also see the connection between the ideas and identify the major and minor details. By summarizing the main ideas and putting them into your own words, you will be able to remember information better. Here's how to create a good summary in preparation for taking a test:

1. **Read the assigned material, your class notes, or your instructor's presentation slides.** Underline or mark main ideas as you go, make explanatory notes or comments about the material, or make an outline on a separate sheet of paper. Predict test questions based on your active reading.

2. **Make connections between main points and key supporting details.** Reread to identify each main point and the supporting evidence. Create an outline in the process.

3. **Review underlined material.** Put those ideas into your own words in a logical order.

4. **Write your ideas in a draft.** In the first sentence, state the purpose of your summary. Follow this statement with each main point and its supporting ideas. See how much of the draft you can develop from memory without relying on your notes.

5. **Review your draft.** Read it over, adding missing details or other information.

6. **Test your memory.** Put your draft away, and try to repeat the contents of the summary out loud to yourself or to a study partner who can let you know whether you have forgotten anything.

7. **Schedule time to review your summary and double-check your memory shortly before the test.** You might want to do this with a partner, but some students prefer to review alone. Some instructors might be willing to help you in this process and give you feedback on your summaries.

Mnemonics. **Mnemonics** (pronounced "ne MON iks") are different methods or tricks to help with remembering information. Mnemonics tend to fall into four basic categories:

1. **Acronyms.** Acronyms are new words created from the first letters of a list or group of words you are trying to remember. For example, a mnemonic acronym for the Great Lakes is HOMES, which stands for Huron, Ontario, Michigan, Erie, and Superior.

2. **Acrostics.** An acrostic is a verse in which certain letters of each word or line form a message. Many students are taught the following to remember the planets in their order from the sun: My Very Excellent Mother Just Served Us Nachos (Mercury, Venus, Earth, Mars, Jupiter, Saturn, Uranus, Neptune).

3. **Rhymes or songs.** Do you remember learning "Thirty days hath September, / April, June, and November. / All the rest have 31, / Excepting February alone. / It has 28 days' time, / But in leap years 29"? If so, you were using a mnemonic rhyming technique to remember the number of days in each month.

4. **Visualization.** You can use visualization to connect a word or concept with a visual image. The more ridiculous the image, the more likely you are to remember the word or concept. For example, if you want to remember the name of George Washington, you may think of a person you know by the name of George. You should then picture that person washing a ton of dishes. Now every time you think of the first president of the United States, you see George washing a ton of dishes.[3]

Mnemonics provide a way of organizing material, a sort of mental filing system. They probably aren't needed if what you are studying is logical and organized, but they can be really useful when material doesn't have a pattern of its own. Although using mnemonics can be helpful in remembering the information, it takes time to think up rhymes, associations, or visual images which have limited use when you need to analyze or explain the material.

---

[3]Example from Jim Somchai, "Memory and Visualization," EzineArticles.com, accessed December 20, 2015, ezinearticles.com/?Memory-and-Visualization&id=569553.

YOUR TURN ❯ STAY MOTIVATED

Do your friends complain that you keep forgetting the times you had planned to meet? Have you forgotten your mother's birthday? Do you have trouble remembering the names of people introduced to you? Improving your memory is actually a lot of fun. There are many memory games available that you can play for a few minutes every day; some of them can be accessed online or on your mobile device. Check out these free apps: Brain Workout for Android, Music Game for iPhone, or Lumosity.

STUDYING TO UNDERSTAND AND REMEMBER

Studying will help you accomplish two goals: understanding and remembering. While memory is a necessary tool for learning, what's most important is that you study to develop a deep understanding of course information. When you really comprehend what you are learning, you will be able to place names, dates, and specific facts in context. You will also be able to exercise your thinking abilities.

Here are some methods that might be useful to you as you're trying to remember detailed information:

- **Pay attention and avoid distractions.** This suggestion is the most basic but the most important. If you're sitting in class thinking about everything except what the professor is saying, or if you're reading and you find that your mind is wandering, you're wasting your time. Force yourself to focus. Review your responses to the questions in Figure 7.1.

- **Be confident that you can improve your memory.** Recall successes from the past when you learned things that you didn't think you could or would remember. Choose memory improvement strategies that best fit your preferred learning styles: aural, visual, reading, kinesthetic. Identify the courses where you can make the best use of each memory strategy.

- **Overlearn the material.** Once you think you understand the material you're studying, go over it again to make sure that you'll remember it for a long time. Test yourself, or ask someone else to test you. Repeat what you're trying to remember out loud and in your own words. Explain it to another person.

- **Make studying a part of your daily routine.** Don't allow days to go by when you don't open a book or keep up with course assignments. Make studying a daily habit!

- **Check the Internet.** If you're having trouble remembering what you have learned, Google a key word and try to find interesting details that will engage you in learning more about the subject. Many first-year courses cover such a large amount of material that you might miss some interesting details unless you look for them yourself. As your interest increases, so will your memory about the topic. Make sure to check multiple online sources.

- **Go beyond memorizing words, and focus on understanding and then remembering the big concepts and ideas.** Keep asking yourself questions like "What is the main point here? Is there a big idea?" Whenever you begin a course, review the syllabus, talk with someone who has already taken the course, and take a brief look at all the reading assignments. Having the big picture will help you understand and remember the details of what you're learning. For example, the big picture for a first-year college success course is to give students the knowledge and strategies to be successful in college.

- **Look for connections between your life and what's going on in the content of your courses.** Course content might seem unrelated to you and your goals, but if you look more carefully, you'll find many connections between course material and your daily life. Seeing those connections will make your courses more interesting and will help you remember what you're learning. For example, if you're taking a sociology class and studying marriage and the family, think about how your own family experiences relate to those described in your readings or in the lectures.

- **Get organized.** If your desk or your digital files are organized, you won't waste time trying to remember where you put a particular document or what name you gave to a file. And as you rewrite your notes, putting them in an order that makes sense to you (for example, by topic or by date) will help you learn and remember them.

> **An Elephant (Almost) Never Forgets**

While elephants apparently do have pretty good memories, they're like the rest of us in that they sometimes forget. Work to develop your memory by using the specific strategies in this chapter. One of the most important strategies you can use is trying to understand the big picture behind bits and pieces of information.

© Shannon Burns

"Is this the memory seminar?"

YOUR TURN > WORK TOGETHER

With a small group of your classmates, share your thoughts on the importance of being organized. How would you describe both your living space and your digital environment?

- **Reduce the stress in your life.** Many college students experience stress because they have to juggle college, work, and family life—and not necessarily in that order! Stress-reducing habits such as eating well and getting enough exercise and sleep are especially important for college students. Remember, too, that your college probably has a counseling center or a health center where you can seek help in dealing with whatever might be causing stress in your daily life.

- **Collaborate.** In your first year of college, join a group of students who study together. Your instructors or the college learning center can help organize study groups. Study groups can meet throughout the term or can get together only to review for midterm or final exams.

- **Get a tutor.** Tutoring is not just for students who are failing. Often the best students ask for help to make sure that they understand course material. Most tutors are students, and at most colleges, tutoring services are free.

You've learned in this chapter that memory and concentration play very important parts in achieving success in college. They help you understand, remember, and deeply learn the material so that you can apply that learning to your career and life.

< Group Effort

One way to enhance your memory is to study with others. Each of you can check specific facts and details and share strategies you use for remembering them. You can also motivate and support one another.

Digital Vision/Photodisc/Getty Images

USE THE CLOUD

Computer labs, laptops, tablets, and smartphones give you the opportunity to work from almost everywhere. What can you do to keep all your important digital files in one place so that you'll never be without them?

THE PROBLEM

You're at the computer lab, and you don't have the files you need. This time you forgot your flash drive; last time, you had your tablet and not your laptop. And what if your devices get damaged or lost?

THE FIX

Save your files to a cloud storage site and have access to them from any Internet-connected computer or tablet. The cloud is basically the Internet, which is simply a network of servers. Through an Internet connection, you can access whatever applications, files, or data you have stored in the cloud—anytime, anywhere, from any device.[4]

HOW TO DO IT

Sign up for a free account from a cloud storage site. These sites allow you to save files to an online location. You'll have your own private storage space that can be accessed only with a password. Some sites are designed for documents (Word files, PDFs, PowerPoint presentations), while others allow easy storage for both print files and audio/video. Cloud storage is great for collaborative projects because you can choose to share some or all of your files with your classmates and friends. The following is a list of sites with free storage (though most require payment to increase your storage size):

Pixsooz/Shutterstock.com

1. **Dropbox (dropbox.com)** is probably the best-known cloud storage site. Dropbox has a Web interface that you and others can access from any computer and save to your own computer. This makes Dropbox look like any other folder on your computer; however, when you add files, it actually adds them to your online folder. Dropbox is available as a stand-alone app on iPhone, iPad, and Android devices and also works with other document-editing mobile apps.

2. **Google Drive (drive.google.com)** allows users to store and share documents up to 5 GB. A great feature of Google Drive is that you can edit documents in real time with your friends and classmates. If you're writing a group paper, all of your co-authors can sign into Google Drive and view the same document. You are able to edit it together, and there is a chat window, so you can have a conversation while editing. Google Drive allows for storage of both audio and video. Like Dropbox, Google Drive is also available as a stand-alone app and integrates well with iPhone, iPad, and Android apps.

3. **MediaFire (mediafire.com)** is newer than Dropbox and Google Drive. MediaFire's key feature is 50 GB of free storage space. Users are able to work together in the cloud and access their files using stand-alone apps on iPhone, iPad, and Android devices.

---

[4]Rama Ramaswami and Dian Schaffhauser, "What Is the Cloud?," *Campus Technology*, accessed August 31, 2015, campustechnology.com/articles/2011/10/31/what-is-the-cloud.aspx.

THINK

Doing well on exams is important, but being able to understand and remember what you learn is a more important life skill in general. How do you think these skills may help you in your current or future job?

_____

_____

_____

_____

_____

WRITE

In this chapter, you read about some memory myths and facts. Did anything you learned surprise you? Have you ever believed in any of the myths? If so, which ones? How can the information about memory and the strategies for improving your memory discussed in this chapter help you change your study habits?

_____

_____

_____

_____

_____

APPLY

Now that you have read and discussed this chapter, consider how you can apply what you have learned to your academic and personal life.

1. Give mnemonics a try. Choose a set of class notes that you need to study for an upcoming quiz or exam. As you study, choose a concept and create your own acronym, acrostic, rhyme, song, or visualization to help you remember.
2. Choose a photo, song, or object that reminds you of a person, life event, or time period. Describe what it is about the photo, song, or object that reminds you of something else. Describe your memory in as much detail as possible and explain how it makes you feel.

Below are suggestions for resources that are available at many colleges and the online resources that are available to everyone.

AT YOUR COLLEGE

VISIT . . .	IF YOU NEED HELP . . .
Learning Center	developing effective memory strategies. Visit your campus learning center and ask if the staff members offer any specific workshops or one-on-one assistance with memory.
Fellow college students	finding tips for remembering the material in different courses.
Your college library	finding books on the topic of memory. Download or check out a book on memory and see what you can learn. Here are some ideas: Higbee, Kenneth L. *Your Memory: How It Works and How to Improve It*, 2nd rev. ed. New York: Marlowe, 2001. Lorayne, Harry. *Memory Mastery.* Hollywood: Frederick Fell Trade, 2010. O'Brien, Dominic. *You Can Have an Amazing Memory: Learn Life-Changing Techniques and Tips from the Memory Maestro.* London: Watkins, 2011. Scotts, Jason. *How to Improve Your Memory & Increase Your Brain Power in 30 Days: Simple, Easy & Fun Ways to Improve Memory Now (Ultimate How To Guides).* Kindle Edition, retrieved from Amazon.com, 2013.

ONLINE

GO TO . . .	IF YOU NEED HELP . . .
Memory Techniques from San Antonio College: alamo.edu/memory	finding memorization techniques.
Memory-Improvement-Tips.com: memory-improvement-tips.com/	improving your memory.
Brain Metrix: brainmetrix.com/	learning more about training your brain.
Lumosity: lumosity.com	improving your memory by playing memory games.

MY COLLEGE'S RESOURCES

 **LaunchPad**
macmillan learning

LaunchPad for *Understanding Your College Experience* is a great resource. Go online to master concepts using the LearningCurve study tool and much more. **macmillanhighered.com/gardnerunderstanding**

8 Taking Tests Successfully

PRE-READING ACTIVITY: Taking tests is an important and unavoidable part of your college experience. For the following statements, mark whether you agree or disagree, and write down the reason for your response.

Tests do not measure students' learning.

Agree ☐   Disagree ☐

Reason:

It is possible to control test anxiety.

Agree ☐   Disagree ☐

Reason:

Smart students are not nervous before taking tests.

Agree ☐   Disagree ☐

Reason:

Test anxiety will go away if students ignore it.

Agree ☐   Disagree ☐

Reason:

If students study before a test, they feel less nervous.

Agree ☐   Disagree ☐

Reason:

PROFILE

Carlos Rivera, 26
Health Sciences Major, *Georgia Perimeter College of Georgia State University*

Bruce Laurance/The Image Bank/Getty Images

Carlos Rivera was born in Guatemala and has lived in Georgia since he was ten years old. After a few years as a car mechanic, he decided to enroll in Georgia Perimeter College in Atlanta because he realized college was important for his goals and his financial future. He chose Georgia Perimeter because of his interest in its medical programs, and so far his favorite course has been biology. After graduating from Georgia Perimeter College, Carlos plans to become a radiologic therapist and help others. Since enrolling, Carlos has taken a straightforward approach to preparing for exams that has served him well. "I review the material periodically throughout the term and the day before exams," he explains. "Typically, I try to get plenty of sleep during the week of exams."

Carlos recounts a challenge he overcame: "I came into one required course with a negative attitude. I didn't know why I needed to take the class, and I didn't pay attention." When he received his first exam grade, Carlos wasn't pleased. "It was definitely not what I was used to," he says. However, he returned to class with an open mind and made an effort to take an interest in the course and to explore how the materials applied to his life and studies. By applying the same strategies he'd used in his other classes to prepare for exams, he was able to improve his grade.

His advice to other first-year students? "Don't slack off, thinking you can make up the work later in the year. Do well from the start—you never know when you may need some room for error later on. If something seems hard, face it and try your best. Most of the time, things are not as difficult as they may seem at first. You can do anything you want with a little perseverance and determination."

"You can do anything you want with a little perseverance and determination."

To access the Learning-Curve study tool, Video Tools, and more, go to LaunchPad for *Understanding Your College Experience.* macmillanhighered.com /gardnerunderstanding

You can prepare for tests and exams in many ways. Sometimes you'll have to recall names, dates, and other specific bits of information. Many instructors, especially in courses such as literature and history, will also expect you to have a good overall understanding of the subject matter. Even in math and science courses, your instructors want you not only to remember the correct theory, formula, or equation but also to understand and apply what you have learned. Knowing your preferred learning style, managing your time and energy, and using study and memory strategies will help you prepare for any kind of test or exam you are facing. This chapter provides you with several strategies to prepare for and take tests and exams successfully. It also describes types of tests and test questions you may encounter and includes tips for managing test anxiety as well as maintaining academic honesty.

8.1

GETTING READY . . .

Believe it or not, you actually begin preparing for tests on the first day of the term. Your lecture notes, assigned readings, and homework are all part of that preparation in addition to rest, diet, exercise, attitude, and more. As you get closer to the test day, you should know how much additional time you will need for review, what material the test will cover, and what format the test will take. It is very important to double-check the exam dates on the syllabus for each class, as in Figure 8.1, and to incorporate

FIGURE 8.1 ❯ Exam Schedule from Sample Course Syllabus

History 111, US History to 1865
Fall 2016

Examinations
Note: In this course, most of your exams will be on Fridays, except for the Wednesday before Thanksgiving and the final. This is to give you a full week to study for the exam and permit me to grade them over the weekend and return the exams to you on Monday. I believe in using a variety of types of measurements. In addition to those scheduled below, I reserve the right to give you unannounced quizzes on daily reading assignments. Also, current events are fair game on any exam! Midterm and final exams will be cumulative (on all material since the beginning of the course). Other exams cover all classroom material and all readings covered since the prior exam. The schedule is as follows:

Friday, 9/9: Objective type

Friday, 9/23: Essay type

Friday, 10/7: Midterm: essay and objective

Friday, 11/4: Objective

Wednesday, 11/23: Essay

Friday, 12/16: Final exam: essay and objective

these dates into your overall plans for time management—for example, in your daily and weekly to-do lists. You should always build additional time into your schedule for test preparation and start reviewing the material early as emergencies can happen a day or two before the exam date. You may have to work extra hours or take care of your sick child, spouse, or parent (or yourself) and not have enough time to study, and as a result, you may not perform well on the test.

Prepare for Test Taking

Tests are usually a major portion of your grade in college, so proper preparation for them is essential. Of course you need to understand the material, but there are many ways you can prepare for exams in addition to your regular study routines.

Find Out about the Test. Ask your instructor about the test format, how long it will last, and how it will be graded. Find out the types of questions, the content that will be covered, and how much time you will have to complete the exam. Talk with your instructor to clarify any misunderstandings you might have about your reading or lecture notes. Adjunct instructors may not have offices or office hours, but you can usually talk to them before or after class. Some instructors might let you view copies of old exams so that you can see the types of questions they use. Never miss the last class before an exam; your instructor might use part or all of that class session to summarize and review valuable information.

Design an Exam Plan. Use information about the test as you design an exam plan. Create a schedule that will give you time to review for the exam without waiting until the night before. Develop a to-do list of the major steps you need to take to be ready, and schedule review dates. Be sure that your schedule is flexible enough to allow for unexpected distractions or emergencies. If you are able to schedule your study sessions over several days, your mind will continue to process the information between these sessions, which will help you during the test. Be sure you have read and learned all the material by one week before the exam. That way, you can use the final week to review. In that final week, set aside several one-hour blocks for review and make specific notes on what you plan to do during each hour. Also, let your friends and family know when you have important exams coming up and how that will affect your time with them.

Use Online Quizzing. Many textbooks have websites available that offer a number of study tools such as flash cards, videos, or online quizzes. Ask your instructors about these sites and also check the preface of your textbooks for information on accessing these sites. You might also use Google to find them. Students who are using digital textbooks will likely find integrated into every chapter quizzes that allow you to test your understanding of the material. Instructors often track completion of these quizzes.

Join a Study Group. Joining a study group is one of the best ways to prepare for exams. Group members can share and review the most important topics, quiz one another on facts and concepts, and gain support from other serious students. Some instructors will provide time in class for the formation of study groups, or you might choose to approach classmates on your own. Your campus learning center may also have a system for organizing study groups. You can always ask your instructor, academic adviser, or college's tutoring or learning center to help you find other interested students and decide on guidelines for the group. Study groups can meet throughout the term, or they can just review for midterms or final exams. Group members should prepare questions or discussion points before the group meets. If your study group decides to meet just before exams, allow enough time to share notes and ideas.

Talk to Other Students. Other students, especially those who have taken a course you are currently taking from the same instructor, may be able to give you a good idea of what to expect on tests and exams. If your college is small, you shouldn't have any trouble finding students who have taken the same courses you are taking now. If you're at a large college, your instructor may be able to suggest a former student who could serve as a tutor. But keep in mind that your instructor may decide to take a different approach in your class than he or she did in past classes. Instructors are not trying to be "sneaky" or "trick" the students; they sometimes just decide to change their approaches to teaching and testing.

Get a Tutor. Most colleges offer free tutoring services. Ask your academic adviser, counselor, or college learning center about arranging for tutoring. Keep in mind that some of the most successful students seek

❮ Strength in Numbers
Study groups can meet anytime, but studying and reviewing with others can be most helpful just before and just after a test or exam.
Hybrid Images/cultura/Corbis

out tutoring, not just students who are struggling. Most students who receive tutoring do well in their courses. Many learning centers employ student tutors (also called peer tutors) who have done well in the same courses you are taking. These students might have some good advice on how to prepare for tests given by particular instructors. If you do well in a particular course, you could eventually become a peer tutor and be paid for your services. Serving as a peer tutor also deepens your own learning and helps you become more successful.

Prepare for Math and Science Exams

Math and science exams often require additional and sometimes different preparation techniques. Here are some suggestions for doing well on these exams:

- Do your homework regularly even if it is not graded, and do all the assigned practice problems like those shown in Figure 8.2. As you do your homework, write out your work as carefully and clearly as you will be expected to do on your tests. This practice will allow you to use your homework as a review for the test.

- Attend each class, always be on time, and stay for the entire class. Many instructors use the first few minutes of class to review homework, and others may end the class by telling you what will be on the test.

- Build a review guide throughout the term. As you begin your homework each day, write out a problem from each homework section in a notebook that you have set up for reviewing material for that course. As you review later, you can come back to these problems to make sure you have a problem from each section you've studied.

- Throughout the term, keep a list of definitions and important formulas and put these on flash cards. Review several of these as part of every study session. Another technique is to post the formulas and definitions in your living space (for example, on the bathroom wall or around your computer work area). Seeing this information frequently will help you keep it in your mind.

If none of these strategies seems to help you, ask a tutor to give you a few practice exams and review your responses with you.

Prepare Physically

Preparing physically for taking tests is as important as preparing emotionally and academically. The following strategies will help you prepare physically:

- **Maintain your regular sleep routine.** To do well on exams, you will need to be alert so that you can think clearly. And you are more likely to be alert when you are well rested. Last-minute, late-night cramming

FIGURE 8.2 ❯ Solving Practice Problems

Completing plenty of practice problems, like the ones shown here, is a great way to study for math and science classes. So try your hand at all the problems provided in your textbook—even those that your instructor hasn't assigned—and check out websites offering such problems. Excerpt from page 395, *COMAP, For All Practical Purposes: Mathematical Literacy in Today's World*, 9th ed. Copyright © 2013 by W. H. Freeman. Used by permission.

8.6 Continuous Probability Models

48. Books on reserve at a university library can be checked out for at most 2 hours. The density curve for the amount of time the book is checked out is the shaded triangle shown in Figure 8.28.

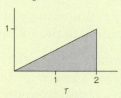

Figure 8.28 Amount of time T that a book is checked out from the reserve shelf, for Exercise 48.

(a) Explain why Figure 8.28 satisfies the definition of a density curve.

(b) What is the probability that the book is checked out for less than 1 hour?

(c) What is the probability that the book is checked out for more than 1 hour?

49. Generate two random real numbers between 0 and 1 and take their sum. The sum can take any value between 0 and 2. The density curve is the shaded triangle shown in Figure 8.29.

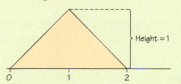

Figure 8.29 The density curve for the sum of two random numbers, for Exercise 49.

(a) Verify by geometry that the area under this curve is 1.

(b) What is the probability that the sum is less than 1? Sketch the density curve, shade the area that represents the probability, and then find that area.

(c) What is the probability that the sum is less than 0.5? Sketch the density curve, shade the area that represents the probability, and then find that area.

50. Suppose two data values are each rounded to the nearest whole number. Make a density curve for the sum of the two roundoff errors, assuming each error has a continuous uniform distribution. (Exercise 49 might help.)

51. On the TV show *The Price Is Right*, the "Range Game" involves a contestant being told that the suggested retail price of a prize lies between two numbers that are $600 apart. The contestant has one chance to position a red window with a span of $150 that will contain the price. On one episode, the price of a piano is between $8900 and $9500. If we assume a uniform continuous distribution (i.e., that all prices within the $600 interval are equally likely), what is the probability that the contestant will be successful?

8.7 The Mean and Standard Deviation of a Probability Model

52. You have a campus errand that will take only 15 minutes. The only parking space anywhere nearby is a faculty-only space, which is checked by campus police about once every hour. If you're caught, the fine is $25.

(a) Give the probability model for the money that you may or may not have to pay.

(b) What's the expected value of the money that you will pay for your unauthorized parking?

53. Exercise 29 gives a probability model for the grade of a randomly chosen student in Statistics 101 at North Carolina State University, using the 4-point scale. What is the mean grade in this course? What is the standard deviation of the grades?

54. In Exercise 28, you gave a probability model for the intelligence of a character in a role-playing game. What is the mean intelligence for these characters?

55. Exercise 30 gives probability models for the number of rooms in owner-occupied and rented housing units. Find the mean number of rooms for each type of housing. Make probability histograms for the two models and mark the mean on each histogram. You see that the means describe an important difference between the two models: Owner-occupied units tend to have more rooms.

56. Typographical and spelling errors can be either "nonword errors" or "word errors." A nonword error is not a real word, as when "the" is typed as "teh." A word error is a real word, but not the right word, as when "lose" is typed as "loose." When undergraduates write a 250-word essay (without checking spelling), the number of nonword errors has the following probability model:

Errors	0	1	2	3	4
Probability	0.1	0.2	0.3	0.3	0.1

does not allow you to get sufficient sleep, so it isn't an effective study strategy. Most students need seven to eight hours of sleep the night before the exam.

• **Follow your regular exercise program.** Exercise is a positive way to relieve stress and to give yourself a needed break from long hours of studying.

- **Eat right.** Eat a light breakfast before a morning exam, and avoid greasy or acidic foods that might upset your stomach. Limit the amount of caffeinated beverages you drink on exam day because caffeine can make you jittery. Choose fruits, vegetables, and other foods that are high in energy-rich complex carbohydrates. Avoid eating sweets before an exam; the immediate energy boost they create can be quickly followed by a loss of energy and alertness. Ask the instructor whether you may bring a bottle of water with you to the exam session.

Prepare Emotionally

Just as physical preparation is important, so is preparing your attitude and your emotions. You'll benefit by paying attention to the following ideas:

- **Know your material.** If you have given yourself enough time to review, you will enter the classroom confident that you are in control. Study by testing yourself or quizzing others in a study group to be sure you really know the material.

- **Practice relaxing.** Some students experience upset stomachs, sweaty palms, racing hearts, or other unpleasant physical symptoms of test anxiety. The section on test anxiety later in this chapter includes an anxiety quiz; if that quiz reveals that test anxiety is a problem for you, consult your counseling center about relaxation techniques. Some campus learning centers also provide workshops on reducing test anxiety.

- **Use positive self-talk.** Instead of telling yourself, "I never do well on math tests" or "I'll never be able to learn all the information for my history essay exam," make positive statements, such as "I have always attended class, done my homework, and passed the quizzes. Now I'm ready to do well on the test!"

- **Be resilient.** If you have had a poor grade on a particular kind of test before, know that you can bounce back. Don't let one bad grade get you down.

YOUR TURN > WORK TOGETHER

Do you sometimes predict that you'll do poorly on a test or exam, even when you've studied hard? Discuss with a small group of your classmates how a positive attitude can help you do your best.

TAKING THE TEST

Throughout your college career, you will take tests in many different formats, in many subject areas, and with many different types of questions. It may surprise you to find that your first-year tests are likely to be more challenging than those in later years because, as a new student, you are still developing your college test-taking skills throughout your first year. The following are test-taking tips that apply to any test situation:

1. **Write your name.** Usually you will have to write your name on a test booklet or answer sheet. Some instructors, however, may require you to fill in your student ID number.

2. **Look over the whole test and stay calm.** Carefully read all the directions before beginning the test so that you understand what to do. Ask the instructor or exam monitor for clarification if you don't understand something. Be confident. Don't panic. Answer one question at a time.

3. **Make the best use of your time.** Quickly review the entire test and decide how much time you will spend on each section. Be aware of the point values of different sections of the test. If some questions are worth more points than others, you need to spend more of your time answering them.

4. **Jot down idea starters before the test.** Check with your instructor ahead of time to be sure that it is OK to write some last-minute notes on the test or on scrap paper. If so, before you even look at the test questions, turn the test paper over and take a moment to write down the formulas, definitions, or major ideas you have been studying. This will help you go into the test with confidence and knowledge, and your notes will provide quick access to the information you may need throughout the test.

5. **Answer the easy questions first.** Expect that you won't completely understand some questions. Make a note to come back to them later. If different sections have different types of questions (such as multiple-choice, short-answer, and essay questions), first finish the types of questions that are easiest for you to answer. Be sure to leave enough time for essay questions.

6. **If you feel yourself starting to panic or go blank, stop whatever you are doing.** Take a deep breath, and remind yourself that you will be OK and you do know the material and can do well on the test. If necessary, go to another section of the test and come back later to the item that triggered your anxiety.

7. **Try to answer each question, even if only in part.** You may not be able to answer all the questions fully; provide as much information as you can remember. Particularly for math and science test questions, you may get some credit for writing down equations and descriptions of

how to solve the problem even if you cannot fully work them out or if you run out of time before finishing them.

8. **If you finish early, don't leave immediately.** Stay and check your work for errors. Reread the directions one last time. Don't get spooked by seeing other students leave the room. They may be leaving because they didn't do nearly as well as you!

8.3 TYPES OF TESTS

While you are in college, you will come across many types of tests. Some may be used in particular subjects such as English or math; others can be used in any class you might take. This section discusses the different test types and presents helpful tips for each one.

Problem-Solving Tests

In science, mathematics, engineering, and statistics courses, some tests will require you to solve problems showing all the steps. Even if you know a short-cut, it is important to document how you got from step A to step B. For these tests, you must also be careful to avoid errors in your scientific notation. A misplaced sign, parenthesis, or bracket can make all the difference.

If you are allowed to use a calculator during the exam, it is important to check that your input is accurate. The calculator does what you tell it to, and if you miss a zero or a negative sign, the calculator will not give you the correct answer to the problem.

Read all directions carefully. Whenever possible, after you complete the problem, work it in reverse to check your solution. Also check to make sure that your solution makes sense. You can't have negative bushels of apples, for example, or a fraction of a person, or a correlation less than negative 1 or greater than 1.

Machine-Scored Tests

For some tests you may have to enter your answers on a Scantron form (see Figure 8.3). The instructor will feed those forms into a machine that scans the answers and prints out your score. When taking any test, especially a machine-scored test, carefully follow the directions. In addition to your name, be sure to provide all other necessary information on the answer sheet. Each time you fill in an answer, make sure that the number on the answer sheet corresponds to the number of the item on the test.

Although scoring machines have become more sophisticated over time, they might still misread additional marks or incomplete bubbles on your answer sheet. When a machine-scored test is returned to you, check your answer sheet against the scoring key, if one is provided, to make sure that you receive credit for all the questions you answered correctly.

FIGURE 8.3 > Example of a Scantron Answer Sheet

Each time you fill in a Scantron answer sheet, make sure that the number on the answer sheet corresponds to the number of the item on the test. And make sure that all bubbles are filled in completely. Vixit/Shutterstock.com

Computerized Tests

Computerized tests are often taken in a computer lab or testing center and are usually not administered online (this chapter's Tech Tip will help you prepare for online tests, which you'll encounter more and more). Computerized tests can be significantly different from one another depending on the kind of test, the academic subject, and whether the test was written by the instructor, by a textbook company, or by another source. Be sure to take advantage of any practice test opportunities to get a better sense of what the tests will be like. The more experience you have with computerized tests, the more comfortable you will be taking them (the same is true with the other test types).

Some multiple-choice computerized tests might allow you to scroll through all the questions; others might allow you to see only one question at a time. After you complete each question, you might have to move on to the next question without being able to return to earlier ones.

For computerized tests in math and other subjects that require you to solve each problem, be sure to check each answer before you submit it. Also, know in advance what materials you are allowed to have on hand, such as a calculator and scratch paper, for working the problems.

Laboratory Tests

In many science courses, you will have laboratory tests that require you to move from one lab station to the next to solve problems, identify parts of models or specimens, or explain chemical reactions. To prepare for lab tests, always attend lab, take good notes, and study your lab notebook carefully before the test.

You might also have lab tests in foreign language courses that can include both oral and written sections. Work with a partner or study group to prepare for oral exams. Have group members ask one another questions that require using key vocabulary words.

Open-Book and Open-Notes Tests

Although you may like the idea of being able to refer to your book or notes during an exam, open-book and open-notes tests are usually harder than other tests, not easier. You won't really have time to read whole passages during an open-book exam.

Study as completely as you would for any other test, and do not be fooled into thinking that you don't need to know the material. But as you study, you can develop a list of topics and the page numbers where they are covered in your text or in your lecture notes. Type a three-column grid (or use an Excel spreadsheet) with your list of topics in alphabetical order in the first column and corresponding pages from your textbook and lecture notebook in the second and third columns so that you can refer to them quickly when necessary.

During the test, keep up with your time. Don't waste time looking up information in your text or notes if you are sure of your answers. Instead, wait until you have finished the test, and then, if you have extra time, go back and look up answers and make any necessary changes.

Take-Home Tests

Some instructors may allow you to take tests outside class and refer to your textbook, notes, and other resources. Take-home tests are usually more difficult than in-class tests. Read the directions and questions as soon as you receive the test to estimate how much time you will need to complete it. Remember that your instructor will expect your essay answers to look more like out-of-class papers, proofread and edited, than like the essays you would write during an in-class test.

It is probably no surprise that issues of academic honesty can arise for take-home tests. If you usually work with a study group or in a learning community for the course, check with the instructor in advance to determine if any type of group work is allowed on the test.

YOUR TURN › WORK TOGETHER

Which types of tests described above do you prefer, and why? And do you perform better on your preferred test types? Share with another student the strategies you use when preparing for these tests.

TYPES OF QUESTIONS

Your instructors choose not only what types of exams they give you but also what types of questions you should answer to demonstrate what you are learning in the course. You may take an exam that has one or multiple types of questions. This section includes strategies to help you answer different types of questions successfully.

Essay Questions

Essay exams include questions that require students to write a few paragraphs in response to each question. Many college instructors have a strong preference for essay questions for a simple reason: They require deeper thinking than other types of questions. Generally, advanced courses are more likely to include essay exams. To be successful on essay exam questions, follow these guidelines:

1. **Budget your exam time.** Quickly go over the entire exam, and note the questions that are the easiest for you to answer. Estimate the approximate amount of time you should spend on each essay question based on its point value. Remember, writing long answers to questions that have low point values can be a mistake because it takes up precious time you might need for answering questions that count more toward the total grade. Be sure you know whether you must answer all the questions or choose among questions. Wear a watch to monitor your time, and don't forget to leave a few minutes for a quick review.

2. **Actively read the whole question.** Many well-prepared students write good answers to questions that were not asked—when that happens, they may lose points or even fail the exam. Many other students write good answers to only part of the question—they also may lose points or even fail the exam.

3. **Develop a brief outline of your answer before you begin to write.** Make sure that your outline responds to all parts of the question. Use your first paragraph to introduce the main points; use the other paragraphs to describe each point in more depth. If you begin to lose your concentration, you will be glad to have the outline to help you regain your focus. If you find that you are running out of time and cannot complete an essay question, provide an outline of key ideas at the very least. Instructors usually assign points on the basis of your coverage of the main topics from the material. That means you will usually earn more points by responding briefly to all parts of the question than by addressing just one part of the question in detail. You might receive some credit for your outline even if you cannot finish the essay.

4. **Write concise, organized answers.** Some students answer essay questions by quickly writing down everything they know on the topic.

But long answers are not necessarily good answers. Answers that are too general, unfocused, or disorganized may not earn high scores. At the same time, don't forget to give examples so that your instructor can see that you really do understand the big ideas and can illustrate them.

5. **Know the key task words in essay questions.** Being familiar with key task words that may appear in an essay question will help you frame your answer more specifically. Table 8.1 lists common key task words. If your instructor allows you to do so, consider circling or underlining key words in the question to make sure you know how to organize your answer.

TABLE 8.1 ▶ Key Task Words in Essay Questions

Analyze	Break the whole topic into parts in order to explain it better; show how the parts work together to produce the overall pattern.
Compare	Identify similarities in ideas, events, or objects. Don't just describe the elements; state how they are alike.
Contrast	Identify the differences between ideas, events, or objects. Don't just describe the ideas; state how they are different.
Criticize/ Critique	Judge something; give your opinion. Criticism can be positive, negative, or mixed. A critique should generally include your own judgments (supported by evidence) and those of experts who agree with you.
Define	Give the meaning of a word or an expression.
Describe	Give more information about the topic.
Discuss	Give broad statements backed up by detailed information. Discussion often includes identifying the important questions related to an issue and trying to answer these questions.
Evaluate	Discuss the strengths and weaknesses of an idea or a position. When you evaluate, you stress how well something meets a certain standard.
Explain	Clarify a statement. Explanations generally focus on why or how something has come about.
Justify	Argue in support of some decision or conclusion by showing evidence or reasons that support the argument. Try to support your argument with both logical and concrete examples.
Narrate	Relate a series of events in the order they occurred, as you do when you tell a story.
Outline	Present a series of main points in order. Some instructors want a formal outline with numbers and letters.
Summarize	Give information in brief form, without examples and details. A summary is short but covers all the important points.

Multiple-Choice Questions

Multiple-choice questions provide any number of possible answers, often between three and five. The answer choices are usually numbered (1, 2, 3, 4, . . .) or lettered (a, b, c, d, . . .), and the test-taker is supposed to select the correct or the best one. Preparing for multiple-choice tests requires you to actively review all of the material that has been covered for a particular period such as a week or a month. Reviewing flash cards, summary sheets, mind maps, or the recall column in your lecture notes is a good way to cover large amounts of material.

Take advantage of the many cues that multiple-choice questions include. Be careful about words in the question such as *not, except, all,* and *but* to make sure that the answer you choose fits the question. Also read each answer choice carefully; be suspicious of choices that use words such as *always, never,* and *only.* These choices are often (but not always) incorrect. Often the correct answer is the option that is the most comprehensive.

In some multiple-choice questions, the first part of the question is an incomplete sentence (called the stem) and the answer choices complete the sentence. In these questions, any answer choices that do not use correct grammar are usually incorrect. For example, in Figure 8.4, "Margaret Mead was an" is the stem. Which of the four options is grammatically wrong and can be ruled out?

FIGURE 8.4 ❯ Example of a Multiple-Choice Question

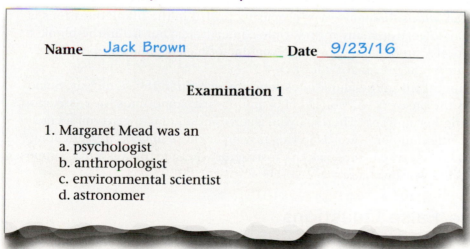

To avoid becoming confused by answer choices that sound alike, predict your own answer to the question before reading the options. Then choose the answer that best matches your prediction.

If you are totally confused by a question, place a check mark in the margin, leave it, and come back later. Sometimes a question later in the exam may provide a clue for the one you are unsure about. If you have absolutely no idea, look for an answer that at least has some pieces of information. If there is no penalty for guessing, fill in an answer for every question, even if it is just a guess. If there is a penalty for guessing, don't just choose an answer at random; leaving the answer blank might be a wiser choice. Finally, always go back, if you have time at the end, and double-check that you chose the right answer for the right question, especially if you are using a Scantron form.

YOUR TURN > DISCUSS IT

Many college instructors do not give essay exams in first-year courses and instead use multiple-choice questions. What do you think are some of the advantages and disadvantages of multiple-choice questions? Share your reactions and ideas with the whole class.

Fill-in-the-Blank Questions

Fill-in-the-blank questions consist of a phrase, sentence, or paragraph with a blank space indicating where the student should provide the missing word or words. In many ways, preparing for fill-in-the-blank questions is similar to getting ready for multiple-choice items, but fill-in-the-blank questions can be harder because you do not have a choice of possible answers right in front of you.

Not all fill-in-the-blank questions are written in the same way. Sometimes the answers will consist of a single word; sometimes the instructor is looking for a phrase. There may be a series of blanks to give you a clue about the number of words in the answer, or there may be just one long blank. If you are unsure, ask the instructor whether the answer is supposed to be one word or more.

True/False Questions

True/False questions ask students to determine whether the statement is correct or not. Remember that for a statement to be true, every detail of the sentence must be correct. That is why questions containing words such as *always*, *never*, and *only* tend to be false, whereas less definite terms such as *often* and *frequently* suggest the statement might be true. Read through the entire exam to see whether information in one question will help you answer another. Do not begin to second-guess what you know or doubt your answers just because a sequence of questions appears to be all true or all false.

Matching Questions

Matching questions are set up with terms in one column and descriptions in the other, and you must make the proper pairings. Before matching any items, review all of the terms and descriptions. Then match the terms you are sure of. As you do so, cross out both the term and its description, and use the process of elimination to assist you in answering the remaining items. To prepare for matching questions, try using flash cards and lists that you create from the recall column in your notes.

8.5

OVERCOMING TEST ANXIETY

Test anxiety takes many different forms. Part of dealing with test anxiety is understanding why it happens and identifying its symptoms. Whatever the reason for test anxiety, you should know that it is common among college students.

Test anxiety has many causes. It can be the result of the pressure that students put on themselves to succeed. Some stress connected with taking exams is natural and can motivate you to perform better. However, when students put too much pressure on themselves or set unrealistic goals, the result can be stress that is no longer motivating.

The expectations of parents, a spouse or partner, friends, and other people who are close to you can also create test anxiety. Some students, for example, are the first in their families to attend college and thus feel extra pressure that can be overwhelming.

Finally, some test anxiety is caused by lack of preparation. Knowing that you are not prepared, that you have fallen behind on assigned reading, homework, or other academic commitments, is usually the source of anxiety. It is logical to be anxious when you know you aren't prepared. This situation becomes even more difficult if the units of the course are cumulative—that is, if they build on one another, as in math and foreign languages, or if the final exam requires understanding all the course material.

Some test anxiety comes from a negative past experience. Forgetting past failures can be a challenge; however, the past is not the present. If you carefully follow the strategies in this chapter, you are likely to do well on future tests. Remember that a little anxiety is OK, but if you find that anxiety is negatively affecting your performance on tests and exams, be sure to ask for help from your college counseling center. Such centers and their professional counselors have a great deal of experience dealing with test anxiety because it is common in college students. Don't think you are a weirdo because you are test anxious.

Take the following test anxiety quiz to find out more about how you feel before taking tests.

Do you experience feelings of test anxiety? Read each of the following questions. If your answer to a question is "yes," place a check mark in the box. If your answer is "no," leave the box blank.

Mental

☐ Do you have trouble focusing and find that your mind easily wanders while studying the material or during the test itself?

☐ During the test, does every noise bother you—sounds from outside the classroom or sounds from other people?

☐ Do you often "blank out" when you see the test?

☐ Do you remember answers to questions only after the test is over?

Physical

☐ Do you get the feeling of butterflies, nausea, or pain in your stomach?

☐ Do you develop headaches before or during the test?

☐ Do you feel like your heart is racing, that you have trouble breathing, or that your pulse is irregular?

☐ Do you have difficulty sitting still, are you tense, or are you unable to get comfortable?

Emotional

☐ Are you more sensitive and more likely to lose patience with a roommate or friend before the test?

☐ Do you feel pressure to succeed from either yourself or from your family or friends?

☐ Do you toss and turn the night before the test?

☐ Do you fear the worst—that you will fail the class or flunk out of college because of the test?

Personal Habits

☐ Do you often stay up late studying the night before a test?

☐ Do you have a personal history of failure for taking certain types of tests (essay, math)?

☐ Do you drink more than your usual amount of caffeine or forget to eat breakfast before a test?

☐ Do you drink alcohol the night before to calm your jittery nerves?

☐ Do you avoid studying until right before a test, choosing to do other activities that are less important because you don't want to think about it?

How many items did you check? To get your **test anxiety reflection score**, count your total, and then see what level of test anxiety you experience.

13–16 Severe: You may want to see if your college counseling center offers individual sessions to provide strategies for dealing with test anxiety. You have already paid for this service through your student fees, so if you have this level of anxiety, take advantage of help that is available for you.

9–12 Moderate: You may want to see if your counseling center will be offering a seminar on anxiety-prevention strategies. Such seminars are usually offered around midterms or just before final exams. Take the opportunity to do something valuable for yourself!

5–8 Mild: Be aware of what situations—certain types of classes or particular test formats—might cause anxiety and disrupt your academic success. If you discover a weakness, address it now before it is too late.

1–4 Slight: Almost everyone has some form of anxiety before tests, and it actually can be beneficial! In small doses, stress can improve your performance, so consider yourself lucky.

Symptoms of Test Anxiety

Test anxiety can appear in many ways. Some students feel it on the very first day of class. Other students begin showing symptoms of test anxiety when it's time to start studying for a test. Others do not get nervous until the night before the test or the morning of an exam day. And some students experience symptoms only while they are actually taking a test.

Symptoms of test anxiety can include:

- butterflies in the stomach, queasiness, nausea
- mild to severe headaches
- an increased heart rate
- hyperventilation, which is breathing unusually deeply or rapidly because of anxiety
- shaking, sweating, or muscle cramps
- "going blank" during the exam and being unable to remember the information

Test anxiety can block the success of any college student, no matter how intelligent, motivated, and prepared that student is. Therefore, it is important to seek help from your college's counseling service or another professional if you think that you have severe test anxiety. If you are not sure where to go for help, ask your adviser or instructor, but seek help promptly! If your symptoms are so severe that you become physically ill, you should also consult your physician or your campus health center.

Types of Test Anxiety

Students who experience test anxiety don't necessarily feel it in all testing situations. For example, you might do fine on classroom tests but feel anxious during standardized examinations such as a college placement test. One reason such standardized tests can create anxiety is that they can change your future. One way of dealing with this type of test anxiety is to ask yourself: What is the worst that can happen? Remember that no matter what the result, it is not the end of the world. How you do on standardized tests might limit some of your options, but going into these tests with a negative attitude will certainly not improve your chances.

Test anxiety can often be subject-specific. For example, some students have math test anxiety. It is important to understand the differences between anxiety that arises from the subject itself and general test anxiety. Perhaps subject-specific test anxiety relates to old beliefs about yourself, such as "I'm no good at math" or "I can't write well." Now is the time to try some positive self-talk and realize that by preparing well, you can be successful even in your hardest courses. If the problem continues, talk to a counselor to learn about strategies that can help you deal with such fears.

Strategies for Dealing with Test Anxiety

In addition to studying, eating right, and getting plenty of sleep, you can try a number of simple strategies for overcoming the physical and emotional impact of test anxiety:

- **Breathe.** If at any point during a test you begin to feel nervous or you cannot think clearly, take a long, deep breath and slowly exhale to restore your breathing to a normal level.

- **Stretch.** Before you go into the test room, especially before a long exam, stretch your muscles—legs, arms, shoulders, and neck—just as you would when preparing to exercise.

- **Have good posture.** Pay attention to the way you are sitting. As you take the test, sit with your shoulders back and relaxed rather than hunched forward. Try not to clutch your pencil or pen tightly in your hand; take a break and stretch your fingers now and then.

- **Create positive mental messages.** Pay attention to the mental messages that you send yourself. If you are overly negative, turn those messages around. Give yourself encouraging, optimistic messages.

- **Keep your confidence high.** Do not allow others (classmates, partners, children, parents, roommates, and friends) to reduce your confidence. If you belong to a study group, discuss strategies for relaxing and staying positive before and during tests.

Getting the Test Back

Students react differently when they receive their test grades and papers. Some students dread seeing their tests returned with a grade; other students look forward to it. Either way, unless you look at your answers (the correct and incorrect ones) and the instructor's comments, you will have no way to evaluate your own knowledge and test-taking strengths. If you want to ask any questions about your grade, this is an excellent reason to visit your instructor during his or her office hours or before or after class; your concern will show the instructor that you want to succeed.

YOUR TURN ❯ STAY MOTIVATED

What do you do when an instructor returns an exam to you? Do you just look at the grade, or do you review the items you answered correctly and incorrectly? Review your graded tests because doing so will help you do better next time. You might find that your mistakes were the result of not following directions, being careless with words or numbers, or even thinking too hard about a multiple-choice question. Mistakes can help you learn, so refer to your textbook and notes to better understand the source and reason for each mistake. If you are a member of a study group, plan a test review with other group members; this allows you to learn from your mistakes as well as those of the others in the group.

CHEATING AND PLAGIARISM

Different colleges define cheating in different ways. Some include the following activities in their definition of cheating: looking over a classmate's shoulder for an answer, using a calculator when it is not permitted, obtaining or discussing an exam (or individual questions from an exam) without permission, copying someone else's lab notes, purchasing or using term papers over the Internet, watching the video instead of reading the book, and copying computer files. Whatever your college's rules about cheating, you must follow them.

Many colleges do not allow certain activities in addition to lying and cheating. Here are some examples of prohibited behaviors:

- intentionally inventing information or results
- submitting the same piece of academic work, such as a research paper, for credit in more than one course
- giving your exam answers to another student to copy during the actual exam or before that exam is given to another class
- bribing anyone in exchange for any kind of academic advantage
- helping or trying to help another student commit a dishonest act

Why Students Cheat and the Consequences of Cheating

Students cheat mainly when they believe they cannot do well on their own. Some college students developed a habit of cheating in high school or even elementary or middle school and do not trust their own ability to succeed in classes. Other students simply don't know the rules. For example, some students incorrectly think that buying a term paper isn't cheating.

Cultural and college differences may cause some students to cheat. In other countries and at some U.S. colleges, students are encouraged to review past exams as practice exercises. Some colleges permit sharing answers and information for homework and other assignments with friends. Make sure you know the policy at your college.

Pressures from others—family, peers, and instructors—might cause some students to consider cheating. And there is no doubt that we live in a competitive society. But in truth, grades are nothing if you cheat to earn them. Even if your grades help you get a job, it is what you have actually learned that will help you keep that job and be promoted. If you haven't learned what you need to know, you won't be ready to work in your chosen field.

Sometimes lack of preparation will cause students to cheat. Perhaps they tell themselves that they aren't really dishonest and that cheating just "one time" won't matter. But if you cheat one time, you're more likely to do it again.

> Stop! Thief!

When students are seated close to each other while taking a test, they may be tempted to let their eyes wander to someone else's answers. Don't let this happen to you. Cheating is the same as stealing. Also, don't offer to share your work or make it easy for other students to copy your work. Reduce temptation by covering your answer sheet.

Although you might see some students who seem to be getting away with cheating, such behaviors can have severe and life-changing results. In some cases, students who have cheated on examinations have been suspended or expelled; graduates have had their college degrees revoked.

Here are some steps you can take to reduce the likelihood of problems with academic honesty:

- **Know the rules.** Learn the academic code for your college by going to its website or checking in the student handbook.

- **Set clear boundaries.** Refuse when others ask you to help them cheat. This might be hard to do, but you must say no. Leave your cell phone in your book bag; instructors are often suspicious when they see students looking at their cell phones during an exam.

- **Improve time management.** Be well prepared for all quizzes, exams, projects, and papers.

- **Seek help.** Find out where you can get help with study skills, time management, and test taking. If your skills are in good shape but the content of the course is too hard, consult your instructor, join a study group, or visit your campus learning center or tutorial service.

- **Withdraw from the course.** Your college has a policy about dropping courses and a deadline to drop without penalty. You might decide to drop only the course that's giving you trouble. Some students choose to withdraw from all classes and take time off before returning to school if they find themselves in over their heads or if a long illness, a family crisis, or something else has caused them to fall behind. But before withdrawing, ask about college policies in terms of financial aid and other scholarship programs. See your adviser before you decide to withdraw.

- **Reexamine goals.** Stick to your own realistic goals instead of giving in to pressure from family members or friends to achieve impossibly high standards.

YOUR TURN › DISCUSS IT

Some students think it is acceptable to get answers from another student who took the exam earlier in the term or in a prior term. What do you think?

About Plagiarism

Plagiarism is taking another person's work or ideas and presenting them as your own. Plagiarism is unacceptable in a college setting. Just as taking someone else's property is considered physical theft, taking credit for someone else's ideas is considered intellectual theft. In written reports and papers, you must give credit anytime you use (a) another person's actual words; (b) another person's ideas or theories, even if you don't quote them directly; or (c) any other information that is not considered common knowledge.

Occasionally, politicians, public figures, writers, and journalists who have plagiarized have jeopardized their careers. In fall 2014, Senator John Walsh of Montana had his master's degree from the U.S. Army War College revoked because of plagiarism. He later left the 2014 Senate race. In spring 2013, Fox News analyst Juan Williams was criticized for plagiarizing material from a Center for American Progress report in a column he wrote for a political insider publication, but he blamed his research assistant. Even a few college presidents have been found guilty of borrowing the words of others and using them as their own in speeches and written documents. Such discoveries may result not only in embarrassment and shame but also in lawsuits and criminal actions.

Because there is no universal rule about plagiarism, ask your instructors about the guidelines they set in their classes. Once you know the rules, plagiarism is easy to avoid. Keep careful notes as you do your research, so that later on you don't mistake someone else's words or ideas for your own. Finally, be sure to check out your college's official definition of plagiarism, which you will find in the student handbook, college catalog, college website, course syllabi, or first-year course materials. If you have any questions about what is and isn't acceptable, be sure to ask someone in charge. "I didn't know" is not a valid excuse.

It should go without saying (but we'll say it anyway) that intentional plagiarism is a bad idea on many levels. Aside from the possibility of being caught and the potential for punishment—a failing grade, suspension, or even expulsion—submitting a paper purchased from an Internet source, copying and pasting passages from someone else's paper, or lifting material from a published source will cause you to miss out on the discovery and skill development that research assignments are meant to teach.

CONQUER ONLINE TESTS

THE PROBLEM — You don't know how to take an online test—a test that is administered online—and you are going to have to take several online tests this term.

THE FIX — Learn to avoid rookie errors that can trip you up.

HOW TO DO IT

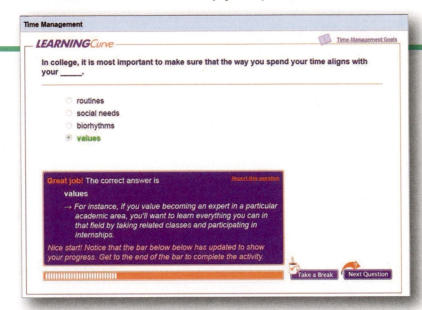

1. **Study with other people.** Whether an online test is part of a self-paced online course or a face-to-face course, start a study group, either in person or online, as far in advance of the exam as possible.

2. **Get organized.** An online, open-book quiz or test can take longer than a normal test if you're not sure where to locate the information you need. When you prepare, study like you would for a normal, in-class, timed test; your notes and books should be for occasional reference only. Don't think you can learn everything you need to know on the day of the test.

3. **Resist the temptation to surf the Web for answers.** The answer you pick might not be what your instructor is looking for. It's much better to check your notes to see what you were taught in class.

4. **Work together.** If your instructor allows collaboration on tests, open up an instant message window with a fellow student. Take the test together, and take it early.

5. **Stay focused.** When you're taking an online test, it's easy to fall prey to real-life diversions like Facebook, iTunes, or a sudden urge to rearrange your closet. Whatever you do, take the test seriously. Go somewhere quiet where you can concentrate—not Starbucks. A quiet, remote spot in the library is ideal.

6. **Budget your time.** Keep an eye on the clock so that you'll be sure to finish the entire test. Tackle the easy questions first. Once you get the easy questions out of the way, you can revisit the harder ones.

7. **Practice using the test interface.** Ask your instructor if you can practice with a "zero points" quiz, so you can familiarize yourself with the testing site and the question setup. You don't want to be nervous about how the site works while you are answering questions on a test that will affect your grade.

8. **Ask about special rules.** Online tests can be set up differently than regular tests. Find out in advance if there's a penalty for wrong answers, if you can retake the test, and if you can go back and change an answer.

9. **Plan for an intermittent connection.** There's always the risk of losing your Internet connection in the middle of the test. To be on the safe side, type your answers and essays into a Word document. Then leave time at the end of the test session to cut and paste them into the test itself.

10. **Use all the time allotted.** If you finish early, take a few minutes to check your answers and spelling carefully (that's good advice for traditional tests, too).

EXTRA STYLE POINTS

Use study guides or a study session from each class to create your own online practice test. If you use Google Drive, you can create a file called a "form," which allows you to create a test, quiz, or survey that you can use with your study group. Everyone in the group can use it at times that are convenient for them, rather than only when the group can get together.

THINK

As you were reading the tips for improving your performance on exams and tests, were you surprised to see different tips for various subjects, such as math and science, and for different kinds of questions, such as multiple-choice and essay? What did you find to be the most useful information in this chapter? What material was unclear to you?

_____

_____

_____

_____

_____

_____

WRITE

Do you consider yourself to be a good test taker or a poor one? Why? Do you experience test anxiety? If you do, what might be the reasons? What did you learn in this chapter that either explains your inability to relax while taking tests or can help you relax and improve your test grades?

_____

_____

_____

_____

_____

_____

APPLY

1. Identify an upcoming test or exam. What time of day is it scheduled, and what type of test will it be? What strategies have you read in this chapter that will help you prepare for and take this test?
2. What course do you find most difficult? If you are anxious about taking tests in this class, what positive self-messages can you use to help yourself stay focused?

USE YOUR RESOURCES

Below are suggestions for resources that are available at many colleges and the online resources that are available to everyone.

AT YOUR COLLEGE

VISIT . . .	IF YOU NEED HELP . . .
Learning Center	preparing for tests. Almost every college has a learning center whose specialty is to help you study for tests. The best students, good students who want to be even better, and students with academic difficulties use learning centers and tutoring services. These services are offered by both full-time professionals and highly skilled peer tutors and are usually free. Ask about online resources available through the center or college library.
Counseling Center	finding workshops and individual or group counseling for test anxiety. Sometimes these services are also offered by the campus health center. Ask your instructor where you can find counseling services at your college.
Fellow students	finding a tutor or joining a study group. Students who work with tutors and in study groups are much more likely to be successful. Often the best help we can get is the closest to us. Keep an eye out in your classes and extracurricular activities for the best students—those who appear to be the most serious, purposeful, and directed.

ONLINE

GO TO . . .	IF YOU NEED HELP . . .
Center for Teaching and Learning at Florida Atlantic University: fau.edu/ctl/#	finding a list of tips to help you prepare for exams. This site also offers tips to study more effectively, tips for success outside the classroom, and other resources.
Study Guides and Strategies: studygs.net/tstprp8.htm	getting tips for reducing test anxiety.

MY COLLEGE'S RESOURCES

LaunchPad for *Understanding Your College Experience* is a great resource. Go online to master concepts using the LearningCurve study tool and much more. **macmillanhighered.com/gardnerunderstanding**

9 Collecting, Evaluating, and Using Information

PRE-READING ACTIVITY: Describe your experiences with writing before you started college. How have you used writing in school or at work? Do you enjoy writing, or does the thought of doing research and writing a research paper cause you to panic? How do you feel about speaking in front of a group of people? Do you prefer that to writing papers? Why or why not? Write your responses to these questions in the space provided below.

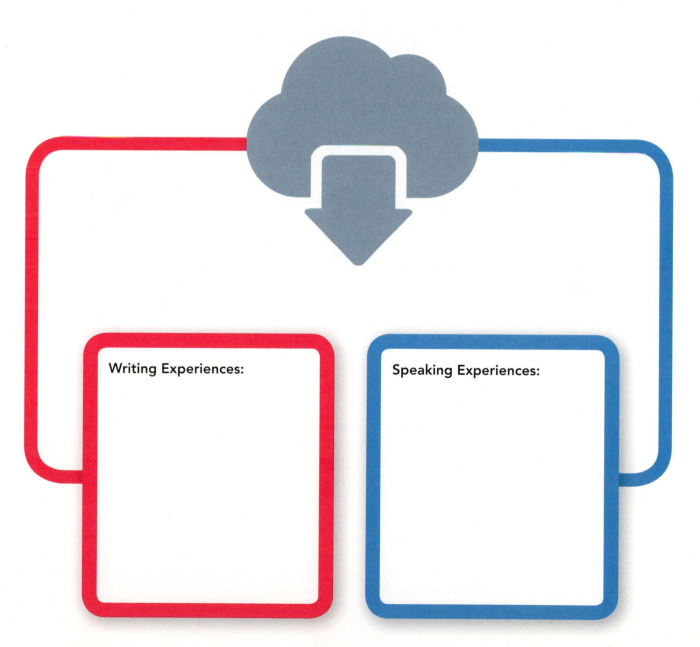

Writing Experiences:

Speaking Experiences:

PROFILE

Victoria Walter, 43
Business Administration Major, *Santa Fe College, Florida*

 Victoria Walter found that life was changing around her. After 25 years of marriage, she saw her two sons off to college and wondered what was next for her. So Victoria decided to enroll in a business administration program at Santa Fe College, a community college in Gainesville, Florida, while also working 40 hours a week as a department manager at a major retail store. After graduation, she would like to transfer to the University of Florida to continue her education. "If all goes according to plan," she says, "I will graduate alongside my sons! Not that I am competing with my sons, but knowing they're in college too keeps me motivated."

When it comes to doing library research, Victoria has learned a lot of skills in her first-year college success course. However, she often struggles with collecting enough information on her topic and communicating the information in writing or in oral presentations to the class. She learned that she could ask a librarian for help in identifying information sources, but she found it a bit difficult to make it clear which ideas were hers and which ideas came from other sources. "After I attended a workshop in the library,

"After I attended a workshop in the library, I developed a better understanding of how to cite my sources."

I developed a better understanding of how to cite my sources," she noted. Victoria's biggest challenge, however, is organizing the facts and details she needs to support her point. She has worked to overcome this challenge, and one of the most effective strategies for Victoria has been creating an outline before she begins writing. "This really helps me stay on track and focus on my topic," she explains. "Also, I always review my written material to ensure that I have covered all key points before completing the paper."

Victoria found that sharing her ideas with a classmate or family member as she develops her paper is helpful. "I noticed that when I write papers," she says, "I tend to write as if I am speaking with someone." She also discovered that she needs someone to proofread her final papers before she submits them.

As far as presenting her ideas in front of a group, Victoria feels extremely nervous. She has learned that preparing notes and practicing in front of her husband or a mirror helps her with controlling her nerves during the presentation.

Already happy with the path her life is taking, Victoria thinks that college will help further her ambitions. "I would like to become an executive manager at my current place of employment. I'll be the manager that other employees come to for job information and employment questions."

To access the Learning-Curve study tool, Video Tools, and more, go to LaunchPad for *Understanding Your College Experience.* macmillanhighered.com /gardnerunderstanding

As Victoria's story illustrates, when you write papers and prepare oral presentations, the ability to find the information you need and to make sense of it is important. Finding information, writing, and speaking are basic requirements for all college courses. Instructors want to see how you form your thoughts about your topic instead of providing just a summary of the information. They are interested in seeing which ideas you are accepting, which you are rejecting, and how you relate the concepts and come to a new understanding of the topic. In short, they want to see you think deeply about the information you find. These skills are particularly important in today's world, where processing information is part of daily life and career, and the more skilled you are, the better able you'll be to explore or confirm your life purpose and plans for the future.

INFORMATION LITERACY

9.1

Information literacy, the number one job skill demanded by most twenty-first-century employers, is the ability to find, interpret, and use information to meet your needs; it includes computer literacy, media literacy, and cultural literacy:

- **Computer literacy** is the ability to use electronic tools for conducting searches and for communicating and presenting to others what you have found and analyzed. This ability involves using different computer programs, digital video and audio tools, and social media.

- **Media literacy** is the ability to think deeply about what you see and read through both the content and context of television, film, advertising, radio, magazines, books, and the Internet.

- **Cultural literacy** is knowing what has gone on and is going on around you in society. You have to understand the difference between the American Civil War and the Revolutionary War, U2 and YouTube, Eminem and M&Ms so that you can keep up with everyday conversations and with your college reading material.

Information matters. It helps people make good choices. The choices people make often determine their success in careers, their happiness as friends and family members, and their well-being as citizens of our planet.

YOUR TURN > DISCUSS IT

In a small group, discuss how information literacy can contribute to people's success in today's world.

Learning to Be Information Literate

People are amazed at the amount of information available to them everywhere, especially online. Many think that because they checked out some links they found on a search engine, they are informed or can easily become informed. Most of us, though, are unprepared for the number of available sources and the amount of information that we can find at the press of a button. What can we do about information overload? To become an informed and successful user of information, keep three basic goals in mind:

1. **Know how to find the information you need.** Once you have figured out where to look for information, you'll need to ask good questions and learn how to search information systems, such as the Internet, libraries, and databases. You'll also want to get to know your college librarians who can help you ask questions, decide what sources you need to investigate, and find the information you need.

2. **Learn how to interpret the information you find.** It is important to find information, but it is even more important to make sense of that information. What does the information mean? Have you selected a source you can understand? Is the information correct? Can the source be trusted?

3. **Have a purpose for collecting information and then do something with it once you have it.** Even the best information won't do much good if you don't know what to do with it. True, sometimes you'll hunt down a fact simply to satisfy your own curiosity. But more often, you'll communicate what you've learned to someone else. First you should decide how to put your findings into an appropriate format such as a research paper for a class or a presentation at a meeting. Then you need to decide what it is that you want to accomplish. Will you use the information to make a decision, solve a problem, share an idea, prove a point, or something else?

In this chapter we'll explore ways to work toward each of these goals—doing so is really what college is all about.

Research: What It Is and What It Isn't

In the past, you might have completed assignments that asked you to find a book, journal article, or Web page related to a particular topic. While finding information is an essential part of research, it's just one step, not the end of the road. Research is not just copying a paragraph from a book or putting together bits and pieces of information without adding any of your own comments. In fact, such behavior could easily be considered plagiarism, a form of cheating that could result in a failing grade or worse (plagiarism is discussed later in this chapter). At the very least, repeating information or ideas without thinking about or interpreting them puts you at risk of careless use of old, incorrect, or one-sided resources.

Research is a process that includes steps used to collect and analyze information to increase understanding of a topic or issue. Those steps are asking questions, collecting and analyzing data related to those questions, and presenting one or more answers. Good research is information literacy in action. If your instructor asks you to select and report on a topic, you might search for information about it, find a dozen sources, evaluate them, interpret them, select a few and remove a few, organize the ones you wish to keep, select related portions, write a paper or prepare a presentation that cites your sources, write an introduction that explains what you have done, draw some conclusions of your own, and submit the results. That's research—the conclusion that you make based on your research is new information. It takes determination and persistence to go through all the steps that good research requires. Some steps will be difficult and time-consuming, and you might be tempted to take shortcuts. Learning to persist at these kinds of tasks and processes in college will pay off in your career as this kind of work will come more easily to you, and you will be more successful.

CHOOSING, NARROWING, AND RESEARCHING A TOPIC

9.2

Assignments that require the use of library materials can take many forms and will be a part of most of your classes. You'll learn several ways to search for information later in the chapter. Before you start searching, however, you need to have an idea of exactly what you're looking for.

Choosing a topic is often the hardest part of a research project. Your instructor may assign a general topic, but to get motivated to begin your research, you'll need to narrow it down to a particular area that interests you enough to research it. Imagine, for example, that you have been assigned to write a research paper on the topic of climate change. What steps should you take? Your first job is to get an overview of your topic. You can begin by conducting a Google search. Once you've found some basic information to understand your topic, you have a decision to make: What aspects of the subject will you research? Soon after you start researching your topic, you may realize that it is really large (for example, simply typing "climate change" into Google will return millions of hits) and that it includes many related subtopics. You can use this new information to create keywords. A **keyword** is a word or phrase that tells an online search tool what you're looking for. You can create a list of keywords; brainstorming different terms and subtopics within your general topic will help you find resources for your topic. For example, for the topic "climate change," keywords may include "ocean level rise," "greenhouse effect," "ozone layer," "glacier recession," or "carbon emissions." Even those terms will generate a large number of hits, so you will probably need to narrow your search topic several times.

What you want are twelve or so focused and highly relevant hits on an aspect of the topic that you can use to write a well-organized essay. Begin by figuring out what you already know and what you would like to learn more about. Perhaps you know a little about climate change causes and effects and you're curious about its impacts on animals and plants; in that case you might decide on a two-part topic: impacts on animals and impacts on plants. By consulting a few general sources, you'll find that you can narrow a broad topic to something that motivates you to learn more and is a manageable size. And when you feel motivated to learn more, you are more likely to earn a better grade. You may end up focusing on the impact of climate change on one particular animal or plant in one specific geographic area.

If you are having trouble coming up with keywords, one place to begin your research is an **encyclopedia,** a book or an electronic database with general knowledge on a range of topics. You have probably used an encyclopedia recently—you may use one all the time without thinking about it: Wikipedia. A *wiki* is a type of website that allows many different people to edit its content. This means that information on wikis can be constantly changing. Many instructors feel that the information on Wikipedia cannot be guaranteed to be reliable because anyone can change it; they instead want students to use sources that have gone through a formal editing and reviewing process. Your instructors might even forbid Wikipedia; if so, avoid it altogether. Even if an instructor permits the use of Wikipedia, it's best to use it only as a *starting point* for your research. Do not plan on citing Wikipedia in your final paper. Rather, check the references at the bottom of Wikipedia pages, or otherwise verify claims made at Wikipedia on another more trustworthy site.

Even with an understanding of various types of sources, it can be difficult to determine what exactly you need for your assignment. Figure 9.1 provides an overview of when to use different common research sources and gives examples of what you'll find in each source.

YOUR TURN > WORK TOGETHER

With a classmate decide where you would go to find information about an environmental issue affecting your neighborhood. Use the chart in Figure 9.1 to determine what kind of information each source provides.

FIGURE 9.1 › Using Common Research Sources

This chart differentiates the most common research sources. You will access these types of sources for classwork and also for your personal life.

INFORMATION TIME LINE		
Source	When to access information	What it offers
Newspapers (print and online)	Daily/hourly after an event	Primary-source, firsthand discussions of a current event, and of what happened at the time of the event; short articles
Magazines	Weekly/monthly after an event	Analysis by a journalist or reporter of an event days or weeks after it occurred; longer articles than in newspapers; informally credits sources; might include more interviews or research as well as historical context
Scholarly articles	Months after an event	In-depth analyses of issues; research-based scientific studies with formally credited sources, written and reviewed by experts; contains graphs, tables, and charts
Books	Months/years after an event	A comprehensive overview of a topic with broad and in-depth analyses

9.3

USING THE LIBRARY

It may seem hard to get motivated to go to the library. Some of us remember when libraries were cold and unfriendly places. Today libraries are inviting and friendly, and so are the people who work in them. You can use libraries not only to read books and articles but also to find online information and spaces for study. Most libraries also have computers and printers that you can use to complete your assignments. Many libraries now also house tutoring and learning centers and have sections where you can purchase and consume food and beverages, socialize, relax, and work in groups on homework assignments. There may also be areas where students are encouraged to talk with each other and study in groups, and, of course, you will find designated quiet study zones.

Whenever you have research to do for a class, for your job, or for your personal life, visit a library in person or access it online. We can't stress this enough. Although the Internet is loaded with billions of pages of information, don't be fooled into thinking it will serve all of your needs. For one thing, you'll have to sort through a lot of junk to find your way to good-quality online sources. More important, if you limit yourself to the Web, you'll miss out on some of the best materials. Although we often think that everything is electronic and can be found through a computer, a great deal of valuable information is still stored in traditional print formats and your college library database.

Every library has books and journals as well as a great number of items in electronic databases that aren't available on public websites. Librarians at your college work with your instructors to determine the kinds of materials that support their teaching. Most libraries also have other types of information, such as government documents, microfilm, photographs, historical documents, maps, music, and films. A key component of being information literate is determining the kinds of sources you need to satisfy your research questions.

A college library is far more than a document warehouse, however. For starters, most campus libraries have websites and apps that offer lots of help for students. Some provide guidelines on writing research papers, conducting online searches, or navigating the **stacks**—the area of a library in which most of the books are shelved.

Of course, no one library can possibly own everything you might need or enough copies of each item, so groups of libraries share their materials with each other. If your college library does not have a journal or book that looks promising for your project, or the item you need is checked out, you can use **interlibrary loan,** a service that allows you to request an item at no charge from another library at a different college or university. The request process is simple, and the librarians can help you get started.

If it is difficult for you to get to your college library because of your commuting, family, work challenges, or time constraints, or because you are an online student who lives far from the actual campus and its library, you will still have off-campus, online access to library materials through a school-provided ID and password. You can also have online chats with librarians who can help you in real time. To learn more, check out your library's website, or e-mail or phone the reference desk. Be sure to use the handouts and guides that are available at the reference desk or online. You will also find tutorials and virtual tours that will help you become familiar with the collections, services, and spaces available at your library.

> **Library of the Future? No, the Present!**
College libraries are changing to learning commons as information goes digital and space for group work becomes a priority. This facility merges the library, information technology, and classrooms and contains multiple zones for individual, small-group, and team-based learning. What does your college library offer?
Norma Jean Gargasz/Alamy Stock Photo

The 10-Minute Rule

If you have been working hard trying to locate information for a research project for 10 minutes and haven't found what you need, don't give up. Ask a librarian for help. Working with librarians shows that you are comfortable

asking for help and smart enough to use resources available to you—acts that build resilience and are good practice for the workplace, where you'll often have to reach out to others when you need assistance. Let the librarian know what searches you've tried, and he or she will be able to help you figure out new strategies to get to the books, articles, and other sources you need. In addition, the librarian can help you develop strategies to improve your research and writing skills. Doing research without a librarian is like driving cross-country without using Google maps or a navigation system—technically, you can do it, but you will get lost along the way and may not get to your destination on time. Get to know at least one librarian as your go-to expert. College librarians are dedicated to helping students, and they are available to assist students in the library or online.

Library Resources

Many college-level research projects will require you to use a variety of sources to find information and do research. The most commonly used resources that college libraries offer are **scholarly journals** and periodicals, which include original, peer-reviewed research articles written by experts or researchers in a particular academic discipline.

Examples are the *Journal of Educational Research* and the *Social Psychology Quarterly*. The term **peer-reviewed** means that other experts in the field read and evaluate the articles in the journal before it is published. You can find scholarly articles by using an online **database**—a searchable set of information often organized by certain subject areas—or your library's catalog, an online resource accessible on or off campus. You may also be able to find some of the scholarly articles by using Google Scholar as your search engine. This is a specific part of Google that searches only within scholarly journal articles.

A **periodical** is a resource such as a journal, a magazine, or a newspaper that is published multiple times a year. Periodicals are designated either by date of publication or by annual volume numbers and issue numbers (based on the number of issues published in a given year). Peer-reviewed scholarly journals are of course periodicals, but most periodicals are classified as popular rather than scholarly. The articles in *Rolling Stone* (a periodical with a focus on politics and popular culture published twice each month) do not go through the peer-review process as do the articles in scholarly journals. Lack of peer review does *not* disqualify magazines as possible legitimate sources for your research, unless your assignment specifically requires all sources to be scholarly articles or books. Look back at Figure 9.1 for a breakdown of different types of sources.

Books are especially useful for research projects. Often students in introductory classes must write research papers on broad topics like the Civil War. While many scholarly articles have been written about the Civil War, they will not provide the kind of general overview of the topic that is available in books.

One of the biggest benefits of searching for books is the ability to browse. When you find your book on the shelf, look at the other books around it. They will be on the same topic. Many books are also available electronically; some of these e-books can be easily accessed online. Your college library may have books available in this format as well. You can browse the entire e-book chapters and even print a few pages.

Have a discussion with a group of your classmates to answer this question: Is the library a necessary resource for learning in college? Do the members of the group agree or disagree? Share your group's ideas with others in the class. If possible, find some students who have been on campus considerably longer than you, and ask them about how they are making use of the library and librarians.

9.4

EVALUATING SOURCES

The Internet makes research easier in some ways and more difficult in others. Through Internet search engines such as Google and Bing, you have immediate access to a great deal of free information. Keep in mind that many of the entries on any topic are not valid sources for serious research, however, and the order of the search results is determined not by their importance but by search formulas that depend both on popularity and on who pays for Web pages to be on the top of the list. Anybody can put up a website, which means you can't always be sure of the website owner's credibility and reliability. A Web source may be written by anyone—a fifth grader, a famous professor, a professional society, or a person with little knowledge about the topic.

Some students might at first be excited about receiving 243,000,000 hits from a Google search on climate change, but they may be shocked when they realize the information they find is not sorted or organized. Think carefully about the usefulness of the information based on three important factors: relevance, authority, and bias.

Relevance

The first thing to consider in looking at a possible source is whether it is relevant: Does it relate to your subject in an appropriate way? How well does it fit your needs? The answers to these questions depend on your research project and the kind of information you are seeking.

- **Is it introductory?** Introductory information is basic and elementary. It does not require background knowledge about the topic. Introductory sources can be useful when you're first learning about a subject. They are less useful when you're drawing conclusions about a particular aspect of the subject.

- **Is it comprehensive?** The more detail, the better. Look for sources that consider the topic in depth and offer plenty of evidence to support their conclusions.

- **Is it current?** You should usually give preference to recent sources although older ones can sometimes be useful (for instance, primary sources for a historical topic or if the source is still cited by others in a field).

- **Can you conclude anything from it?** Use the "So what?" test: So what does this information mean? Why does it matter to my project?

Authority

Once you have determined that a source is relevant to your project, check that it was created by somebody who is qualified to write or speak on the subject and whose conclusions are based on solid evidence. This, too, will depend on your subject and the nature of your research. For example, a fifth grader would generally not be considered an authority, but if you are writing about a topic such as bullying in elementary schools, a fifth grader's opinion might be exactly what you're looking for.

Make sure you can identify the author and be ready to explain why that author is qualified to write on the subject. Good qualifications might include academic degrees, other research and writing on the subject, or related personal experience.

Determine whether your project calls for scholarly publications, periodicals such as magazines and newspapers, or both. Many journalists and columnists are extremely well qualified, and their work might be appropriate for your needs. But as a general rule, scholarly sources that have been thoroughly reviewed give the work credibility in a college research project.

YOUR TURN > WORK TOGETHER

While you are reading this chapter, conduct an Internet search for the phrase "finding resources for research papers" with a couple of your classmates. What ideas did you find through your Internet search?

Bias

When you are searching for sources, you should realize that all materials have an author who has personal beliefs that affect the way he or she views the world and approaches a topic. This is a normal part of the research process; however, serious authors have adopted ways to ensure that their own opinions don't get in the way of accuracy. You will want to find such objective sources whenever possible; many sources will be heavily biased toward a specific viewpoint or ideology. Consider, for instance, how news outlets like MSNBC and Fox News often present very different, biased viewpoints on political issues.

Research consists of considering multiple perspectives on a topic, analyzing the sources, and creating something new from your analysis. Signs of bias, such as overly positive or overly harsh language, hints of a personal agenda, or a stubborn refusal to consider other points of view, indicate that you should question the credibility and accuracy of a source. Although nothing is wrong with someone having a particular point of view, as a researcher you will want to be aware that the bias exists. You may need to exclude strongly biased sources from your research. For example, if you are writing about climate change, you will want to examine sources for evidence of political or personal agendas. The following questions can help you evaluate your sources:

- Who is the author?
- Why is the author interested in this topic? What is the author's goal in writing about this topic?
- Does the author present facts or personal opinions about the topic?
- Does the author provide evidence that is based on research or information from other sources? Does the author cite these sources?
- Are the conclusions the author made based on sound evidence, or are they just based on the author's personal interests and opinions?
- What do you think is missing from the article?

YOUR TURN › DISCUSS IT

Do you know websites, blogs, newspapers, magazines, or TV networks that you believe are biased? Why do you consider them biased?

9.5

USING YOUR RESEARCH IN WRITING

You have probably heard the saying "Knowledge is power." But knowledge gives you power only if you put it to use in the form of what might be called a product. You have to decide what form that product will take—a piece of writing or a presentation—and what kind of power you want it to hold. Who is your audience, and how will you present the information? What do you hope to accomplish by sharing your conclusions? Remember that a major goal of information literacy is to use information effectively to accomplish a specific purpose. Make it a point to do something with the results of your research. Otherwise, why bother? You researched information to find the answer to a question. Now is the time to formulate that answer and share it with others.

Many students satisfy themselves with a straightforward report that summarizes what they found, and sometimes that's enough. More often, though, you'll want to analyze the information and use that analysis to form your own ideas. To do that, first consider how the facts, opinions, and details you found from your different sources relate to one another. What do they have in common, and how do they differ? What conclusions can you draw from those similarities and differences? What new ideas did they

spark? How can you use the information you have on hand to support your conclusions? Essentially, what you're doing at this stage of any research project is **synthesis,** a process in which you put together parts of ideas to come up with a whole result. By accepting some ideas, rejecting others, combining related concepts, and pulling it all together, you'll create new information and ideas that other people can use.

Your final paper will include analysis and synthesis of the sources you found through your research. You must make sure that you clearly state which thoughts and ideas came from the sources you found, and which are yours.

THE WRITING PROCESS

9.6

Your writing tells others how well you think and understand the ideas you are learning in your courses. In college, you are required to write often. Students have to write lab reports in science courses, reflection papers in response to readings in several courses, and journal entries and one-minute papers in writing courses. Like research, writing takes practice, and it is always a good idea to ask for help. This section will get you started by walking you through the writing process with step-by-step guidelines for effective and efficient writing.

Steps to Good Writing

The writing process typically includes the following steps:

1. Prewriting
2. Drafting
3. Revising

Now, let's look more in-depth at each one of these steps.

Step 1: Using Prewriting to Discover What You Want to Say.
Engaging in prewriting activities is the first step in the writing process. Prewriting simply means writing things down as they come to mind based on the information from the sources you found through your research along with your own ideas, without consciously trying to organize your thoughts, find exactly the right words, or think about structure. It can involve filling a page, whiteboard, or screen with words, phrases, or sentences.

The most commonly used prewriting activity is called **freewriting.** Freewriting is a powerful process for discovering ideas you didn't know you had! Freewriting simply means writing without worrying about punctuation, grammar, spelling, and background. It helps you avoid the temptation to try to write and edit at the same time. It's impossible to write well and simultaneously organize, check grammar and spelling, and offer intelligent thoughts to your readers. If you are freewriting on your computer or tablet, turn off the grammar and spell checkers.

When you freewrite, you might notice that you have more ideas than you can fit into one paper, which is common. Freewriting helps you figure out what you really want to say as you make connections between ideas.

Step 2: Drafting. When you have completed your research with the help of your librarian, gathered a lot of information sources and ideas, and done some freewriting, it's time to move to the drafting stage. Before you start writing your draft, you need to organize all the ideas you generated in the freewriting step and form a **thesis statement,** a short statement that clearly defines the purpose of the paper (see Figure 9.2).

Figure 9.2 › Example of a Thesis Statement

In the example provided, you can see that the student made notes about what she needs to address in her paper to support the thesis.

Thesis: Napoleon's dual personality can be explained by examining incidents throughout his life.

1. Explain why I am using the term "dual personality" to describe Napoleon.
2. Briefly comment on his early life and his relationship with his mother.
3. Describe Napoleon's rise to fame from soldier to emperor. Stress the contradictions in his personality and attitudes.
4. Describe the contradictions in his relationship with Josephine.
5. Summarize my thoughts about Napoleon's personality.
6. Possibly conclude by referring to opening question: "Did Napoleon actually have a dual personality?"

Most students find that creating an outline helps them organize their thoughts, resulting in a clear structure from the thesis to the conclusion (see Figure 9.3 for an example). Once you've set the structure for your paper, you'll add analysis and synthesis of your research findings, and you're well on your way to a final draft. If you have chosen the thesis carefully, it will help you check to see that each sentence relates to your main idea. When you have completed this stage, you will have the first draft of your paper in hand.

Figure 9.3 › Example of an Outline

An outline is a working document; you do not need a complete outline to begin writing. Note how this author has a placeholder for another example; she has not yet decided which example from her research to use.

Outline for a Napoleon Paper

  I. Thesis—Napoleon's dual personality can be explained by examining incidents in his life

 II. Dual Personality

      a. What is it?

      b. How does it apply to Napoleon?

III. Napoleon's Rise to Fame

      a. Contradictions in his personality and attitudes

          i. Relationship with Josephine

         ii. Example #2 (to come)

IV. Summary of my thoughts about Napoleon's personality

 V. Conclusion

      a. Restate and answer thesis

          i. Yes, he had a dual personality because:

              1. Josephine

              2. Example #2

Step 3: Revising. The key to good writing is rewriting or revising, which is the stage at which you take a good piece of writing and do your best to make it great. After you draft your paper, read it once. You may need to reorganize your ideas, add transitions such as *therefore* or *however*, cut unnecessary words from sentences and paragraphs, rewrite some sentences or paragraphs, or use stronger words.

After you revise your paper, put it aside for at least a day and then reread it. Distancing yourself from your writing for a while allows you to see it differently later. You will probably find and correct more grammatical and spelling errors, reorganize your written ideas, and make your writing stronger as a result.

It also might help to share your paper with one or more of your classmates or a family member to get their feedback. You should also check to see if your college provides any writing or editing assistance. Most colleges do in the writing center or a learning center. Once you have talked with your reviewers about their suggested changes, it will be your decision to either accept or reject them.

At this point, you are ready to finalize your writing and turn in your paper. Reread the paper one more time, and double-check spelling and grammar.

Write. Review. Revise.

Good writers spend more time revising and editing their written work than they spend writing the original version. Never turn in your first draft; spend the necessary time to reread and improve your work.

© Radius Images/Corbis

Know Your Audience

Before you came to college, you probably spent much more time writing informally than writing formally. Think about all the time you've spent writing e-mails, Facebook posts, texts, and tweets. Now think about the time you've spent writing papers for school or work. The informal style that you use in writing an e-mail, a text, or a post can become a problem when you try to write a formal research paper. Be sure that you know when you can use abbreviations and when you have to write out an entire word or phrase. When you write research papers in college, you should assume that your audience includes instructors and other serious students who will make judgments about your knowledge and abilities based on your writing. You should not be sloppy or casual when writing a formal paper.

The Importance of Time in the Writing Process

Many students turn in poorly written papers because they skip the first step (freewriting) and last step (rewriting/revising) and make do with the middle one (drafting). The best writing is usually done over an extended period of time, not as a last-minute task.

When planning the amount of time you'll need to write your paper, make sure to add enough time for the following:

- Asking your instructor for clarification of the assignment
- Seeking help from a librarian or from the writing center
- Narrowing or expanding your topic, which might require finding some new sources
- Balancing other assignments and commitments
- Dealing with technology problems

Writing for class projects might be a challenge at first. It is important to leave time to get help from writing center staff or trained peers in the learning center. Also, ask your instructor for examples of papers that have received good grades. You might show your instructor a draft of your paper and ask for his or her comments for improving your paper.

Citing Your Sources

At some point, you'll present your findings whether you are writing an essay, a formal research paper, a script for a presentation, or a page for a website. Remember that you must include a complete **citation,** a reference that enables a reader to locate a source based on information such as the author's name, the title of the work, and the publication date.

Citing your sources serves many purposes. Source citations show your audience that you have based your conclusions on good, reliable evidence. They also provide a starting place for anyone who would like more information about the topic or is curious about how you reached your conclusions. Most important, citing your sources is the simplest way to avoid

plagiarism—taking another person's work or ideas and presenting them as your own. Plagiarism can be a problem on all college campuses, so instructors are now using electronic systems such as Turnitin (**turnitin.com**) to identify passages in student papers that have been plagiarized, as shown in the image below. Many instructors routinely check their students' papers to make sure that the writing is original and that sources are cited. Some students consider plagiarizing because they think that doing so will help them get a better grade, but you can avoid the temptation if you keep in mind the high likelihood of getting caught.

To avoid plagiarism, you should pay careful attention to source citation, which includes many details and can get complicated, but it all comes down to two basic rules you should remember as you write:

1. If you use somebody else's exact words, you must give that person credit.

2. If you use somebody else's ideas, *even if you use your own words to express those ideas*, you must give that person credit.

Your instructors will tell you about their preferred method for citation: footnotes, references in parentheses included in the text of your paper, or endnotes. If you're not given specific guidelines or if you simply want to be sure that you do it right, use a handbook or writing style manual. One standard manual is the *MLA Handbook*, published by the Modern Language Association (**mlahandbook.org**). Another is the *Publication Manual of the American Psychological Association* (**apastyle.org**). You can also download MLA and APA apps on your mobile devices from Google Play or iTunes.

> A Speed Trap for Plagiarizers

If knowing that plagiarism is wrong isn't enough of a reason to prevent you from doing it, how about knowing that you will probably get caught? Turnitin's Originality Check compares submitted papers against billions of Web papers, millions of student papers, and leading library databases and publications. Just as known speed traps usually get you to slow down when you are driving, knowing about systems like Turnitin can help you resist the urge to plagiarize.

Courtesy Turnitin

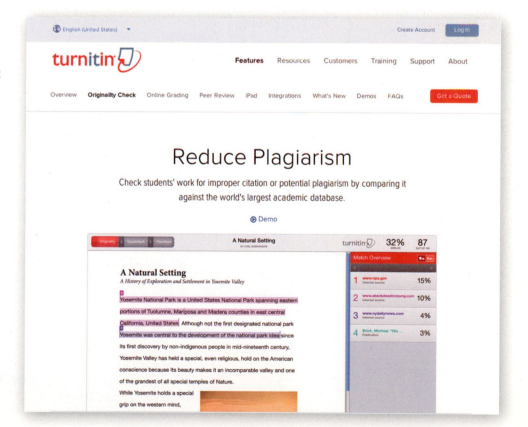

USING YOUR RESEARCH IN PRESENTATIONS

▲ Speak with Confidence.

If you follow the guidelines to successful speaking, you will be able to deliver a meaningful presentation that clearly informs your audience about a topic that matters to them.

© Hill Street Studios/Blend Images/ Corbis

What you have learned in this chapter about writing also applies to public speaking—both are processes that you can learn and master, and each results in a product. Since the fear of public speaking is a common one (it is more common, in fact, than the fear of death), you might be thinking along these lines: What if I plan, organize, prepare, and practice my speech, but my mind goes completely blank, I drop my note cards, or I say something totally embarrassing? Remember that people in your audience have been in your position and will understand your anxiety. Your audience wants you to succeed. Just be positive, rely on your wit, and keep speaking. Just as there is a process for writing a paper, there is a process for developing a good speech. The guidelines in Table 9.1 can help you improve your speaking skills greatly and lose your fear of speaking publicly.

Table 9.1 ❯ Guidelines for Successful Speaking

Step 1: Clarify Your Objective	Begin by identifying the goals of your presentation: What do you want your listeners to know, believe, or do when you are finished?
Step 2: Understand Your Audience	In order to understand the people you'll be talking to, ask yourself the following questions: • Who are my listeners? • What do they already know about my topic? • What do they want or need to know? • What are their attitudes toward me, my ideas, and my topic?
Step 3: Organize Your Presentation	Build your presentation by selecting and arranging blocks of information to help your listeners connect the ideas they already have to the new knowledge, attitudes, and beliefs you are presenting. You can actually write an outline for your speech.
Step 4: Choose Appropriate Visual Aids	Use software programs, such as Prezi or PowerPoint, to prepare your presentations. When creating PowerPoint slides or using Prezi templates, you can insert images and videos to support your ideas while making your presentations animated, engaging, and interactive. You might also choose to prepare a chart, write on the board, or distribute handouts. • Make visuals easy to follow. • Use font colors to make your slides visually attractive. • Explain each visual clearly.

(continued next page)

Step 4: Choose Appropriate Visual Aids (continued)	• Give your listeners enough time to process visuals. • Proofread carefully. • Maintain eye contact with your listeners while you discuss the visuals. Don't turn around and address the screen. Remember that a fancy slideshow can't make up for lack of careful research or sound ideas.
Step 5: Prepare Your Notes	Memorize the introduction and conclusion of your speech, and then use a carefully prepared outline to guide you in between. Practice in advance. Because you are speaking mainly from an outline, your choice of words will be slightly different each time you give your presentation, with the result that you will sound prepared but natural. Try using note cards; number them in case you accidentally drop the stack on your way to the front of the room.
Step 6: Practice Your Delivery	Practice your delivery before an audience: a friend, your dog, even the mirror. If you ask a practice audience (friends or family) to give you feedback, you'll have some idea of what changes you might want to make. Practice your presentation aloud several times to control your anxiety. Consider making an audio or video recording of yourself on your cell phone or mobile device to hear or see your mistakes. Use eye contact and smile.
Step 7: Pay Attention to Word Choice and Pronunciation	As you reread your presentation, make sure that you have used the correct words to express your ideas. Get help ahead of time with words you aren't sure how to pronounce. Try your best to avoid *like, um, uh, you know,* and other fillers.
Step 8: Dress Appropriately	Dress appropriately. Leave the baseball cap, the T-shirt, and the tennis shoes at home. Don't overdress, but do look professional.
Step 9: Request Feedback from Someone in Your Audience	After you have completed your speech, ask a friend or your instructor to give you some honest feedback. Pay attention to suggestions for ways you can improve.

YOUR TURN › DISCUSS IT

Do you enjoy public speaking? Are you an anxious or a confident speaker? What do you usually do to become more comfortable when speaking in front of a group? Make a list of these strategies and be prepared to discuss them with your classmates.

SAY "YES" TO TWITTER

There is more to Twitter than sharing what you had for lunch. It is a great way to gather information, share your interests, and stay connected to what you care about.

THE PROBLEM *You hear Twitter mentioned often, but you don't know why or even how you would use it.*

THE FIX *Dive in! But remember everything you share is public.*

HOW TO DO IT

Twitter is a microblogging site used by millions of people globally. Microblogging is sending live messages, called tweets, from Web-enabled devices. It's called "micro" because you are allowed only 140 characters per message.

1. **Education.** Following leaders in your chosen field helps you stay up-to-date on current issues and gives you the chance to interact with experts. Some instructors are even using Twitter in class as a way for you to engage with course material online.

2. **Job hunting.** Following the official Twitter feed of organizations you want to work for can lead to instant notification of new job opportunities.

3. **Community involvement.** Twitter allows for global conversations on important issues. Live tweeting is very common and allows for international exchange of information in real time.

Diagram of a Tweet

Here is a diagram showing Twitter in action. The key below walks you through each element of the sample tweet.

 ❶

Source: © Jo Kirchherr/Westend61/Corbis

Fiona Curry @fiona_curry **❷**　　**❸**
The Fault in Our Stars by @realjohngreen is my favorite book! #favoritebook **❹**

↰Reply ⇄ Retweet ★ Favorite **❺**

Source: © Gerhilde Skoberne/Corbis

Kevin King @kevinbooklover
RT @fiona_curry The Fault in Our Stars by @realjohngreen is my favorite book! #favoritebook **❻**

Source: © Matelly/Corbis

Tessa Pool @tessapool
.@fiona_curry Mine too! Check out this article via @nytimes on the book and #yalit: http://nyti.ms/1jRNITC **❽**
❼

❶ Tweet author profile image.
❷ Tweet author name and username.
❸ When mentioning somebody in a tweet or addressing your comments to a specific user, use "@username." The name will become a hyperlink to that person's profile, and your message will be visible to them and their followers.
❹ Use hashtags (#) in front of keywords related to the topic of your tweet. They become links that will take you to all tweets using that hashtag.
❺ See something you like? You have options to reply to, "retweet," or "favorite" a tweet.
❻ "Retweeting" means posting someone else's exact tweet to your list of followers. Do this by either prefacing your tweet with "RT @username" or pushing the retweet button at the bottom of their original tweet. Be sure to always give somebody credit for what they share!
❼ When replying to a user, your tweet will begin with @username. Be sure to use a period before @username so that the tweet goes to all of that user's followers.
❽ When sharing a link, use URL shorteners like *bitly.com* or *tinyurl.com* to save space.

THINK

Developing information literacy skills in college is clearly a necessity, but think beyond your college experience. How will improving your information literacy skills help you once you are out of college? Think of a career that you are interested in, and describe how you might use those skills in that career.

WRITE

Did the material in this chapter make you think about libraries and research in a new light? What did you find to be the most useful information in this chapter? What would you like to learn more about?

_____

_____

_____

_____

_____

_____

_____

_____

APPLY

1. It is important to get comfortable with all of the resources in your campus library. Think about a book you love that was turned into a movie (e.g., *Divergent*, *The Hunger Games*, or a book from the Harry Potter series). Search your library catalog to find a downloadable e-book or print copy of the book, an audiobook version, a DVD, or a soundtrack from the movie. Use a newspaper database to find movie reviews or interviews with the author.

2. Choose a national current event. Write it here: _____

_____

Carefully read about it in two places:
a. on your favorite news website (e.g., cnn.com)
b. in a traditional national newspaper (e.g., *New York Times*, *Wall Street Journal*, *Christian Science Monitor*, or *USA Today*). A library will have these newspapers, or you can access them online.

In a Word document, compare and contrast the way the event was described by the online news site and traditional national newspaper you chose.

- Are the authors' names provided?

- Do you find clues that indicate the authors are taking a biased stand in reporting? If so, describe these clues.

- For whom do you think the authors were writing (who is the intended audience)? For example, were they writing for any reader or for people of a certain age or educational level?

- Were the facts presented the same way by both the online source and the print source? Explain your answer.

- Did one source include more details than the other? If so, explain your answer.

- Did the authors include their sources? If so, what were they?

3. Develop a five-slide presentation, using Prezi or PowerPoint, to introduce yourself to your classmates in a new way. You might include slides that contain points about your high school years, your hobbies, your jobs, your family, your baby pictures, and so forth. Use the effective speaking strategies in this chapter to help you outline your presentation. In addition to text, use visuals such as photos, video clips, and art to engage your audience. Map out your slides here:

Slide 1

Slide 2

Slide 3

Slide 4

Slide 5

Below are suggestions for resources that are available at many colleges and the online resources that are available to everyone.

AT YOUR COLLEGE

VISIT . . .	IF YOU NEED HELP . . .
Your instructors	understanding expectations for any writing assignment. Talk to your instructor after class, drop by during office hours, or make a one-on-one appointment.
College Library	working on an assignment. Check out the library website or ask about a calendar of upcoming events. Many libraries have drop-in classes or workshops to help you learn specific skills. Head over to the reference desk and talk with a librarian about the assignment you are working on.
Writing Center	finding effective writing and research tools and writing or revising your paper.
Specialized Collections	finding information specific to your major. Check the main library's website for any specialized libraries or collections such as a biology or nursing collection. Make it a point to visit all of them.
Technology Support Center	dealing with a computer crisis. *Everyone* deals with their computer crashing at some point. It seems that disaster may strike right before a major paper is due. Prepare yourself! Check out your school's technology support services *before* you need them. Attend an orientation, chat with help-desk staff, and review their website so you know where to go when you're in crisis mode.
Departments of Speech and Communications	finding resources and specific courses to help you develop your speaking skills.
Student Activities	learning and practicing speaking skills. When you become active in student organizations, especially those like the student government association and the debate club, you will have many opportunities for speaking in front of a group.

ONLINE

GO TO . . .	IF YOU NEED HELP . . .
The University of Iowa's History Department, which offers tips on common writing mistakes: clas.uiowa.edu/history/teaching-and-writing-center/guides	finding writing tips.
Toastmasters International: toastmasters.org/Resources/Public-Speaking-Tips	finding speaking tips.

Purdue University's online writing lab MLA: owl.english.purdue.edu/owl/resource/747/01/	using MLA citation style.
Purdue University's online writing lab APA: owl.english.purdue.edu/owl/section/2/10/	using APA citation style.
American Psychological Association: apastyle.org/learn/faqs/index.aspx	with answers to the frequently asked questions about APA style.

MY COLLEGE'S RESOURCES

LaunchPad for *Understanding Your College Experience* is a great resource. Go online to master concepts using the LearningCurve study tool and much more. **macmillanhighered.com/gardnerunderstanding**

12 MAKING THE RIGHT CAREER CHOICE

STUDENT GOALS

10 Thinking in College

PRE-READING ACTIVITY: You are determined to lose some weight. You talk to a few friends and family members about different weight-loss options. Most options seem to take a long time and require a lot of effort. A friend shows you a magazine ad for a product that promises a weight loss of 30 pounds in 60 days with no diet or exercise. The price seems to be right, and the ad claims that several famous people have lost weight by using this product.

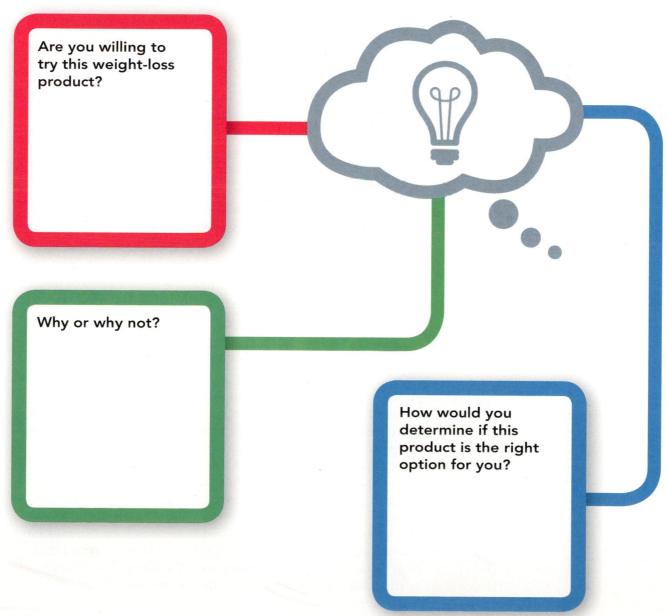

Are you willing to try this weight-loss product?

Why or why not?

How would you determine if this product is the right option for you?

📁 PROFILE ✕

Donna Williford, 41

Health Care Business Informatics Major, *Pitt Community College, North Carolina*

As a student in a health care field at Pitt Community College, Donna Williford understands the importance of critical-thinking skills both inside and outside the classroom. When Donna arrived on campus last fall, she previously had held many jobs that all had one thing in common: the need to think deeply and to make good decisions.

Last year, Donna decided to fulfill a lifelong dream and enroll in college; she doesn't regret waiting until later in life to do so. "I'm more focused now, at 41, than I would have been fresh out of high school," she says. Donna uses that focus to her advantage in college, writing essays and preparing for tests. Donna's ability to think deeply has come in handy more than once, especially when evaluating the quality of sources as she does research. Similarly at work, she has been able to use her thinking skills in her interactions with medical staff and patients who have different backgrounds and needs.

After graduation, Donna hopes to get a job working with computers in the growing field of electronic medical records management, where she plans to continue learning and thinking outside the box. As new technologies are introduced, the medical staff needs to change the ways they work. "Excellent thinking skills will play a vital role in my everyday decisions in the health care field," she says. Donna's one piece of advice for other first-year students is this: "Be open to changes and new ideas because that's what a good life is all about."

> **"Be open to changes and new ideas because that's what a good life is all about."**

 **LaunchPad**
macmillan learning

To access the Learning-Curve study tool, Video Tools, and more, go to LaunchPad for *Understanding Your College Experience.* macmillanhighered.com /gardnerunderstanding

As Donna's story suggests, the most important skill you'll acquire in college is the ability to think for yourself. Courses in every discipline will encourage you to ask questions, to sort through different information and ideas, to form opinions of your own, and to defend them.

Learning to think—using the mind to produce ideas, opinions, decisions, and memories—is part of normal human development. Just as your body grows, so does your ability to think logically and rationally about abstract concepts.

The concept of **critical thinking** might not be new to you; you may have heard the term before. Being a good critical thinker does not mean that you are "critical" or negative in your dealings with others. Rather, the term refers to thoughtful consideration of the information, ideas, and arguments that you encounter in order to guide belief and action—this is the kind of thinking you will do in college, and it's what this chapter is all about. We will explain how developing and applying your critical-thinking skills can make the search for answers an exciting and rewarding adventure.

COLLEGE-LEVEL THINKING

In college, the level of thinking that your instructors expect from you exceeds that which you did in high school, in terms of both the questions that are asked and the answers that are expected. If a high school teacher asked, "What are the three branches of the U.S. government?" there was only one acceptable answer: "Legislative, executive, and judicial." A college instructor, on the other hand, might ask, "Under what circumstances might conflicts arise among the three branches of government, and what does this tell you about the democratic process?" There is no single or simple answer, and that's the point of higher education. Questions with complicated answers will require you to think deeply. The shift to this higher or deeper level of thinking can be an adjustment—it might even catch you off guard and cause you some stress.

Important questions usually do not have simple answers, but to answer them well, you will have to discover many ways of thinking. The Nobel prize–winning economist Daniel Kahneman describes two types of thinking: "fast thinking" and "slow thinking."[1] He characterizes fast thinking as automatic, emotional, stereotyped, and subconscious. This type of thinking is certainly useful in some situations. Sometimes it works to make quick decisions based on what seems easiest, results in the least conflict, or conforms to personal beliefs. Other times, though, you might notice people who depend on others to think for them or think what they believe is true simply because they wish, hope, or feel that it is true without ever examining the underlying assumptions that support those beliefs. People without good thinking skills are easily convinced to buy a product, accept an idea, vote for a political candidate, or do something against their will by those who provide misleading information. Have you ever stopped to consider whether people who don't do any real critical thinking have much control over their lives or have any real power in business or society?

Slow thinking takes more effort, more careful attention, and is more logical, rational, and deep. By improving your slower and more logical thinking abilities and strategies, you will become a better learner and problem solver. Slow thinkers are comfortable with uncertainty. They examine problems; ask questions; suggest new answers that challenge the existing situation; discover new information; question authorities, traditional beliefs, and conclusions (even when presented by "experts"); make independent judgments; and develop creative solutions.

---

[1]Daniel Kahneman, *Thinking, Fast and Slow* (New York: Farrar, Straus and Giroux, 2013).

People who do have good thinking skills tend to be successful, whether it's earning an A, getting a promotion, or making connections in the community. And it shouldn't surprise you that strong thinking skills are among the most valued by college admissions counselors and employers. When employers say they want workers who can find reliable information, analyze it, organize it, draw conclusions from it, and present it convincingly to others, they are describing employees who are good critical thinkers.

Whatever else you do in college, make it a point to develop and sharpen your critical-thinking skills. You won't become a great critical thinker overnight, but you will improve a lot between now and when you graduate from college. With practice, however, you can learn how to tell if information is truthful and accurate. Thinking critically—mastering slow thinking—will help you make better decisions, come up with fresh solutions to difficult problems, and communicate your ideas effectively.

10.2 DEVELOPING STRONG THINKING SKILLS

As you've read, a high-priority goal in college is to develop strong thinking and decision-making skills. Having these skills will help you become a competent and confident individual who is capable of contributing to the larger society by helping solve community and national problems. There are steps you can take to develop these skills.

Ask Questions

The first step of thinking at a deeper level, of true critical thinking, is to be curious. This involves asking questions. Instead of accepting statements and claims at face value, question them. Here are a few suggestions:

- When you come across an idea or a statement that you consider interesting, confusing, or suspicious, first ask yourself what it means.
- Do you fully understand what is being said, or do you need to pause and think to make sense of the idea?
- Do you agree with the statement? Why or why not?
- Can the statement or idea be interpreted in more than one way?

Don't stop there.

- Ask whether you can trust the person or group making a particular claim, and ask whether there is enough evidence to back up that claim (more on this later).
- Ask who might agree or disagree and why.
- Ask how a new concept relates to what you already know.
- Think about where you might find more information about the subject, and what you could do with what you learn.

> **Comparison Shopping**

Use shopping to practice your critical-thinking abilities. You need to ask the right questions to find out if a deal is really a deal.

© Randy Glasbergen www.glasbergen .com

© Randy Glasbergen. www.glasbergen.com

- Ask yourself about the effects of accepting a new idea as truth.
  - Will you have to change or give up what you have believed for a long time?
  - Will it require you to do something differently?
  - Will it be necessary to examine the issue further?
  - Should you try to bring other people around to a new way of thinking?

Consider Multiple Points of View and Draw Conclusions

Before you draw any conclusions about the validity of information or opinions, it's important to consider more than one point of view. College reading assignments might deliberately expose you to conflicting arguments and theories about a subject, or you might encounter differences of opinion as you do research for a project. Your own belief system will influence how you interpret information just as others' belief systems and points of view might influence how they present information. For example, consider your own ideas about the cost of higher education in the United States. American citizens, politicians, and others often voice opinions on tuition and fees at two-year versus four-year colleges and universities and even whether college should be free. What do you think should be done about the cost of college, if anything, and *why* do you hold this viewpoint?

The more ideas you consider, the better your thinking will become. Ultimately, you will discover not only that it is OK to change your mind but also that a willingness to do so is the mark of a reasonable, educated person. Considering multiple points of view means synthesizing material, evaluating information and resources that might contradict each other or offer multiple points of view on a topic, and then honoring those differences.

As you begin to draw conclusions based on the many viewpoints and other types of evidence you've explored, you need to look at the outcome of your inquiry in a more demanding, critical way. In a chemistry lab, it might be a matter of interpreting the results of an experiment. In buying a tablet, it might require evaluating your needs and your budget, asking others about their experiences, and reading buyers' reviews.

If you are looking for solutions to a problem, which ones seem most promising after you have conducted an exhaustive search for materials? If you have found new evidence, what does it show? Does what you are learning motivate you to investigate more about your topic? Do your original beliefs still hold up, or do you think they need to be modified or abandoned? Most important, consider what you would need to do or say to persuade someone else that your ideas are valid. Thoughtful conclusions are the most useful when you can share them with others.

After considering multiple viewpoints and drawing conclusions, the next step is to develop your own views based on credible evidence and facts, while staying true to your values and beliefs. Critical thinking is the process you go through in deciding how to align your experience and value system with your viewpoint. The end-game isn't to arrive at the "right" answer but rather the one that you think is the most practical, or it might be a new idea of your own creation.

YOUR TURN > DISCUSS IT

Our experiences shape the way in which we think about the world around us. Name three people (such as family members, friends, coaches, religious leaders, celebrities, national figures) who have most influenced the way you think. Describe how these individuals' values, actions, expectations, and words have shaped the way you think about yourself and the world. Have any of them influenced your purpose for being in college?

Make Arguments

What does the word *argument* mean to you? If you're like most people, the first image it brings up might be an ugly fight you had with a friend, a yelling match you witnessed on the street, or a heated disagreement between family members. True, such unpleasant confrontations are arguments, but the word also refers to a calm, reasoned effort to persuade someone of the value of an idea.

When you think of it this way, you'll quickly recognize that arguments are central to academic study, work, and life in general. Scholarly articles, business memos, and requests for spending money all have something in common: The effective ones make a general claim, provide reasons to support it, and back up those reasons with evidence. That's what argument is.

It's important to consider different arguments in tackling new ideas and complex questions, but arguments are not all equally valid. Whether examining an argument or making one, a good critical thinker is careful to ensure that ideas are presented in an understandable, logical way.

Challenge Assumptions and Beliefs

To some extent, it's unavoidable to have beliefs based on gut feelings or blind acceptance of something you've heard or read. However, some assumptions should be examined more thoughtfully, especially if they will influence an important decision or serve as the foundation for an argument.

We develop an understanding of information based on our value systems and how we view the world. Our family backgrounds influence these views, opinions, and assumptions. College is a time to challenge those assumptions and beliefs and to think critically about ideas we have always had.

Well-meaning people will often disagree. It's important to listen to both sides of an argument before making up your mind. If you follow the guidelines in this chapter, you will have critical-thinking skills to figure things out instead of depending purely on how you feel or what you've heard. As you listen to a lecture, debate, or political argument about what is in the public's best interest, try to predict where it is heading and why. Ask yourself whether you have enough information to justify your own position.

YOUR TURN ❯ DISCUSS IT

Have you ever read a book or watched a movie introducing ideas that made you question your own thinking or your opinions about something? Discuss your experience in class and explain how those ideas changed your way of thinking.

Examine Evidence

Another important part of thinking critically is checking that the evidence supporting an argument—whether someone else's or your own—is of the highest possible quality. To do that, simply ask a few questions about the argument as you consider it:

- What general idea am I being asked to accept?
- Are good and sufficient reasons given to support the overall claim?
- Are those reasons backed up with evidence in the form of facts, statistics, and quotations?
- Does the evidence support the conclusions?
- Is the argument based on logical reasoning, or does it appeal mainly to emotions?
- Do I recognize any questionable assumptions?
- Can I think of any counterarguments, and if so, what facts can I use as proof?

- What do I know about the person or organization making the argument?
- What credible sources can I find to support the information?

If you have evaluated the evidence used in support of a claim and are still not certain of its quality, it's best to keep looking for more evidence. Drawing on questionable evidence for an argument has a tendency to backfire. In most cases, a little persistence will help you find better sources.

Recognize and Avoid Faulty Reasoning

Although logical reasoning is essential to solving any problem, whether simple or complex, you need to go one step further to make sure that an argument hasn't been compromised by faulty reasoning. Here are some of the most common missteps—referred to as logical fallacies or flaws in reasoning—that people make in their use of logic:

Attacking the person. Arguing against other people's positions or attacking their arguments is perfectly acceptable. Going after their personalities, however, is not OK. Any argument that resorts to personal attack ("Why should we believe a cheater?") is unworthy of consideration.

> **Logic That Just Doesn't Fly**
>
> This cartoon is an obvious example of faulty reasoning. Some conversations or arguments tend to include reasoning like this. Can you think of an illogical leap like this one that someone used in an argument with you? How did you use critical thinking to counter it? Or did your emotions get the best of you?
>
> © Randy Glasbergen
> www.glasbergen.com

PENGUINS ARE BLACK AND WHITE. SOME OLD TV SHOWS ARE BLACK AND WHITE. THEREFORE, SOME PENGUINS ARE OLD TV SHOWS.

GLASBERGEN

Copyright 1997 by Randy Glasbergen.

www.glasbergen.com

Logic: another thing that penguins aren't very good at.

Begging. "Please, officer, don't give me a ticket! If you do, I'll lose my license, and I have five little children to feed, and I won't be able to feed them if I can't drive my truck." None of the driver's statements offer any evidence, in any legal sense, as to why she shouldn't be given a ticket. Pleading *might* work if the officer is feeling generous, but an appeal to facts and reason would be more effective: "I fed the meter, but it didn't register the coins. Since the machine is broken, I'm sure you'll agree that I don't deserve a ticket."

Appealing to false authority. Citing authorities, such as experts in a field or the opinions of qualified researchers, can offer valuable support for an argument. However, a claim based on the authority of someone whose expertise is questionable relies on the appearance of authority rather than on real evidence. We see examples of false authority all the time in advertising: Sports stars who are not doctors, dietitians, or nutritionists urge us to eat a certain brand of food; famous actors and singers who are not dermatologists extol the medical benefits of a costly remedy for acne.

Jumping on a bandwagon. Sometimes we are more likely to believe something that many others also believe. Even the most widely accepted truths can turn out to be wrong, however. At one time, nearly everyone believed that the earth was flat, until someone came up with evidence to the contrary.

Assuming that something is true because it hasn't been proven false. If you go to a library or look online, you'll find dozens of books detailing close encounters with flying saucers or ghosts. These books describe the people who had such encounters as completely honest and trustworthy. Because critics could not disprove the claims of the witnesses, the events are said to have actually occurred. Even in science, few things are ever proved completely false, but evidence can be discredited.

Falling victim to false cause. Frequently, we make the assumption that just because one event followed another, the first event must have caused the second. This reasoning is the basis for many superstitions. The ancient Chinese once believed that they could make the sun reappear after an eclipse by striking a large gong because they knew that on a previous occasion the sun had reappeared after a large gong had been struck. Most effects, however, are usually the result of several causes. Don't be satisfied with easy before-and-after claims; they are rarely correct.

Making hasty generalizations. Sometimes it is tempting to draw a conclusion based on a few anecdotes or limited evidence. For instance, if your high-school-age sister and some of her friends were scrambling to get tickets to a Zendaya concert, could you assume that *all* teenage girls are Zendaya fans? Generalizations based on only a few examples are almost always inaccurate. Can you think of times when you have been guilty of this?

Slippery slope. "If we allow tuition to increase, the next thing we know, it will be $20,000 per term." Such an argument is an example of "slippery slope" thinking. Fallacies like these can slip into even the most careful reasoning. One false claim can derail an entire argument, so be on the lookout for weak logic in what you read and write. Never forget that accurate reasoning is a key factor in succeeding in college and in life.

YOUR TURN > DISCUSS IT

Have you ever used or heard someone use any of these logical fallacies to justify a decision? Do logical fallacies sometimes persuade others of the truth of an argument? Share an example with the class, and discuss why people use logical fallacies.

Now that you have read about critical thinking, it would be beneficial to rate yourself as a critical thinker. Use Figure 10.1 to rate your critical-thinking skills.

FIGURE 10.1 > Rate Your Critical-Thinking Skills

Circle the number that best fits you in each of the situations described below.

Situations	Never		Sometimes		Always
In class, I ask lots of questions when I don't understand.	1 2 3	4 5 6	7 8 9	10
If I don't agree with what the group decides is the correct answer, I challenge the group's opinion.	1 2 3	4 5 6	7 8 9	10
I believe there are many solutions to a problem.	1 2 3	4 5 6	7 8 9	10
I admire those people in history who challenged what was believed at the time, such as "the earth is flat."	1 2 3	4 5 6	7 8 9	10
I make an effort to listen to both sides of an argument before deciding which way I will go.	1 2 3	4 5 6	7 8 9	10
I ask lots of people's opinions about a political candidate before making up my mind.	1 2 3	4 5 6	7 8 9	10
I am not afraid to change my belief if I learn something new.	1 2 3	4 5 6	7 8 9	10
Authority figures do not intimidate me.	1 2 3	4 5 6	7 8 9	10

The more 7–10 scores you have circled, the more you use your critical-thinking skills. The lower scores indicate that you may not be using critical-thinking skills very often or use them only during certain activities.

APPLYING YOUR CRITICAL-THINKING SKILLS

As with any skill that you want to develop, you need to practice thinking critically in order to get good at it. Now that you are aware of what good thinking is, and isn't, you can look for opportunities to improve.

Collaborate

One way to become a better critical thinker is to practice with other people. Researchers who study the thinking of elementary school students, high school students, and college students find that critical thinking and collaboration go hand in hand. Students at all levels are more likely to exercise their critical-thinking abilities when they are confronted by the experiences and opinions of others; that is why it's so important to form and join study groups while you are in college. Having more than one student involved in the learning process generates a greater number of ideas and discussions that can challenge your thinking and assumptions, improving your critical-thinking skills. People think more clearly when they talk as well as listen, which is a very good reason to participate actively in your classes. Creative brainstorming and group discussion encourage original thought. These habits also teach participants to consider alternative points of view carefully and to express and defend their own ideas clearly. As a group negotiates ideas and learns to agree on the most reliable concepts, it moves closer to a conclusive solution.

Both in college and in careers, you will find that collaboration—not only with people in your work setting but also with others around the globe—is essential to almost any career you may choose. Whether in person or through digital communication, teamwork improves your ability to think critically.

YOUR TURN > WORK TOGETHER

Make a list of the ways you can form a successful study group. Compare your ideas with those of several classmates to determine what makes a study group effective.

Be Creative

Another way to develop strong thinking skills is to take advantage of opportunities to be creative. Our society is full of creative individuals who think outside the box, challenge the usual way of doing things, or simply ask questions that others are not asking. Many have achieved fame by using their thinking skills and actions to change the world. Even a single

‹ Get a Second Opinion and a Third

One way to become a better critical thinker is to practice with other people. By getting feedback from others, you can see the possible problems in your own position or approach. Whether debating an issue in a political science class or making a gown in a fashion design course, appreciate how people bring their own life experiences, personal taste, knowledge, and expertise to the table. Most questions do not have clear-cut answers, and there are often several ways to accomplish a task. Getting input can help improve your finished product.

thought can lead to major progress. As you move through your other first-year courses such as sociology, psychology, history, or math, you will encounter assignments that will encourage you to be creative. You will also learn about people who have used their creative-thinking abilities to find a sense of purpose and to become world changers in academic and nonacademic areas.

Below are some critical thinkers of our past and present who made contributions that continue to affect our lives.

- **Abraham Lincoln:** When we think of great leaders, Lincoln often comes to mind. Lincoln was able to think about the relationship between national policy and human rights in new and different ways. By working slowly and deliberately, Lincoln changed American laws and began a long process toward guaranteeing equal rights for all U.S. citizens.

- **Martin Luther King Jr.:** King could be considered one of the greatest activists of all time. When racial segregation ruled in the South, he contributed to the civil rights movement by voicing his concerns and presenting his dream of a different world. He created opportunities for change in many unfair policies and practices.

- **Twitter creators Jack Dorsey, Evan Williams, Biz Stone, and Noah Glass:** Twitter was created in 2006 as a social networking and micro-blogging site to enhance communication around the world through hashtag statements that are limited to 140 characters each. In spite of early public resistance, the site quickly gained popularity and changed our way of communicating in times of national and international crisis due to its quick information-sharing ability.

- **Steve Jobs:** As an innovative thinker, Jobs shaped the way our society views technology and digital capabilities. He was resilient and did not give up even when faced with challenges such as losing his position as the head of Apple at one time.
- **Lady Gaga:** Pushing her artistic expression through fashion and activism, Lady Gaga projects an identity that challenges gender expectations and voices her belief in equality for all individuals.

YOUR TURN > STAY MOTIVATED

People who make a difference in their communities, nation, or the world stay motivated; they are resilient. They don't quit, even when they experience tough times. Can you think of religious leaders, politicians, athletes, or entrepreneurs who have maintained their motivation to achieve success? What can you learn from them about the way that resilience helps people stay motivated?

Learn to Solve Problems

Your success both in college and in your future life will depend on how well you make decisions and solve problems. Making decisions and solving problems involve thinking logically, weighing evidence, and formulating conclusions. Here are some examples of situations that you might experience in college that will require these skills:

- Deciding how to schedule your research and writing time when you have two papers due on the same day
- Finding a way to get your family to compromise on a suitable lights-out time because you're not getting the sleep you need
- Finding time for exercising with your busy schedule in order to stay healthy and avoid weight gain
- Deciding whether to study at home on the weekends or go to the library to study
- Understanding the advantages and disadvantages of accessing information sources, including social media and online news outlets and periodicals

These situations provide opportunities for you to improve your problem-solving skills. On a more personal level, the college years also represent a time in your life when you get to know yourself. You will begin to develop or change your own positions on societal and political issues, learn more about what is important to you, and develop into a contributing citizen of your country and also the world.

In college, you'll be exposed to ideas and often-conflicting opinions about contemporary issues such as same-sex marriage, military operations, immigration, global human rights, animal rights, comprehensive sex education, food safety, the state of public education in the United States, student loan debt and loan forgiveness, and economic inequality. The list goes on and on. Before accepting any opinion on any issue as "the truth," look for evidence that supports different positions on these debates. In fact, look for opportunities to participate in such debates. In most colleges, these opportunities are available to students.

YOUR TURN ▸ WORK TOGETHER

Think of a problem you had to solve in the past and how you were able to do it. Then with another classmate or in a small group, share your problems and solutions.

10.4 BLOOM'S TAXONOMY AND THE FIRST YEAR OF COLLEGE

Benjamin Bloom, a professor of education at the University of Chicago, worked with a group of other researchers to design a system of classifying goals for the learning process. This system is known as Bloom's Taxonomy, and it is now used at all levels of education to define and describe the process that students use to understand and think critically about what they are learning.

Bloom identified six levels of learning, as you can see in Figure 10.2. The higher the level, the more critical thinking it requires.

FIGURE 10.2 ▸ The Six Levels of Learning of Bloom's Taxonomy

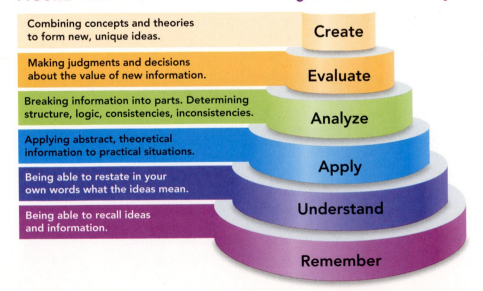

Combining concepts and theories to form new, unique ideas. — **Create**

Making judgments and decisions about the value of new information. — **Evaluate**

Breaking information into parts. Determining structure, logic, consistencies, inconsistencies. — **Analyze**

Applying abstract, theoretical information to practical situations. — **Apply**

Being able to restate in your own words what the ideas mean. — **Understand**

Being able to recall ideas and information. — **Remember**

You have been using the levels of Bloom's Taxonomy throughout your education, perhaps without being aware of it. As you work through the courses in your first year of college, you will recognize material you've learned before, and you will practice your skills of defining and remembering. You'll become aware that the skills on Bloom's first level aren't going to get you very far. To retain new information, you'll need to move to level 2, understanding the information clearly enough so that you can describe the concepts to someone else. Many of your classes will require you to apply what you learn to your experience and to new situations (level 3)—as you engage with material in this way, your comprehension grows as does your ability to retain new knowledge. Next you'll move on to level 4 to analyze—break down information into parts—and level 5, where you evaluate new ideas, making decisions and judging them. As you reach the sixth, or highest, level, you create something new by combining information, concepts, and theories.

Let's take a closer look at Bloom's Taxonomy by taking a concept you're likely to encounter in your first year of college—diversity—and matching your cognitive development of the concept to Bloom's Taxonomy:

Level 1 (Remember): Read a dictionary definition of the word *diversity*.

Level 2 (Understand): Explain the concept of diversity to another student without reading the dictionary definition.

Level 3 (Apply): Write about all the types of human diversity that exist within the student body at your college and possible categories of human diversity that are not represented there.

Level 4 (Analyze): Conduct two separate analyses to break down the issue into components or questions. The first analysis will look at why your institution has large numbers of certain types of students. The second analysis will consider why your institution has small numbers of other types of students.

Level 5 (Evaluate): Write a paper that combines your findings in level 4 and hypothesizes what components of your college culture either attract or repel certain students.

Level 6 (Create): In your paper, describe your college's "diversity profile" and suggest new ways for your campus to support diversity.

If you pay close attention, you will discover that Bloom's Taxonomy is often the framework that college instructors use to design classroom activities and out-of-class assignments. Be aware of how you use each of these levels to build your critical-thinking skills. No matter what the topic is, this framework will help move you to deeper understanding and an ability to apply what you learn to other situations and concepts.

USE YOUR THINKING SKILLS IN CONDUCTING RESEARCH

College instructors expect their students to be able to conduct research when they write papers or create projects. In high school or a casual setting, doing research usually means going to a search engine like Google, Bing, or Ask.com. Many of us do this so automatically that we say, "Let me 'Google' that." Is a Google search all professors are looking for when they ask you to conduct research?

THE PROBLEM *You need to conduct research for a paper, but you're not sure how to evaluate the types of information found on the Internet.*

THE FIX *Use a critical-thinking system to conduct your research.*

HOW TO DO IT

Start with good questions. If you are researching a topic, such as "marijuana legalization," generate some questions you have about that subject rather than just going to Google and typing "marijuana" into the search box:

- What is the history of marijuana use in the United States?
- Why was marijuana use made illegal in the first place?
- Where has it been legalized and why?
- What have been some of the positive and negative outcomes of making it legal?

Generating questions will save you time by clarifying what you need to know, so you will recognize useful results and ignore the ones that won't help you.

Use databases. Your school pays for research databases, which collect a variety of credible, scholarly research. When you use research databases, you can be sure that the information is reliable, and you can refine your search terms to produce 20 or 30 good returns, as opposed to 20 or 30 million that you will have to sort through. Most databases are available online with login information that your college can provide, so you can use them anytime from home or on your laptop.

Use a variety of locations to confirm information. When you see the same information in a variety of credible sources, you can start to trust its accuracy. Remember that there are still useful sources of information in print form that are not yet available online.

Consider the quality of the information. Where did it come from? Who said it and why? How current is it? Has anything major happened in this area since this information was published?

ONE STEP FURTHER

Get in the habit of reading (not just watching) a variety of news and information sources. If you get news only from TV or links posted on Facebook, you will miss some important stories. Remember this: Professionals need to be up-to-date in their own areas of interest and expertise, but they also must be able to understand larger current events happening in the world around them. You must have broad knowledge in order to place your specific professional knowledge in context.

THINK

In your opinion, is it harder to think critically than to base your arguments on how you feel about a topic? Why or why not? What are the advantages of finding answers based on your feelings? What about those that are based on critical thinking? How might you use both approaches in seeking answers?

WRITE

One major shift from being a high school student to being a college student is the level of critical thinking your college instructors expect of you. How would you describe critical thinking to a high school student or one of your middle or high school children?

APPLY

1. After reading this chapter, think of professionals (doctors, engineers, marketing professionals) for whom problem solving and critical thinking are necessary. Choose one career, and describe why you think critical thinking is a necessary and valuable skill in that area. Also, try to think of any careers where critical thinking is not involved. Which of these careers has more or less appeal to you and why?
2. Describe an experience you have had since coming to college that has challenged you to think about an issue in a new and different way.

Below are suggestions for resources that are available at many colleges and the online resources that are available to everyone.

AT YOUR COLLEGE

VISIT . . .	IF YOU NEED HELP . . .
College catalog	taking argument courses and critical thinking courses. Such courses will help you develop the ability to form logical arguments and avoid logical fallacies.
Student Activities Center	joining a debate club or team.
Library	finding resources for improving your critical thinking skills. For example, *Twelve Angry Men* by Reginald Rose (New York: Penguin Classics, 2006) is a reprint of the original teleplay, which was written in 1954 and made into a film in 1958. It is also available on DVD. The stirring courtroom drama pits twelve jurors against one another as they argue the outcome of a murder trial in which the defendant is a teenage boy. While critical thinking is needed to arrive at the truth, all the jurors except one use noncritical arguments to arrive at a guilty verdict. However, the analysis of that one holdout produces a remarkable change in their attitudes.

ONLINE

GO TO . . .	IF YOU NEED HELP . . .
ICYouSee Guide to Critical Thinking: icyousee.org/think /think.html	finding a guide to critical thinking about what you see on the Web.
Google	with critical thinking. Google "help with critical thinking" for some helpful resources like those available through the Foundation for Critical Thinking. Evaluate your search results using the skills you learned in this chapter.

MY COLLEGE'S RESOURCES

LaunchPad for *Understanding Your College Experience* is a great resource. Go online to master concepts using the LearningCurve study tool and much more. **macmillanhighered.com/gardnerunderstanding**

11 Maintaining Wellness and Relationships in a Diverse World

PRE-READING ACTIVITY: By now you know that college is demanding. Successful students are the ones who pay attention to the many aspects of wellness that affect success in college, including stress management, diet, exercise, weight management, sleep, and building relationships in a diverse environment. This chapter covers all these topics with the goal of helping you understand how they are connected. List some challenges you have already encountered in each of these areas, and how you overcame them.

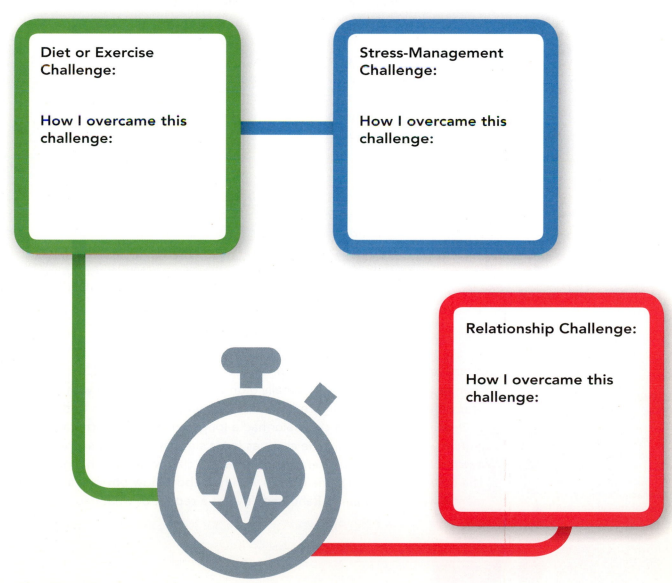

Diet or Exercise Challenge:

How I overcame this challenge:

Stress-Management Challenge:

How I overcame this challenge:

Relationship Challenge:

How I overcame this challenge:

PROFILE

Rahm Patel, 19

Accounting Technology Major, *Palm Beach State College, Florida*

When Rahm Patel started attending Palm Beach State College, he was expecting to have a lot of fun. After the first week of classes when he received the syllabus for each course, he could tell he was going to have to work hard. "To make more study time, I cut back on going to the gym each week," he explained. "I started skipping lunch to save time and ate snacks from vending machines between classes instead."

He also found himself sleeping less and eating more junk food during the exam weeks. It was a perfect storm. As Rahm stopped exercising and started eating junk food and sleeping poorly, stress and anxiety got the better of him. It all came to a head just before a scheduled class presentation. He knew he wasn't ready to do his best, so he e-mailed his instructor and asked for an extension, which his instructor granted. But even with the extension, Rahm's presentation did not go well. His lack of preparation was obvious to the instructor and the other students. Along with a grade of C minus, the instructor, Dr. Cruz, also attached a personal note that read:

> "I realized that eating right, exercising, and sleeping would help me be less anxious and more in control in all of my classes."

Dear Rahm,

I know you are not happy about your performance in class today and your grade. I also was very disappointed in your presentation, especially since I had granted you an extension. I have also noticed that you seem tired and distracted and have fallen asleep in class on more than one occasion. If you continue on this path, your final course grade will suffer. I would like to suggest that you make an appointment to see a college counselor to talk over what's going on in your life and how you can turn this around before it's too late.

Dr. Cruz

"I was really embarrassed that Dr. Cruz had noticed how I had changed," Rahm admitted. "I really didn't have a relationship with any of my instructors, but I figured I better take her advice and go to the counseling center." The counselor had a long conversation with Rahm, and he was honest about the changes in his sleeping, eating, and exercise habits and how his overall attitude about classwork had changed. The counselor shared some articles with him about how physical and mental wellness connect. Rahm didn't want a repeat of what had

 **LaunchPad**
macmillan learning

To access the Learning-Curve study tool, Video Tools, and more, go to LaunchPad for *Understanding Your College Experience.* macmillanhighered.com /gardnerunderstanding

happened. "I realized that eating right, exercising, and sleeping would help me be less anxious and more in control in all of my classes," said Rahm.

After reading the articles and working with the counselor, he developed a new plan for gaining more control over his life. The counselor also advised Rahm to visit Dr. Cruz during office hours to get to know her and to discuss how he could improve his performance in class. In their meeting, Dr. Cruz promised to work with Rahm on his presentation skills and to help him become more organized in his study strategies. Rahm was pleasantly surprised by how much he enjoyed his visit with his instructor.

Like Rahm, many college students need help in managing their lives when they enter college. This chapter focuses on helping you manage significant components of your life while in college: your personal wellness and relationships with the people you encounter throughout your college experience and beyond. When life is busy or when all your energy is focused on one thing in particular, you might find yourself off balance, not paying enough attention to yourself or the many people around you. By taking a broad view of your life and where it's going, you can see where you need to make adjustments.

The first year of college can be one of life's most interesting and challenging transitions. Much of what you experience will be new—new friends, new freedoms, and new responsibilities. The college experience shouldn't only be about studying. To make the most of the college years, it's important to spend time with friends and enjoy activities your college has to offer. The freedoms you experience in this new environment bring challenges and risks, and you need to learn to handle them. Your success in and after college depends on your ability to make sensible decisions about your personal habits and behaviors, to learn to maintain important relationships and cultivate new ones, and to achieve balance; that is what this chapter is all about.

11.1

UNDERSTANDING WELLNESS

Wellness is a concept that includes the care of your mind, body, and spirit. It includes reducing stress in positive ways, keeping fit, fostering your spirituality, deepening your self-knowledge, maintaining good sexual health, and taking a safe approach to alcohol—assuming that you are of legal age to consume it.

Take this short quiz. As you consider each question, rate yourself on a scale of 1–5, with 1 being "never" and 5 being "always."

_____ 1. Are you able to manage your stress successfully?

_____ 2. Do you eat a wide range of healthy foods?

_____ 3. Do you exercise several times a week?

_____ 4. Do you get 7 or more hours of sleep each night?

_____ 5. Do you ask for help from friends, family, or professionals when you need it?

_____ 6. Are you practicing safe sexual behaviors?

_____ 7. Do you avoid abusing alcohol or other substances?

_____ 8. Do you have time to relax?

What areas did you mark as 4 or 5? _____

What areas did you mark as 1 or 2? _____

As you read the preview of the many components of wellness described in this chapter, pay special attention to the areas that you scored as 1 or 2 so that you can get yourself on track.

Managing Stress to Maintain Wellness

Everyone experiences stress at one time or another—it's a normal part of being a human being—but the level of stress affecting college students can decrease their academic success. Consider the level of stress you feel today. Rate your current level of stress on a scale of 1–5: 1 is "little or no stress" and 5 is "extremely stressed."

My current stress level: _____

If your stress level is a 3 or higher, describe the symptoms of stress that you are experiencing.

_____

_____

Why you are feeling this level of stress?

_____

_____

If your stress level is a 1 or 2, what are some of the reasons?

_____

_____

When you are stressed, your body undergoes physiological changes. Your breathing becomes rapid and shallow; your heart rate increases; the muscles in your shoulders, forehead, neck, and chest tighten; your hands become cold or sweaty; your stomach becomes upset; your hands and knees may shake; your mouth goes dry; and your voice may sound strained. Over time, stress can develop into chronic health issues such as irritable bowel syndrome, common colds, migraines, and fatigue.

A number of psychological changes also occur when you are under stress. You might experience a sense of confusion, trouble concentrating, memory lapses, and poor problem solving. As a result of stress, you may also make decisions that you regret later. High stress levels can lead to emotions such as anger, anxiety, depression, fear, frustration, and irritability, which might cause you to be unable to go to sleep at night or to wake up frequently. These stress-related changes can turn into more serious psychological problems such as anxiety disorder, depression, or panic attacks.

Stress has many sources, but two seem to be prominent: life events and daily hassles. Life events are those that represent major adversity, such as the death of a parent, spouse, partner, or friend. Researchers believe that an accumulation of stress from life events, especially if many events occur over a short period of time, can cause physical and mental health problems. Daily hassles are the minor irritants that we experience every day, such as losing your keys, having three tests on the same day, arguing with your roommate, or worrying about money. The best starting point for handling stress is to be in good physical and mental shape. If you pay attention to your body and mind, you will be able to recognize the signs of stress before they become uncontrollable.

YOUR TURN > STAY MOTIVATED

Do you get stressed before an exam or a presentation? Some level of stress might motivate you to do well, but a high stress level can have the opposite effect. The next time you are stressed before a test or presentation, note how you feel, both physically and mentally. Are you more energized, more alert? Or does your stress negatively affect your concentration or self-confidence? Manage your stress so that it helps, not hurts, your preparation and performance. If your stress is out of control, seek help from the campus counseling center.

Modifying your lifestyle is the best overall approach to stress management. You have the power to change your life so that it is less stressful. This power rests on an important, but simple, concept known as locus of control. Locus of control suggests that all of us are able to control some elements of our daily lives. When you identify the parts of your life that do not serve you well, make plans for change, and then carry out those plans, you are using your locus of control. One example of your locus of control includes deciding when to get up in the morning: if being late for class stresses you out, get up 10 or 15 minutes earlier. Another example is how you prepare for tests: If you have a lot of test anxiety, learn and practice test-taking skills. Many daily stresses result from decisions that you make yourself using your locus of control, and they all have a cumulative impact on what happens to you, either positive or negative, over a lifetime. As you learn from mistakes, you learn to believe in yourself and you develop greater resilience.

Another way students can take control of their lifestyle is by knowing their boundaries and making priority lists. This might mean saying "no" to friends or family members who distract you from your tasks and obligations—for instance, telling a friend that you have to stay in to study instead of giving him or her a ride. It is OK to say "no," and you don't have to feel guilty about doing so. Students have many obligations (classes, work, their family, and peers), and they have to work hard to manage all their obligations and still maintain good grades.

Check your college website, counseling center, health center, student newspaper, or fitness center for workshops that teach stress management and relaxation techniques. You'll also find apps, websites, books, and other resources that guide you through many options.

YOUR TURN ❯ WORK TOGETHER

With a group of students in your class, review the list of ways to lower your stress level. Discuss the ideas that make the most sense for you. On the basis of your experience, which ideas would your group suggest to other college students?

The Importance of Good Nutrition

There is also a clear connection between what you eat and drink, your overall health and well-being, and stress. Eating a lot of junk food will add pounds to your body and reduce your energy level, and with less energy you are less likely to want to exercise. When you can't keep up with your work because you're slow or tired, you will experience more stress.

Many of us find that gaining weight is really easy; a few days of donuts, pizza, and soft drinks can pack on unexpected pounds. Losing weight, even a small amount, is far more difficult. Let's face it—food is one of life's greatest pleasures, and having the self-discipline to say "no" to a giant piece of birthday cake is difficult. Weight gain also will reduce your energy and interest in exercise.

If you are gaining weight and losing energy, what can you do about your eating habits? It might not be easy at first, but if you start making small positive changes, you can build toward a new way of eating. You will not only feel better but also be healthier and probably happier. Here are some commonsense suggestions:

- Limit snacks to healthy options, such as fruits, vegetables, yogurt, and small portions of nuts, such as pistachios, almonds, cashews, or walnuts.

- Be careful about "fad" diets. Before using diet pills or beginning a diet regimen such as the Paleo, Atkins, or South Beach diet, check with your physician. These diets may show results quicker than maintaining a balanced diet and exercising, but they might cause you to miss essential nutrients, especially if you are an athlete. Simply changing your portion sizes can be a first step toward weight loss.

- Eat plenty of vegetables and fruits daily. Opt for these over fruit juices, which tend to be high in sugar.

- Drink plenty of water. Drinking 64 ounces of water a day helps flush your system, keep your skin healthy, and manage weight. A rule of thumb: To keep hydrated, drink water before and after a workout and between meals.

- Add variety to your meals. Cafeterias can offer several options, and the most important strategy is to eat a balanced and well-portioned meal that includes protein, vegetables, grains, salad, and fruit. Stay away from fried and sugary foods. Choose grilled or broiled lean meat and fish instead. A good reference is ChooseMyPlate.gov, the icon for which is shown in Figure 11.1. Watch your portion sizes. Avoid large, jumbo, or king-size fast-food items and all-you-can-eat buffets.

FIGURE 11.1 ❭ MyPlate Eating Guidelines

The MyPlate icon was introduced by the federal government in 2011 to replace the Food Guide Pyramid. **ChooseMyPlate.gov** provides tips and recommendations for healthy eating and understanding the plate's design.

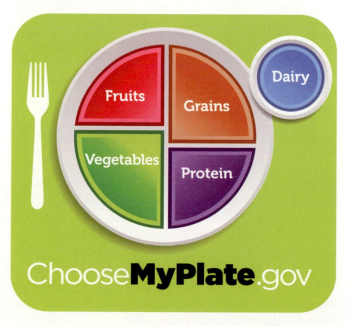

- Eat a healthy breakfast! Your brain will function better if you eat a power-packed meal first thing in the morning. Try oatmeal, smoothies, eggs, and foods high in protein to help you focus and boost your metabolism for the rest of the day.

- Always read the nutrition label on packaged foods. Be skeptical of marketing on labels. Instead, look for the number of grams of fat, sugars, protein, and carbohydrates. Check the sodium content: Sodium (table salt) will make you retain water, which increases your weight, and can possibly increase your blood pressure. Do not let "nonfat/lowfat" options entice you. Often, these products contain chemicals and unhealthy by-products that are worse for you than their full-fat counterparts.

- If possible, take time to cook your own food, bring your lunch, and pack your own snacks. Preparing your own meals and snacks is almost always healthier and more cost-effective than eating out or buying snack food at convenience stores.

❯ A Serving Is a Slice, Not the Whole Pizza

Have you ever found yourself staring at the remains of a pizza like this one and realizing that you're a bit out of control? Start to rein yourself back in. Stop at the grocery store on the way home to pick up some healthy snacks. Throw out half-eaten bags of chips. Take a long walk or give yourself an extra half hour in the morning to take another walk or jog. It's never the wrong time or too late to take better care of yourself, and no step in the right direction is too small.

© Image Source/Corbis

Risky Eating Habits. Although we advise you to think about what you eat from day to day, we also advise you not to overthink your diet. Remember that the key to good health is achieving balance, and an obsession with food intake may be a sign that things are out of balance. Over the last few decades, an increasing number of both male and female college students have been developing eating disorders such as anorexia nervosa (an extreme fear of gaining weight), bulimia (overeating followed by self-induced vomiting or laxative use), or binge eating disorder (compulsive overeating long past the feeling of being full).

Anyone who is struggling with an eating disorder should seek immediate medical attention. Eating disorders can be life-threatening if they are not treated by a health care professional. Contact the National Eating Disorder Association (**nationaleatingdisorders.org**) to find a professional in your area who specializes in the treatment of eating disorders. For help on campus with possible eating disorders, check out your counseling and/or health centers. This is a common phenomenon with stressed-out college students.

Caffeine. Caffeine is probably the best example of a commonly ingested substance that is linked to high stress levels. College students, like many adults, use caffeine to help with productivity. Caffeine increases alertness and reduces feelings of fatigue if used moderately. Up to 400 milligrams (mg) of caffeine a day appears to be safe for most healthy adults. That's roughly the amount of caffeine in four cups of brewed coffee, ten cans of cola, or two "energy shot" drinks. However, too much caffeine can cause nervousness, headaches, irritability, upset stomach, and sleeplessness—all symptoms of stress. It is important to monitor your daily use of caffeine. Many students consume energy drinks, which can contain more than the recommended amount of caffeine. Be careful to limit your caffeine intake. Using coffee or energy drinks when you're studying for exams, or even to get through the day, can become a crutch. Find other sources of energy, especially low-cost sources, like jogging or power napping.

The Effect of Alcohol and Other Substances on Wellness

In this section, our purpose is not to make judgments, but to warn you about the ways in which irresponsible use of legal and illegal substances can cause serious harm to your health and well-being and have a major negative impact on your college experience and success, not to mention your overall life. For college students, tobacco, alcohol, and marijuana are the substances most commonly used and abused. It is important to observe the laws that pertain to such use to avoid legal consequences. In the United States, the age at which you can legally consume alcohol is 21; and recreational marijuana use is legal only in a few states. The minimum legal age to purchase tobacco products has increased to 21 in California and Hawaii as well as dozens of localities in eight states across the United States.

Alcohol Use. Because 65 percent of college students drink alcohol in a given month, with a large percentage drinking too much,[1] it is important that all students learn about the effects of alcohol consumption. Alcohol can turn even people who don't drink into victims, such as people who are killed by drunk drivers or family members who suffer as a result of the destructive behavior of an alcoholic relative. You might have heard news reports about college students who died or were seriously or permanently

---

[1]Aaron White and Ralph Hingson, "The Burden of Alcohol Use: Excessive Alcohol Consumption and Related Consequences among College Students," *Alcohol Research: Current Reviews* 35, no. 2 (2013). http://pubs.niaaa .nih.gov/publications/arcr352/201-218.htm.

injured as a result of excessive drinking. Just one occasion of heavy or high-risk drinking can lead to serious problems.

People experience the pleasurable effects of alcoholic beverages as the alcohol begins to affect several areas in the brain. How fast you drink makes a difference. Your body gets rid of alcohol at a rate of about one drink—defined as one 12-ounce beer, one 5-ounce glass of wine, or 1.5 ounces of hard liquor— per hour. Drinking more than one drink an hour may cause a rise in blood alcohol content (BAC) because the body is absorbing alcohol faster than it can eliminate it. We should also note here that popular home remedies for sobering up, like drinking coffee or water or taking a cold shower, don't work.

At BAC levels of .025 to .05, a drinker tends to feel animated and energized. At a BAC level of around .05, a drinker may feel rowdy or boisterous. This is where most people report feeling a buzz from alcohol. At a BAC level between .05 and .08, alcohol starts to act as a depressant, so as soon as you feel that buzz, remember that you are on the brink of losing coordination, clear thinking, and judgment.

Driving is seriously impaired at BAC levels lower than the legal limit of .08. In fact, an accurate safe level for most people may be half the legal limit, or .04. As BAC levels climb past .08, people become progressively less coordinated and less able to make good decisions. Most people become severely uncoordinated with BAC levels higher than .08 and may begin falling asleep, falling down, or slurring their speech.

Most people pass out or fall asleep when their BAC level is above .25. Unfortunately, even after you pass out and stop drinking, your BAC level can continue to rise as alcohol in your stomach is released to the intestine and absorbed into the bloodstream. Your body may try to get rid of alcohol by vomiting, but you can choke on your vomit if you are unconscious, semi-conscious, or severely uncoordinated. Worse yet, at BAC levels higher than .30, most people will show signs of severe alcohol poisoning, such as an inability to wake up, slowed breathing, a fast but weak pulse, cool or damp skin, and pale or bluish skin. Anyone exhibiting these symptoms needs medical assistance immediately.

Now that we have discussed the dangers of excessive drinking, here are some simple harm-reduction approaches to consuming alcohol:

- **Slow down drinking.** One way to maintain a "buzz"—the euphoric sensation you experience from drinking—is by drinking one beer per hour or less. Pacing yourself and limiting your drinks help prevent you from attaining a high BAC level. It may also help prevent you from being sexually assaulted.

- **Eat while you drink.** Sometimes eating while you consume alcohol helps slow down your drinking and slows down the processing of alcohol. Body weight and gender play a large role in this as well.

- **Drink water.** Alcohol dehydrates your body, so it is important to drink plenty of water while consuming alcohol.

- **Designate a driver before you go out.** Walking is always a better option than driving a vehicle, but if you are going to take a vehicle to a destination with alcohol, you should always designate a sober driver before you leave.

Tobacco and Marijuana. Tobacco is a legal drug that contains nicotine, a highly addictive substance, and is the cause of many serious medical conditions, including heart and lung diseases and some forms of cancer. One concern that particularly relates to college students is *social smoking—* smoking when hanging out with friends, drinking, or partying. Becoming addicted to cigarettes often derails plans to stop social smoking after graduation.

You may have noticed advertisements for electronic cigarettes (e-cigarettes or e-cigs) or seen them in stores. According to the U.S. Food and Drug Administration, e-cigarettes are battery-operated products designed to deliver nicotine, flavors, and other chemicals in the form of vapor. "Vaping," or using e-cigarettes, has not been fully studied, so consumers currently don't know the potential risks.

Although only a small percentage of college students use smokeless tobacco, the habit is no less addicting than smoking is. One dip delivers the same amount of nicotine as three or four cigarettes. Smokeless tobacco contains 28 known cancer-causing substances and is associated with many of the same health risks as cigarette smoking.

A final reason for smokers to quit, or for others never to start, is the cost (see Table 11.1). If you are a smoker, contact your campus health or counseling centers for more information about quitting.

TABLE 11.1 ❯ Average Cost of Smoking across the United States

Half-Pack-a-Day Smoker
$5.51/pack × 3.5 packs/week = $19.29/week
$19.29/week × 52 weeks/year = $1,002.82/year
$1,002.82/year × 4 years of college = $4,011.28
IN 25 YEARS, YOU WILL HAVE SPENT $25,070.50
Pack-a-Day Smoker
$5.51/pack × 7 packs/week = $38.57/week
$38.57/week × 52 weeks/year = $2,005.64
$2,005.64/year × 4 years of college = $8,022.56
IN 25 YEARS, YOU WILL HAVE SPENT $50,141.00

Recently, Colorado, Washington, Oregon, Alaska, and Washington, D.C., became the first places in the United States to legalize recreational marijuana use for individuals 21 years or older. It is still not legal in other states or federally, however. As with tobacco, there are health risks associated with smoking it. Some impacts of marijuana use include an increase in anxiety, paranoia, short-term memory loss, and depression. In addition, marijuana smoke increases your risk for lung cancer, much like tobacco. It is important to know the risks and acknowledge your state and federal laws.

Exercising to Maintain Wellness

Exercise is an excellent stress-management technique, the best way to stay fit, and an important element in effective weight management. Whether it's walking to class, going to the campus recreation center, or going for a bike ride, it is important to get outside and be active every day. Any kind of exercise benefits your body and spirit and is a great choice for stress and weight management. Choose activities that you enjoy so that you look forward to your exercise time, and make it a regular part of your routine. People who exercise report higher energy levels, less stress, better sleep, healthier weight, and an improved self-image compared with people who do not exercise.

Besides doing wonders for your body, aerobic exercise keeps your mind healthy. When you do aerobic exercise, your body produces hormones called beta-endorphins. These natural narcotics cause feelings of contentment and happiness and help manage anxiety and depression. Your mood and general sense of competence improve with regular aerobic exercise.

Think about ways to combine activities and use your time efficiently. Maybe you can leave your car at home and walk or ride a bike to class. If you must drive, then park at the far end of the parking lot to get in extra steps. Try going to the gym with a friend and asking each other study questions while on the treadmill. Take the stairs whenever possible. Wear a pedometer or a tracker like Fitbit, or use pedometer apps such as S Health or Stepz on your phone, and aim for a certain number of steps each day. If you're a parent, run around with your kids. Many campuses have fitness centers that offer exercise equipment and organized sports. The most important thing about exercise is that you stay active and make it part of your day-to-day life.

Knowing your BMI is a good way to understand your optimum size. According to the U.S. Centers for Disease Control and Prevention (CDC), BMI is calculated by weight and height, and provides an effective way to screen for health issues. You can use an automatic BMI calculator such as that available at **nhlbi.nih.gov/health/educational/lose_wt/BMI/bmicalc .htm**, or you can do the calculation yourself. For an adult, calculate BMI by dividing weight in pounds (lbs.) by height in inches (in.) squared and multiplying by 703.

> **Example:** Weight = 150 lbs., Height = 5'5" (65")
> **Calculation:** $[150 \div (65)^2] \times 703 = 24.96$

Per **cdc.gov**, a BMI of under 18.5 indicates "underweight," 18.5 to 24.9 is "normal," 25 to 29.9 is "overweight," and 30 or higher is "obese."

The Importance of Sleep

Getting adequate sleep is another way to protect yourself from stress. According to a 2013 Gallup poll, almost 50 percent of individuals aged eighteen to twenty-nine get less than the recommended seven hours of sleep per night.[2]

---

[2]Gallup, "In U.S., 40% Get Less Than Recommended Amount of Sleep," http://www.gallup.com/poll/166553/less-recommendedamount-sleep.aspx, accessed 4/18/16.

> **Catch Some Zzzzs**

Brief naps, 20 minutes or so, can revive you. When you aren't getting enough sleep, you cannot do your best. Establish good sleeping habits and grab opportunities for power naps when you can, like this student who arrived early for his next class.
© Randy Faris/Corbis

Lack of sleep can lead to anxiety, depression, and academic problems. Researchers found that students who studied all week but then stayed up late partying on the weekends forgot as much as 30 percent of the material they had learned during the prior week. Try the following suggestions to establish better sleep habits:

- Avoid long daytime naps that last longer than 30 minutes.
- Try reading or listening to relaxing music before going to bed.
- Exercise during the day.
- Get your clothes, school materials, and food for the next day together before you go to bed.
- Sleep in the same room and bed every night.
- Set a regular schedule for going to bed and getting up.
- Track your sleep by using tools such as Fitbit or wellness apps.

Managing Your Emotional Health to Maintain Wellness

Your emotional or mental health is an important component of your overall health. Particularly in the first year of college, some students have difficulty establishing positive relationships with others, dealing with pressure, or making wise decisions. Other students are optimistic and happy, and seem to believe in their own abilities to address problems successfully. Your ability to deal with life's challenges is based on your emotional intelligence (EI). Emotional intelligence is part of your personality; if you take a psychology course in college, you will learn more about it.

Taking care of your emotional health is a big part of maintaining wellness. When one's emotional health declines, the consequences can be very serious.

Depression. According to the National Institute of Mental Health, an estimated 17 million adult Americans suffer from depression during any one-year period.[3] College students are at especially high risk for both depression and suicide because of the major life changes and high stress levels some of them experience during the college years.

Depression is not a weakness; it is an illness that needs medical attention. Many college students suffer from some form of depression. The feelings are often temporary and may be situational. A romantic breakup, a disappointing grade, or an ongoing problem with another person can create feelings of despair. Although most depression goes away on its own, if you or a friend has any of the following symptoms for more than two weeks, it is important to talk to a health care provider:

- feelings of helplessness and hopelessness
- feeling useless, inadequate, bad, or guilty
- self-hatred, constant questioning of one's thoughts and actions
- loss of energy and motivation
- loss of appetite
- weight loss or gain
- difficulty sleeping or excessive need for sleep
- loss of interest in sex
- difficulty concentrating for a significant length of time

‹ Difficulty Coping

Many events in life can trigger feelings of despair. Know the signs of depression. If you or someone you care about seems to be having trouble, reach out. College campuses have resources to help.

© Wavebreak Media Ltd/Veer/Corbis

---

[3]See "Depression" at the website of the American Psychological Association, http://www.apa.org/topics/depress/recover.aspx, accessed 4/18/16.

One trigger for depression is simply the process of starting college. As you begin, you may not know enough about this new way of life to know what to expect. This may trigger short-term depression and anxiety. You can receive free and confidential assistance on many campuses either through a counseling or health center.

Suicide. The CDC reports that students aged 15 to 24 are more likely than any other group to attempt suicide.[4] Most people who commit suicide give a warning of their intentions. The following are common indicators of someone's intent to commit suicide:

- recent loss and inability to let go of grief
- change in personality—sadness, withdrawal, indifference
- expressions of self-hatred
- change in sleep patterns
- change in eating habits
- a direct statement about committing suicide (e.g., "I might as well end it all.")
- a preoccupation with death

If someone you know threatens suicide or displays any of these signs, here are some ways you can help:

- Talk to the person who is depressed; urge him or her to seek assistance.
- Listen.
- Find self-help resources online or available through the campus library and share them with the individual.
- Share your concerns with others who could be supportive of this person.
- Bring your concerns about this person to the attention of an advisor or counselor.
- Find out whether there is a counseling center on campus and if so, get information on what services are available, and offer to go with your friend.

Finally, remember no shame is attached to having high levels of stress, depression, anxiety, or suicidal tendencies. Unavoidable life events or physiological imbalances can cause such feelings and behaviors. Proper counseling, medical attention, and in some cases prescription medication can help students cope with depression and suicidal thoughts.

Cyberbullying. In recent years, cyberbullying has been on the rise, not just in grade school and high school, but on college campuses as well. Experts define **cyberbullying** as "any behavior performed through electronic or digital media by individuals or groups who repeatedly communicate hostile or aggressive messages intended to inflict harm or discomfort on others."[5] According to a recent study, the prevalence of cyberbullying

---

[4]See "Suicide Facts at a Glance," from the Division of Violence Prevention of the Centers for Disease Control, http://www.cdc.gov/ViolencePrevention/pdf/Suicide-DataSheet-a.pdf, accessed 4/18/16.

[5]P. K. Smith et al., "Cyberbullying: Its Nature and Impact in Secondary School Pupils," *Journal of Child Psychology and Psychiatry*, no. 49 (2008): 375–76.

among college populations ranges from 10 to 28.7 percent.[6] These may seem like low numbers, but cyberbullying can go unreported because of embarrassment or privacy concerns. Tragic cyberbullying stories that have resulted in the victim's clinical depression or suicide have been reported in recent years.

Cyberbullying is a serious issue that harms individuals in many ways. It is a crime that should be dealt with immediately. If someone you know has experienced cyberbullying, or if you have been a cyberbullying victim, you should report it as soon as possible. Several foundations and resources are available to help students report cyberbullying:

- **stopbullying.org**
- the Megan Meier Foundation, **meganmeierfoundation.org**
- National Crime Prevention Council, **ncpc.org**

YOUR TURN › WORK TOGETHER

Google "college students and cyberbullying." As you read through the articles that you find, write down common reasons and causes of cyberbullying. Bring your notes to class and share them with other students in a small group. Discuss why college students are at risk for cyberbullying, depression, and suicide, and share ideas for what colleges can do to decrease this risk.

---

[6]Carlos P. Zalaquett and SeriaShia J. Chatters, "Cyberbullying in College: Frequency, Characteristics, and Practical Implications," *SAGE Open* (Jan.–Mar. 2014): 1–8. Web.

MANAGING YOUR RELATIONSHIPS

How well you are able to manage your emotions is directly related to the quality of the relationships in your life, which has a direct impact on your ability to maintain personal wellness. We all do better with a strong support system in place. The relationships you maintain and develop in college will have positive effects on your success. While you are making new friends, you continue to have relationships with your parents, spouse, children, or other family members. Sometimes the expectations of family members change, and negotiating such changes is not always easy. If you are fresh out of high school, you might feel that your parents still want to control your life. If you have a spouse or partner, going to college will give you a new identity that might seem strange or threatening to your partner. If you have children, they might not understand what's going on as you try to balance your need for study time with their need for your undivided attention.

If your friends or others close to you also go to college, you will have a great deal to share and compare. But if your friends are not college students, they, too, might feel threatened as you take on a new identity. Romantic relationships can support you or can create major conflict and heartbreak, depending on whether your partner shares your feelings and whether the relationship is healthy.

Friendships in and beyond College

One of the best things about going to college is meeting new people from different backgrounds and interests. You learn as much or more from other students you meet as you learn from instructors. Although not everyone you hang out with will become a close friend, you will likely find a few special relationships that might even last a lifetime. One thing that researchers on higher education's effects know for sure is that the greatest impact on students during college is the impact of other students. This suggests two things: (1) These relationships are hugely important; and (2) you need to choose these relationships intentionally and carefully as you are more likely to become similar to the people with whom you associate.

YOUR TURN > WORK TOGETHER

Make a list of any stories you heard or ideas you developed about college students and instructors before coming to college. Share these ideas in a small group. See how many stories or rumors were common among students in the group. Talk about whether these stories are proving to be accurate or inaccurate in your college experience.

Digital Communication and Relationships

So much of our communication with others occurs through e-mail, text and photo messaging, mobile apps, and posting on social networking sites. Online communication enables us to connect with others, whether we're forming new friendships or romantic relationships or maintaining established ones. Online communication also gives us a broad sense of community.

Social networking sites and apps such as Facebook, Twitter, Instagram, Vine, Viber, Telegram, WhatsApp, and Snapchat are popular with college students; it's likely that you use sites and apps such as these throughout the day to keep up with your friends. While social media outlets have both positives and negatives, one thing is certain: As students enter college, most do not carefully examine what they share through social media. Online statements, posts, and messages can have a strong impact, so you should be careful about everything you put into public view. Students often ignore the fact that what goes online or is shared through a mobile app lives on forever, although some sites claim differently. Today it is common for many employers to check job applicants' online image before they offer them jobs. Given how often we use technology to communicate with others, it becomes critically important to use it properly. When you do, you are strengthening, and not weakening, your relationships. Table 11.2 provides some helpful suggestions for improving online communication.

TABLE 11.2 > Best Practices for Online Communication

Key Points to Remember	Best Practices
1. Match the seriousness of your message to your communication medium.	*Online* is best for transmitting quick reminders or messages that require little time and thought to craft. *Offline* is better for sharing personal information such as engagement announcements or news of health issues.
2. Online communication is not necessarily more efficient.	If your message needs a quick decision or answer, a phone call or a face-to-face conversation may be better. Use online communication if you want the person to have time to respond.
3. Presume that your posts are public.	If you wouldn't want a message to be seen by the general public, don't post it or send it online.
4. Remember that your posts are permanent.	Even after you delete something, it still exists on servers and may be accessible.
5. Practice the art of creating drafts.	Don't feel pressured to answer an e-mail immediately. Taking time to respond will result in a more competently crafted message.
6. Protect your online identity.	Choose passwords carefully and limit the personal information you put online.
7. Protect yourself when online correspondence turns into face-to-face communication.	Exercise caution and common sense when meeting any online acquaintances in person.

Source: Adapted from Steven McCornack, *Reflect & Relate: An Introduction to Interpersonal Communication*, 3rd ed. (Boston: Bedford/St. Martin's, 2013), 24–27.

Serious Relationships

College presents an opportunity not only to make lots of new friends but also to start, maintain, or end a romantic relationship. You might already be in a long-term committed relationship, or you might look for one in college. For some older students, it is even possible that ending a long-term relationship, like a marriage, may be a trigger for returning to college. Given that college allows you to meet people from different backgrounds who share common interests, you might find it easier to meet romantic partners in college than you ever have before. Whether you choose to commit to one serious relationship or keep yourself open for meeting others, you'll grow and learn a great deal about yourself and those with whom you become involved.

Protecting Yourself and Others against Sexual Assault and Violence

Sexual assault that happens on college campuses is a problem that has existed for many years. Everyone is at risk of becoming a victim of sexual assault, but the majority of victims are women. The results of a recent study conclude that during their first year in college, one in seven women will have experienced incapacitated assault or rape and nearly one in ten will have experienced forcible assault or rape.[7] According to statistics, more than 80 percent of these survivors will be assaulted or raped by someone they know[8]—and most will not report the crime. Alcohol is a factor in nearly 75 percent of the incidents.[9]

Interventions to reduce sexual violence on campus are urgently needed. In 2013, the federal government instituted an initiative called the Campus Save Act. The act mandates that all colleges and universities must provide sexual assault, violence, and harassment education to students. The Campus Save Act provides an amendment to the Clery Act of 1990, which the federal government implemented after a female college student was raped and killed. The Clery Act requires postsecondary institutions to report sexual and other crimes and related statistics. Colleges can report cases of sexual misconduct, but as always, the student's information must remain confidential. You can find out more about the Campus Save Act by visiting **campussaveact.org**, contacting your campus security or public safety office, or contacting your student judicial office. It is always up to the survivor to decide how he or she would like to proceed after a sexual assault has occurred.

Whether sexually assaulted by an acquaintance or by a stranger, a survivor can suffer long-term traumatic effects as well as depression, anxiety, and even suicide. Many survivors essentially blame themselves, but the

[7]Kate B. Carey, Sarah E. Durney, Robyn L. Shepardson, and Michael P. Carey, "Incapacitated and Forcible Rape of College Women: Prevalence across the First Year," *Journal of Adolescent Health* 56 (2015): 678–80, http://i2.cdn.turner.com/cnn/2015/images/05/20/carey_jah_proof.pdf.

[8]C. P. Krebs, C. H. Lindquist, T. D. Warner, B. S. Fisher, and S. L. Martin, *The Campus Sexual Assault (CSA) Study* (Washington, DC: National Institute of Justice, 2007).

[9]Meichun Mohler-Kuo, George W. Dowdall, Mary P. Koss, and Henry Wechsler, "Correlates of Rape While Intoxicated in a National Sample of College Women," *Journal of Studies on Alcohol* 65, no. 1 (2004): 37–45, http://www.jsad.com/doi/10.15288/jsa.2004.65.37.

only person at fault for a sexual assault is the perpetrator. If you are a survivor of sexual assault, regardless of whether you choose to report it to the police, it is useful to seek help by contacting a counselor, a local rape crisis center, campus public safety or police department, student health services, women's student services, or a local hospital emergency room. Here are some steps you can take to help a sexual assault survivor:

- Remain empathetic and nonjudgmental.
- Keep information private and ensure the survivor confidentiality.
- Listen.
- Ask the survivor how he or she would like to proceed—discuss options like contacting campus police or the campus counseling center.
- Seek out advice from a professional on how to help the survivor.
- Stay in touch and follow up to see if the survivor is getting the help he or she needs.

If you observe a sexual assault or a potential sexual assault, make your presence known. Don't be a bystander; intervene in any way you can. Create a distraction, and if you need help, ask for help.

Marriage, Committed Relationships, and/or Parenting during College

Can you sustain a committed relationship during college? Can you be a successful college student and a good parent at the same time? The answer to each question, of course, is "yes," although meeting everyone's needs—yours, your spouse's, your partner's, your parents', your children's—is not easy. If you are married or in a committed relationship, namely one in which you are living together, with or without children, you need to become an expert at time management. If you do have children, make sure you find out what resources your college offers to help you with daycare or after-school care, particularly if you are a single parent or have the entire responsibility for raising your child or children.

Sometimes going to college can create conflict with a spouse or partner as you take on a new identity and a new set of responsibilities. Sometimes jealousy may be a factor when the student talks about new friends and impressive instructors. Financial problems are likely to put extra pressure on your relationship, so both you and your partner have to work hard at paying attention to each other's needs. Be sure to involve those in your household in your decisions and reassure them of their continuing significance to you. Bring them to campus at every opportunity, and let your partner read your papers and other assignments—your children also if they are old enough. Introduce your partner to some of the new acquaintances you are making at college, so he or she does not feel shut out or isolated. Finally, set aside time for your partner and children just as carefully as you schedule your work and your classes.

Relationships with Family Members

If you come from a cultural background that values family relationships and responsibilities above everything else, you will have to find a way to balance your home life and college. In some cultures, if your grandmother or aunt needs help, that might be considered just as important—or more important than—going to class or taking an exam. Some instructors might help you if you have occasional problems with meeting a deadline because of family obligations, but you cannot expect that they will. It's important that you explain your situation; your instructors cannot guess what you need. As the demands on your time increase, it is important that you talk with family members to help them understand your role and responsibilities as a student and ask for their help and support.

Not every family is ideal. If your parents or other members of your family are not supportive, find other people who can help you create the family you need. Seek help from the counseling center if you find yourself in the middle of a difficult family situation.

YOUR TURN > WORK TOGETHER

In a small group, talk about how your family members are adjusting to your college experience. Are they supportive, fearful, meddling, remote? How do their attitudes and reactions affect your motivation with regard to college? Share strategies with other students for handling issues that arise and staying motivated, even when family issues seem to get in the way.

Connecting through Involvement

Students who become involved with at least one campus organization are more likely to complete their first year and remain in college because they are more engaged and involved in the campus activities and events and get to connect with a lot of students, instructors, and other college employees. Consider your interests and the high school activities you enjoyed most, and choose some to explore at your college. You might want to join a sports team, perform community service, or run for a student government office, or you might prefer to join a club or an organization.

Almost every college has organizations you can join; usually, you can check them out through activity or club fairs, printed guides, open houses, Web pages, and social media outlets such as Twitter, Instagram, or the college's Facebook page. Find out what the organization is like, what the expectations of time and money are, and whether you feel comfortable with the members.

You can also get involved in the surrounding community. Consider volunteering for a community service project such as caring for animals at a shelter, serving the homeless at a soup kitchen, or helping build or renovate homes for needy families. Your college might offer service opportunities as part of first-year courses.

Remember that one of the best things about going to college is meeting new people from different backgrounds and interests. You learn as much or more from other students you meet as you learn from instructors. Although not everyone you hang out with will become a close friend, you will likely find a few special relationships that might even last a lifetime.

Be careful not to overextend yourself when it comes to campus activities. While it is important to get involved, joining too many clubs or organizations will make it difficult to focus on any given activity and will interfere with your studies. Future employers will consider a balance in academics and campus involvement an important quality in applicants.

Working

One of the best ways to develop relationships on your campus is to get an on-campus job. Generally, your on-campus supervisors may be much more flexible than off-campus employers in helping you balance your study demands and your work schedule. You might not make as much money working on campus as you would in an off-campus job, but the relationships you'll develop with important people who care about your success in college and who will write those all-important reference letters make on-campus employment well worth it. Consider finding a job related to your major. For example, if you are a computer science major, you might be able to work in a computer lab. That work could help you gain knowledge and experience and make connections with experts in your field. If an on-campus job is not available, or you don't find one that appeals to you, an off-campus job can allow you to meet new people in the community.

11.3

THRIVING IN DIVERSE ENVIRONMENTS

So far in this chapter, you have learned strategies for managing the various aspects of wellness and have a better understanding of how doing so helps you maintain healthy relationships in your life. A logical next step is to increase your awareness of differences and similarities among people, which is an important component of building healthy relationships. While you're in college, you'll meet students who are different from you in race, ethnicity, culture, economic status, sexual orientation, and religion. These differences will provide you with many opportunities to experience diversity.

Diversity is the difference in social and cultural identities among people living together. In spite of their differences in life story and worldview, most college students have similar goals and dreams. Sharing your differences and similarities with others can enrich your entire life.

A college serves as a microcosm of the real world—a world that requires us all to work, live, and socialize with people from different ethnic and cultural groups and in close proximity. In 2014 and 2015, through events in Baltimore, Chicago, Ferguson, Missouri, and Charleston, South Carolina, we were reminded that racial differences continue to create misunderstanding, hate, and violence even in the twenty-first century.

For many students, college is the first time they have interacted with people across the diversity spectrum who see the world differently based on their life experience. That makes college a good place to understand your perspectives on diversity, explore your own feelings and prejudices (we all have them), and build a respectful understanding of how and why people often have different views.

Familiarizing yourself with differences can greatly expand your experiences in the classes you take, the organizations you join, and the relationships you have. This work, although difficult at times, will add to your educational experiences, personal growth, and development. Thinking critically about your personal values and belief systems will also allow you to have a greater sense of belonging and to make a positive contribution to our multicultural society.

∧ Expand Your Worldview

How has going to college changed your experience with diversity? Are you getting to know people of different races or ethnic groups? Do your classes have both traditional-aged and returning students? Make it a point to seek out people who are different from you, and share your personal stories and worldviews.

Purestock/Alamy Stock Photo

YOUR TURN > DISCUSS IT

Look around your classroom. What kinds of diversity do you see? What other kinds of diversity might exist but can't be seen? With a small group of students, discuss why some college students have an interest in diversity, both seen and unseen, and why other students avoid the topic. Share your ideas with the whole class.

Other Differences You Will Encounter in College

When you think about diversity, you might first think of differences in race or ethnicity. Although it is true that those are two forms of diversity, you will most likely experience many other types of diversity in college and in the workplace, including age, religion, economic status, physical challenges, learning challenges, and sexuality.

Age. Although some students enter college around age eighteen, others choose to enter or return at an older age. Age diversity in the classroom gives everyone the opportunity to learn from others who have different life experiences. A campus where students of different ages are in classes together can be an invigorating learning environment.

Religion. Religion is a specific fundamental set of beliefs and practices generally agreed on by a number of persons or sects. Freedom to practice one's religion has been central to the American experience. In fact, many settlers of the original thirteen colonies came to North America to escape religion-based discrimination. However, religion-based discrimination still exists, and people may come under attack based on their religious affiliations. For example, in light of the recent terrorist attacks at the national and international levels, many Muslim students have felt threatened and afraid of being subject to potential hate crimes. In 2015, a female Muslim student was attacked on a college campus while receiving hate-related comments because of her religion. It is important to understand that most Muslims do not subscribe to terrorist groups' ideologies and, in fact, despise terrorism.

Embrace opportunities on your campus to learn about religions that are different from yours. Doing so will help you overcome any misperceptions you have of others and will make you a more open-minded person able to appreciate global differences.

Economic Status. The United States is a country of vast differences in wealth. This considerable economic diversity can be either a positive or a negative aspect of college life. On the positive side, you will be exposed to, and can learn from, students from a wide range of economic statuses. Meeting others who have grown up with either more or fewer opportunities than you did is part of learning how to live in a democracy.

Try to avoid developing exaggerated feelings of superiority or inferiority. You have more in common with other students than you think. Now your individual efforts, dreams, courage, determination, and ability to stay focused can determine your success.

Learning and Physical Challenges. Although the majority of college students have reasonably average learning and physical abilities, the numbers of students with physical or learning disabilities are rising on most college campuses, as are the services that are available to them. Physical disabilities can include deafness, blindness, paralysis, or specific disorders such as cerebral palsy or multiple sclerosis. Other students have some form of learning disability that makes college work a challenge. People who have physical or learning disabilities want to be treated just as you would treat anyone else—with respect. If a student with a disability is in your class, treat him or her as you would any student; too much eagerness to help might be seen as an expression of pity.

If you have, or think you might have, a learning disability, visit your campus office for students with disabilities for a diagnosis and advice on getting extra help for learning problems. Unlike in high school, students with disabilities themselves need to inform this office if they require accommodations.

◆ Learning with a Disability

Many college students have a learning or physical disability, but that does not stop them from studying and graduating. All colleges provide support services to students who have documented disabilities.

Monika Wisniewska/Shutterstock

Sexuality. The word *sexuality* refers to the people to whom you might be sexually, or even romantically, attracted. You are familiar with the terms *gay*, *straight*, *homosexual*, *heterosexual*, and *bisexual*. In college, you may meet students, staff members, and instructors who have a different sexual orientation than you. Sexual orientation can be difficult to talk about, and it is important that you respect all individuals whom you meet. Check to see if your campus has a center for the lesbian, gay, bisexual, transgendered, and questioning/queer (LGBTQ) community. If there are educational events about sexual identity on your campus, consider going to hear some speakers and expanding your worldview.

Stereotyping: Why We Believe What We Believe

Many of our beliefs are the result of our personal experience. Others are a result of a **stereotype,** a generalization, usually exaggerated or oversimplified and often offensive, that is used to describe or distinguish a group.

A negative experience with individual members of a particular group may result in stereotyping people in that group. We may acquire stereotypes about people we have never met before or have accepted a stereotype without even thinking about or questioning it. Children who grow up in an environment in which dislike and distrust of certain types of people are openly expressed might adopt those very judgments even if they have had no direct interaction with those being judged. Spending time with people who view the world in a way you may never have considered contributes to your college experience and helps you avoid stereotyping.

> ### YOUR TURN ▸ TRY IT
>
> Think back to the earliest messages you received from family members or friends about how you should react to people who are different from you. Which messages still positively or negatively affect your behavior? Which messages have you revised? Jot down some thoughts.

Overcoming Discrimination, Prejudice, and Insensitivity

If you have ever been treated unfairly because of your race, gender, background, or other characteristics, that memory should motivate you to help stand up for others who are victims of discrimination. Taking action on behalf of others will help you replace negative memories with positive action.

Almost all colleges consider it part of their purpose to provide a welcoming and inclusive campus environment for all students. Because of acts of violence, intimidation, and stupidity occurring in many locations including college campuses, college administrations have established policies against any and all forms of discriminatory actions, racism, and insensitivity. Many campuses have adopted zero-tolerance policies that prohibit verbal and nonverbal harassment as well as hate crimes such as physical assault, vandalism, and intimidation.

Some students instigate hate crimes because of deeply held negative views or fears about people who represent a different race, ethnic group, or sexual orientation. Other students might "follow the crowd" or feel pressured by peers to participate in organized harassment of a certain group. Commit to becoming involved in making your campus a safe place for all students. If you have been a victim of a racist, insensitive, or discriminatory act, report it to the proper authorities.

❮ Commit to Coexist

In a college environment, students often learn that there are more commonalities than differences between themselves and others. By learning to coexist respectfully and peacefully, students can take the first step toward building a better world.

Rawpixel.com/Shutterstock.com

Challenge Yourself to Experience Diversity

Diversity enriches us all, and understanding the value of working with others and the importance of an open mind will enhance your educational and career goals. Your college campus is diverse, and so is the workforce you will enter or in which you currently are. You will be much better equipped to succeed professionally if you are the kind of employee who can work well with diverse people. Use your desire for success to fuel your motivation to understand and appreciate diversity and to learn about various groups in and around your community, at both college and home. Understanding viewpoints different from yours and learning from such differences will help you see similarities where you didn't think they existed. Work hard to overcome feelings of awkwardness or being uncomfortable. Small steps toward greater appreciation of diversity builds resilience and confidence that will serve you well over a lifetime, especially if your personal and professional life makes your world bigger. Participate in campus events that include ethnic and cultural celebrations to learn about new and exciting ideas and viewpoints. If you want to learn more about a culture or group, ask a member of that group for information. If you do so in a tactful, genuine way, most people will be happy to share information about their viewpoints, traditions, and history. It is only through allowing ourselves to grow that we really learn.

KEEP TRACK

We all want to be healthy and look fit, but we live in a world that makes us inactive and presents us with convenient but unhealthy food options. Many of us spend lots of time in front of television and computer screens. Even when we aren't watching a particular show or presentation, we view videos on our phones. When we are bored, we have games on our phones that often keep us sitting right where we are. It seems like we are in front of digital screens almost 24 hours a day. So instead of letting technology make you a couch potato, how can you use it to help you become fit and stay fit?

THE PROBLEM

You want to stay healthy, but hours sitting in front of a computer or eating too much fast food are getting in your way.

THE FIX

Enlist technology to get you moving and making healthier choices.

HOW TO DO IT

Learn how to filter out the fiction. When it comes to fitness and nutrition, there's a lot of conflicting advice and bad information out there, and more than a few scams. Zero in on a few reputable, well-vetted sources of information. You can find everything from healthy menu plans to yoga training to bracelets and apps that can help you keep track of what you are eating and how much exercise and sleep you are getting a day.

Use technology to stay fit. Download fitness apps or wear fitness bracelets to keep track of your daily steps and other physical activities, your calorie intake, and your sleep patterns.

Clear some floor space. Make some of the time you spend in front of a screen active time. The Internet can be a valuable ally if you're struggling to find time to work out. Free websites like YouTube and online services like Netflix, which charges a low monthly fee, let you stream a huge variety of workout videos with no need to hit the gym.

Exergame. Video gaming systems like Xbox let you enjoy real-life workouts in the virtual world. Try *Dance Dance Revolution* or virtual baseball, bowling, boxing, golf, or tennis. While you're at it, get your friends or family members to join in.

Fitness Websites	
Site Name	**Web Address**
FitDay	fitday.com
fitness.com	fitness.com
Fitness Partner	primusweb.com /fitnesspartner
Livestrong	livestrong.com
Men's Fitness	mensfitness.com
Nutrition Data	nutritiondata.self.com
WeightWatchers	weightwatchers.com

Health-Related Phone Apps	
App Name	**Function**
FitStar	Makes workout dynamic
Argus	Tracks physical activity
Human Tracks	Tracks casual activity
Fooducate	Features shopping guide to help you buy good food
Diet Point Weight Loss	Helps track food/calorie intake
Spark People	Connects you to a range of health sites

ONE STEP FURTHER

Use your electronic calendar to send periodic alerts to your mobile device throughout your school day and workday to take breaks or work out. When you are studying, working, or attending classes, it is very easy to forget to give your body time to be active. You don't necessarily have to go to the gym. Sometimes a brisk walk or 15 minutes of stretching and relaxed breathing can reset your body and your mind.

11

THINK
WRITE
APPLY

THINK

If you could make only three recommendations to a new first-year college student about managing his or her wellness in college, what would they be?

WRITE

Describe some of the ways in which your life has changed since you started attending college. How have you handled these changes? What has been the most difficult aspect of your college life so far? Why?

APPLY

1. Identify one area in your life in which you need to make changes to become healthier. How do you think becoming healthier will improve your performance in college? What are the challenges you face in becoming healthier?
2. College can be stressful at times. What are your sources of stress in college? How are you managing your stress? List the strategies you apply in reducing your stress.
3. College life offers many opportunities to meet new people and to develop a new support network. But finding friends and mentors you can trust is not always easy. What steps have you taken so far to meet new people and build a network of support in college? What can you do in the future to expand your support network?
4. Check out some of your fellow students' profiles on a social media site such as Facebook or Twitter. What kinds of personal information do they share? What kinds of issues are they writing about? Do you think it is important for college students to be careful about the kind of information they post on social media sites? Why or why not?
5. Use your college course catalog to identify courses that focus on topics of multiculturalism and diversity. Why do you think academic departments have included these issues in the curriculum? How would studying diversity help you prepare for different academic fields and careers?

Below are suggestions for resources that are available at many colleges and the online resources that are available to everyone.

AT YOUR COLLEGE

VISIT . . .	IF YOU NEED HELP . . .
Counseling Center	thinking and talking about your relationships and making the most appropriate decisions. It is normal to seek such assistance. This kind of counseling is strictly confidential (unless you are a threat to yourself or others) and usually is provided at no charge, which is a great benefit.
Health Center	seeking prevention and/or treatment.
Campus support groups	finding support groups led by professionals for dealing with problems related to excessive alcohol and drug use, abusive sexual relationships, and other issues. Your campus counseling center can help you identify support groups at your college or in your community.
Student organizations	getting into a group with other students that share the same interests with you.

ONLINE

GO TO . . .	IF YOU NEED HELP . . .
Columbia University: goaskalice.com	getting advice about college student health issues.
American Institute of Stress: stress.org	dealing with stress.
The American Dietetic Association: eatright.org	finding information on healthy eating and nutrition.
The American Cancer Society: cancer.org	finding out how tobacco affects your health and learning more about the health effects of tobacco.
The Center for Young Women's Health: youngwomenshealth.org/collegehealth10.html	getting helpful advice on sexual health as well as other issues.
Substance Abuse and Mental Services Administration: samhsa.gov	finding up-to-date information about substance abuse and mental health.
Drug-Rehab: drug-rehab.org	finding a private, nonprofit referral service for drug and alcohol rehab treatment.
The Centers for Disease Control and Prevention: cdc.gov	accessing reliable information on disease control.

The National Suicide Prevention Lifeline: 1-800-273-TALK, suicidepreventionlifeline.org	answering questions about suicide prevention.
National Eating Disorders Association: nationaleatingdisorders.org	understanding eating disorders.
U.S. Government's Nutrition Information: nutrition.gov	accessing nutrition information.
The University of Chicago's Student Counseling Virtual Pamphlet Collection: dr-bob.org/vpc/	solving relationship problems.
The University of Texas Counseling Center on Healthy Romantic Relationships during College: cmhc.utexas.edu/healthyrelationships.html	accessing information that explores the ups and downs of romantic relationships.
The Clery Center for Security on Campus: clerycenter.org/campus-sexual-violence -elimination-save-act	finding information on the Campus Sexual Violence Elimination (SaVE) Act.
Diversity Web: diversityweb.org	finding resources related to diversity on campus.
Tolerance.org	accessing resources for dealing with discrimination and prejudice both on and off campus.

MY COLLEGE'S RESOURCES

LaunchPad for *Understanding Your College Experience* is a great resource. Go online to master concepts using the LearningCurve study tool and much more. **macmillanhighered.com/gardnerunderstanding**

12 Making the Right Career Choice

PRE-READING ACTIVITY: One of the reasons most students attend college is to learn skills that they can apply to a job or career. What kind of job or career do you want after you complete your studies? What kind of life do you want to lead after college? Explain three reasons for attending college.

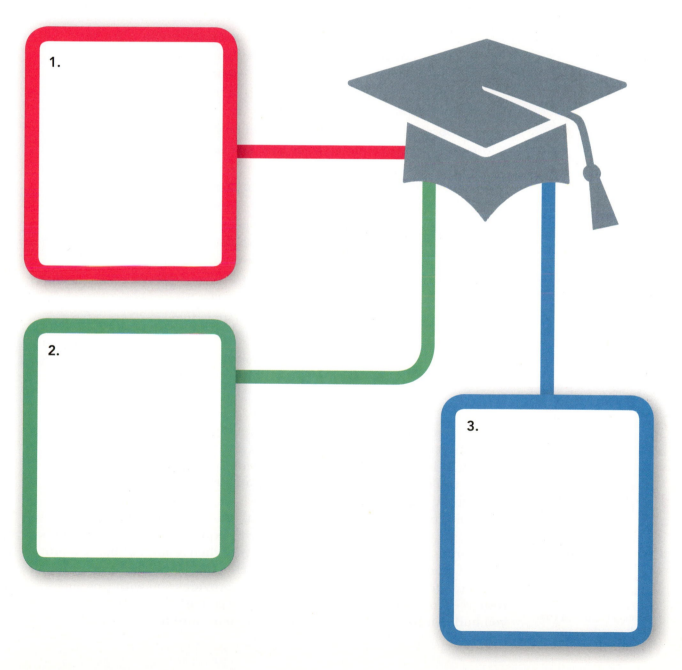

1.

2.

3.

12.1 Careers and the New Economy

12.2 Self-Exploration in Career Planning

12.3 Planning for Your Career

12.4 Getting Experience

12.5 Job Search Strategies

12.6 Skills Employers Seek

12.7 Staying on the Path to Success

"Choose a career that you will love for the rest of your life."

 PROFILE

Rebecca Hall, 25
English Major, *Tidewater Community College*, Virginia

Henrik Sorensen/Getty Images

Rebecca Hall grew up all over the world, moving with her parents, who were in the military, from state to state and even to countries like France before settling in Virginia. She graduated from high school in 2010 and decided to take time off from academics before heading to college. She began working as a waitress, but after realizing she was losing sight of her career goals, she decided to enroll at Tidewater Community College and study English. She knew she would need a degree to provide for herself, but why English? "My favorite classes so far have been English classes," Rebecca explains. "I love the critical-thinking aspects and the ability to write analytically on the topics that are presented in class."

Rebecca has since taken that love of English and writing and transformed the passion into a career goal. She wants to teach English at the high school level. She plans to finish her two-year degree at Tidewater Community College and then transfer to Old Dominion University.

When she is not in school, Rebecca takes a little time out to enjoy hiking. She also finds time to work 8 hours a week as a peer tutor in the campus writing center, where she helps students with editing and proofreading their papers.

Her advice to first-year students is, "Choose a career that you will love for the rest of your life. If you are not happy doing it now, you will most likely not be happy doing it 20 years from now."

Your decision to attend college increases your possibilities for employment and will likely contribute to a great career path. College is a time for gaining academic knowledge and exploring career opportunities to help you grow from a student into a productive member of the global economy.

Some students know what career path they want to follow before they even begin college. Others enter college to explore career options by taking courses in different subject areas. Even when students choose a program of study or major, they may not be clear on how their selected majors relate to their future careers. This chapter provides you with tips and resources for career planning. Visiting your college career center can help you build on the material in this chapter, so be sure to use this valuable resource.

 **LaunchPad**
macmillan learning

To access the Learning-Curve study tool, Video Tools, and more, go to LaunchPad for *Understanding Your College Experience.* macmillanhighered.com /gardnerunderstanding

CAREERS AND THE NEW ECONOMY

For some people, the reason for attending college is to get a good job. For others, the reason is to fulfill the dream of getting a college education. For many students who are first in their families to attend college, it's both. Getting a degree, whether associate's or bachelor's, or completing a certificate program, helps students qualify for better jobs or prepares them to continue their studies at a four-year college or university or in a graduate or professional program. Higher education, in and of itself, improves critical-thinking and problem-solving skills and changes a person's societal status to a college-educated individual.

Over the past few years, the global economy has experienced extreme ups and downs. Economic uncertainty is a reality, and although earning a college degree is one of the best ways you can increase your chances of gaining employment, it is important to make decisions about your major and career path based on information about yourself and the long-term demands of the job market.

> **YOUR TURN > DISCUSS IT**
>
> Discuss with another student how the current economy affects your thinking about your future career.

Characteristics of Today's Economy

The following characteristics define today's economy:

- **Global.** Many corporations are multinational; they look for cheap labor, capital, and resources both within and outside the United States. College graduates in the United States now compete for jobs with others around the world, particularly in industries that involve the fields of science, technology, engineering, and mathematics (STEM).

- **Unstable.** Economic instability is troubling, but having a college education gives you a great advantage over those without degrees. Attending college to earn a degree or certificate in a relatively short time allows you flexibility in an uncertain job market.

- **Innovative.** The economy has always depended on creativity to generate consumer interest in new products and services around the world. The United States, as a leader in industry innovation, needs college graduates who possess creativity and imagination and a desire to move forward.

- **Without boundaries.** In almost every organization, teams need to work together. You might be an accountant and find yourself working with the public relations division of your company, or you might be a nurse who does staff training. The ability to work outside traditional boundaries while expanding your skills, abilities, and knowledge will be essential to your professional success.

- **Ever changing.** Nowadays, new jobs in nearly all industries will demand more education and training. As you previously learned in this book, the most important skill you need to learn in college is how to keep learning throughout your life. To give yourself the best chance at avoiding a negative employment situation, it's important to adapt your skills to the job market that exists. Doing so requires flexibility and the desire to continue to develop yourself.

- **Social.** In a recent survey, employers were asked which attributes they look for on an applicant's résumé. In this world of increasing technology advancements, the biggest group of respondents chose both "leadership" and "the ability to work in a team structure." These skills/qualities are followed by "written communication skills," "problem-solving skills," "strong work ethic," and "analytical/quantitative skills."[1]

These characteristics of the economy—global, unstable, innovative, without boundaries, ever changing, and social—should provide a roadmap for you as you make decisions throughout your college experience.

Building the Right Mindset for the Future

Even after you have landed a job, you will be expected to continue learning and developing yourself. Whether you are preparing to enter a career for the first time or to change careers after many years on the job, keep the following in mind:

- **A college degree does not guarantee employment.** Consider what it will be like competing with hundreds of other college graduates earning the same degree as you and graduating at the same time! With a college degree, however, more opportunities will be available, financially and otherwise, than if you did not have a degree. For those who start an associate's degree and complete it, the reward is considerable. If you transfer to a four-year college or university after you graduate with your associate's degree, the payoff is even greater. Just because you want to work for a certain organization or in a certain field, though, doesn't mean that a job will always be available for you there.

- **You are more or less solely responsible for your career.** Career development is a lifelong process, controlled only by you! Students who realize they are responsible for managing their careers actively throughout their lifetime will be more successful and more satisfied than those who think someone else will come along to manage things for them.

- **To advance your career, you must accept the risks that accompany employment and plan for the future.** As organizations grow or

---

[1]National Association of Colleges and Employers, *Job Outlook 2015* (Bethlehem, PA: National Association of Colleges and Employers, 2015), http://www.naceweb.org/s11122014/job-outlook-skills-qualities-employers-want .aspx, accessed 1/4/2016.

> **Thinking Things Through**

When you're asked about your plans for employment after college, do you feel clueless? If so, you're not alone. Many students come to college without firm career plans. This chapter will give you some new ways to think about your career choices. Your experiences in college will help you make thoughtful decisions about your future.

Blend Images/Peathegee Inc.

downsize in response to economic conditions, you must do your best to prepare for the unexpected. As we have stated at several points in this book, perhaps the most vital skill you can gain in college is learning how to learn. Lifelong learning will help keep you employable and can provide you with many opportunities regardless of the economy.

- **Career choice is not permanent.** College students often view the choice of a career as a big and permanent decision. This is not correct. A career is based on your professional development decisions over a lifetime. In fact, many students with jobs attend college (often after completing a B.A. degree or even an advanced degree) to change their careers because of professional or personal reasons. There is no one right occupation just waiting to be discovered. Rather, there are many career choices you might find satisfying. The question to consider is this: What is the best choice for me now?

Now the good news: Hundreds of thousands of graduates find jobs every year, even in difficult economic times. It might take them longer to get where they want to be, but persistence pays off. If you start preparing now and continue to do so while in college, you'll have time to build a portfolio of academic and other learning experiences (e.g., on-campus clubs and groups, cooperative [co-op] programs, internships, work-study jobs) that will begin to add to your career profile.

YOUR TURN > TRY IT

Ask another student about his or her career goals. Why has she or he chosen that career path? Does that person seem passionate about this career? Why or why not?

SELF-EXPLORATION IN CAREER PLANNING

Are you confident in your skills and abilities? Do you know exactly what you want or can accomplish? How well you know yourself and how effectively you can do the things you need to do are central to your success not only as a college student but also as a person. **Self-assessment** is the process of gathering information about oneself in order to make informed decisions.

Self-assessment is a good first step in setting your academic and career goals. While you might know what you like to do and what you are good at doing, you may lack a clear idea of how your self-knowledge can help you explore different career possibilities. Factors that can affect your career choices include your values, skills, aptitudes, personality, and interests.

Values

Your **values,** formed through your life experiences, are those things you feel most strongly about. For career planning, values generally refer to what you most want in a career in relation to how you want to live. For example, some people value job security, money, and a regular schedule. Others value flexibility, excitement, independence, variety, and particular work environments such as the outdoors. Some career choices pay higher salaries than others but may require hard work and long hours.

Thus, knowing your personal wishes and needs in relation to your values is important. You might find that what you value most is not money but rather the chance to work for a specific cause or the opportunity to have a particular lifestyle. In general, being aware of what you value is important because a career choice that is closely related to your core values is likely to be the best choice. If your values are not in line with the values of the organization where you work, you might be in for trouble.

❮ A Passion for Helping People?

Do you enjoy working with the public? Are you interested in helping sick people? Do you want to work in a health-related field? Does a career in the health professions align with your values, interests, and personality? If you're not sure, you might want to reconsider your plans.
© Jose Luis Pelaez Inc/Blend Images/Corbis

Aptitude and Skills

Aptitude is your natural or acquired proficiency in a particular area, which makes it easier for you to learn certain skills and do certain things. The ability to do something well can usually be improved with practice. You may bring different skills to multiple situations, and it is important to know both your strengths and weaknesses. Skills typically fall into three categories:

1. **Personal.** Some skills come naturally or are learned through personal experience. Examples of these skills are honesty, punctuality, teamwork, self-motivation, and conflict management.

2. **Workplace.** Some skills can be learned on the job; others are gained through training designed to increase your knowledge or expertise in a certain area. Examples include designing websites, bookkeeping, and providing customer service.

3. **Transferable.** Some skills gained through your previous jobs, hobbies, or even everyday life can be transferred to another job. Examples include planning events, motivating others, paying attention to detail, and organizing workspaces.

When you shine a light on your aptitudes, you can discover a path in which your strengths become your best intellectual assets. By identifying your skill set, you can turn your current skills into career possibilities.

Personality

Your **personality** refers to the combination of your characteristics or qualities that combine to form your character—how you think, feel, and behave. Your personality makes you who you are and can't be ignored when you make career decisions. The quiet, orderly, calm, detail-oriented person will probably make a different work choice than the aggressive, outgoing, argumentative person will. Using an assessment tool such as the well-known and widely used Myers-Briggs Type Indicator can help you understand how you make decisions, perceive the world, and communicate with others.

Getting a good sense of your values, skills, aptitudes, personality, and interests will help you make a career choice that leads to success and satisfaction. Each of us defines success and satisfaction in our own way. The process is complex and personal. Two factors can change how we feel about our success and happiness: knowing that we are achieving the life goals we've set for ourselves and finding that we gain satisfaction from what we're receiving from our work.

YOUR TURN > WORK TOGETHER

Work with a classmate and discuss the jobs you have had, either for pay or as a volunteer. Which of your jobs was your favorite? Which did you dislike? Be prepared to discuss your reasons in class and to offer thoughts about what your previous work experiences tell you about your preferences for work in the future.

PLANNING FOR YOUR CAREER

The process of making a career choice begins with creating a career plan, and college is a good time to start, if you haven't already. Here are some important steps to take:

- **Take a variety of classes.** You'll want to be introduced to different fields of study.

- **Visit your college's career center in person, and explore its website.** You'll find listings for part- and full-time jobs, internships, co-op programs, and seasonal employment. You'll also find on-campus interviewing opportunities for internships and for full-time employment after graduation. Attend workshops on advanced résumé writing, internship placement, interviewing, and other job search skills. Participate in mock interview activities to improve your interviewing skills.

- **Take as many self-assessments as possible.** Talk to a career counselor about your skills, aptitudes, interests, and career plans. Research possible careers that match your skills, interests, and academic major (see the Tech Tip at the end of this chapter).

- **Prepare a draft of your résumé and have it reviewed by a career counselor or a professional in your desired field.** These individuals can provide you with useful feedback to improve your résumé.

- **Create profiles on professional sites, such as LinkedIn.** Share your skills and experience with potential employers and make professional connections.

‹ Making Connections

Some career fairs may be specific to disciplines such as health care, information technology, or business. Others may be specific to the audience, such as this career fair for military veterans. Attending events like these is part of planning for your career. Career fairs give job candidates the opportunity to make a strong first impression with potential employers.
© Sandy Huffaker/Corbis

- **Get involved in clubs and organizations.** Take on a leadership role in a club or organization that connects with your interests.

- **Attend your college's career fair.** Employers in the area visit your campus to hire students. Get to know more about the employers who hire graduates in your major. Some career fairs may be specific to disciplines such as health care, information technology, or business.

- **Build on your strengths and develop your weaker skills.** Whether in or out of class, find ways to practice what you are good at and get help with what you need to improve.

- **Network.** Connect with instructors, family members, and friends to find contacts in your fields of interest so that you can learn more about those areas. Participate, if possible, in mentoring programs hosted by alumni (past graduates of your college). Spend the summer completing internship, service-learning, and co-op experiences.

- **Volunteer.** Whether you give of your time to a nonprofit organization, a school, or a business, volunteering can help you explore careers and get some experience in an area that interests you.

- **Do occupational and industry research for your field or for geographic areas that interest you.** Look for all the career options within and beyond your field.

- **Visit work environments in person.** Explore career options through informational interviews (interviewing to find out about a career) and job shadowing (observing someone at work with his or her permission).

- **Get a job.** Many students already have jobs when they enter college. Holding a job, especially one related to your major, can add to your classroom learning. In any job, though, you learn essential skills such as teamwork, communication, and time management that are important to employers!

- **Conduct an audit of your own online presence.** Make sure nothing inappropriate is posted about you on Facebook, Instagram, Twitter, or other social media outlets.

You can complete these steps at a different pace or in a different order than your friends do. What you want is to develop your qualifications, make good choices, and take advantage of opportunities on and off campus to learn more about your career preferences. Keep your goals in mind as you select courses and look for employment, but also keep an eye out for special opportunities. The path you think you want to follow might change as you grow.

YOUR TURN ❯ STAY MOTIVATED

Have you explored your college's career center? What did you learn? What other benefits did you gain as a result of your visit? If you haven't made a visit, when in your college experience do you think going to the career center will be most important? Why?

GETTING EXPERIENCE

Now that you have developed a career plan and gotten a handle on your interests, it's time to test the waters. But since employers prefer to hire people with experience, how can you gain experience if they won't hire you without any? There are several ways to gain some experience while you are in college. Engaging in experiential learning opportunities, such as service learning, volunteer activities, internships, co-op programs, and competitions and projects designed for students, can help you gain some experience while you are in college.

Experiential Learning Opportunities

Gaining experience in your field while in college can help you meet people who may later serve as important references for employment. That experience can also teach you things you won't learn in the classroom. Here are a number of ways to pursue such experience:

- **Service learning/volunteer activities.** In service learning, you are required as part of a course to perform service work without pay. You are then asked to reflect and write about the value of this service experience, and you are evaluated by the course instructor. Service learning allows you to apply what you learn in class to actual practice. Some instructors build service learning into their courses, but if this option isn't available, consider volunteering! A little time spent each week can provide many personal and professional rewards, allowing you to continue learning about yourself, your interests, and your abilities.

❮ Linking Classroom and Career

This student studies computer science and works in the college computer labs, helping other students with their technology problems. Imagine what he is learning about his program of study and how his work experience relates to what he learns in his courses.

Goodluz/Shutterstock.com

- **Internships and co-ops.** What you learn in the classroom can be applied to the real world through internships and co-ops. An **internship** is short-term, on-the-job training. As an intern, you might not get paid, but you might be able to receive academic credit. Check with your academic department and career center to find out what internships are available in your major. Remember that with one or more internships on your résumé, you'll be a step ahead of students who do not get this valuable experience. A **co-op** program allows you paid work assignments that provide you with an opportunity to apply what you learn in class to the workplace.

- **Student projects/competitions.** In many fields, students engage in competitions based on what they have learned in the classroom. They might compete against teams from other colleges. In the process, they learn teamwork, communication, and problem-solving skills.

Working in College

Most students have to work while they are in college to support themselves and/or their families. Although balancing work and study is a challenging task, there are many benefits to working while taking classes:

- gaining professional experience
- earning money for tuition, books, and living expenses
- networking/making connections
- learning more about yourself and others
- developing key skills, such as communication, teamwork, problem solving, work ethic, and time management

If you do not already have a job, your first decision will be whether to work on campus or off. If you choose to work on campus, look for opportunities as early in the term as you can. You might be pleasantly surprised by the variety of on-campus opportunities, such as tutoring in the writing or math center, being an attendant in the fitness center, or serving as a student ambassador for the admissions office or career center.

One benefit of on-campus employment is that the work schedules are often flexible. Another benefit is that you might be able to connect with instructors and administrators you can later consult as mentors or ask for reference letters. Plus, your supervisor will understand that you occasionally need time off to study or take exams. Finally, students who work on campus are more likely to graduate from college than are students who work off campus; keep this fact in mind as you think about mixing college and work.

Some on-campus jobs are reserved for work-study students. The federal **work-study** program is a form of government-sponsored financial aid that provides part-time employment to help with college expenses. Once you accept the work-study award on your financial aid notification, you will be sent information regarding the steps you should take for getting a job within the program. Keep in mind that your work-study award will be limited to a certain number of hours and amount of money each term; once you reach your limit in earnings, you can no longer work until the next term begins. Generally, you will have to interview for a work-study position whether on or off campus. Check with your college's financial aid office or career center to get a list of available jobs and to get help preparing your application materials and getting ready for the interview.

In looking for a job, you may decide that you would rather work off campus. An off-campus job might pay better than an on-campus one, or be closer to your home, or be in an organization where you want to continue working after you finish college. The best place to start looking for off-campus jobs is your college career center, which might have listings or websites with off-campus employment opportunities. Feel free to ask a career counselor for suggestions.

Whether you work on or off campus, keep in mind that overextending yourself can negatively affect your college success and your ability to attend class, do your homework, and participate in many other valuable parts of college life, such as group study. Take some time to decide how involved you are able to be, and stay within reasonable limits. Students who work in paid jobs more than fifteen to twenty hours a week have a lower chance of succeeding in college.

12.5

JOB SEARCH STRATEGIES

To find a job while you are in college or after you graduate, you can apply the following job search strategies:

- **Learn the names of the major employers in your college's geographic area:** manufacturers, service industries, resorts, and so on. Once you know who the major employers are, check them out or visit their websites. If you like what you see, visit your career center to arrange an informational interview or job-shadowing opportunity.

- **Check online postings and classified ads** in the local newspaper, either in print or online.

- **Check your college's student newspaper.** Employers who favor hiring college students often advertise their businesses. Some companies also have programs that enable students to earn online degrees while working. Be cautious about work opportunities that seem unrealistic, such as those offering big salaries for working at home or those that ask you to pay an up-front fee for a job. When in doubt, ask your career center for advice.

- **Be aware that many job openings are never posted.** Employers usually prefer to hire people who are recommended to them by current employees, friends, or the person leaving the position. Realize that who you know is important. Your friends who already work on campus or who have had an internship can be the best people to help you when you are ready to search for your job.

Market Yourself

You might think that marketing yourself is what you do when you need a job, but in fact that's not the case at all. Marketing yourself is actually about developing a presence at your college and within your industry. If you can create a name and reputation for yourself, you can shape your own future. You need to stand out from your peers if you want to go far in your career. Think carefully about what you can do outside the classroom, such as becoming a co-op student, an intern, or a volunteer. Taking control of your own image is your responsibility. There is no one who can portray you as accurately as you can portray yourself. Remember to share your career goals with instructors, advisers, friends, and family; they can't help market you if they don't know you! The more others know about your professional goals, the more they are able to help you make professional connections.

> **YOUR TURN > WORK TOGETHER**
>
> Discuss with your classmates what strategies you could use to market yourself to a potential employer. Which of your characteristics or aptitudes would you emphasize? What do your peers plan to do to market themselves?

Build a Résumé

A good résumé is an excellent and necessary way of marketing yourself. Before you finish college, you'll need a résumé, whether it's for a part-time job, an internship, or a co-op position. You will also need to show a résumé to an instructor who agrees to write you a letter of recommendation. There are two résumé formats: chronological and skill focused. Figure 12.1 shows a chronological résumé. You can choose the chronological format to list your jobs and other experiences from the most to least recent. Choose the skills résumé if you can group skills from a number of jobs or projects under several meaningful categories. Your career center can help you choose the format that is right for you based on your experience and future goals.

The average time an employer spends screening résumés for the first time is 7 to 10 seconds. Many employers also use résumé-scanning software to identify key terms and experiences of the applicants who are most important to the employer. If you are a new professional, a one-page résumé is appropriate. Add a second page only if you have truly outstanding skills or work experiences that won't fit on the first page, but consult with your career center for guidance on this point. If you are in college to get retrained and change your career, make sure to update your information on your résumé.

FIGURE 12.1 > Sample Résumé

Sandra Sanchez
1322 8th Avenue, Apt. # 8A
Jersey City, NJ 07087
Cell: 201-555-1212
ssanchez@yahoo.com

Objective

To obtain a position as an IT intern

Qualifications

Dedicated individual with the ability to identify problems, provide solutions, plan and organize tasks, and work in groups

Work Experience

September 2013-September 2015
Hudson County Community College

Computer Lab Assistant
- Assisted students with their computer problems in the lab
- Maintained the computer stations by updating software programs
- Helped to provide an organized learning environment
- Labeled and displayed materials and information related to the lab

August 2011-July 2013
Import/Export Clover Company

Administrative Assistant
- Answered telephone calls
- Assisted the manager with correspondence
- Managed filing, scanning, copying, and other clerical tasks
- Used Outlook calendar function to make appointments and organize events
- Maintained the database

Education

Hudson County Community College, Jersey City, NJ
September 2013-Present
Associate Degree in Computer Science

Union City High School
September 2009-June 2013
Diploma

Languages

English, Spanish

References

Furnished upon request.

Write a Cover Letter

A cover letter is *more important* than a résumé and much harder to write well. When sending a cover letter, think about who will receive it. Different fields will have different requirements. Your academic adviser or career counselor can help you address your letter to the right person, and so can the Internet. Never write, "To whom it may concern." Use the proper formats for date, address, and salutation (Dear _____:). These are details that employers pay attention to, and a mistake in your letter may cost you an interview. Most important of all is to present a letter that is grammatically correct and free of errors. Make sure to ask someone whose writing ability you trust to proofread your cover letter, or better yet, take it to your college's learning center.

A cover letter, written to explain how hiring you will benefit the organization, is an excellent way of marketing yourself to a potential employer. It is important to review the organization's website and find out what skills and experience its employees have. Use the cover letter to highlight your skills for every requirement of the position. Your career center can help you write a cover letter that talks about your education and your experience related to the position. Spending time on writing an excellent cover letter also prepares you for the interview by allowing you to think about how your background matches the needs of that position and the organization.

Interview

The first year of college might not seem like a time to be concerned about interviews. However, students often find themselves in interview situations soon after arriving on campus, sometimes online through Skype, Zoom, Adobe Connect, imo, or other digital conferencing products. You might be looking for positions in student government, finding an on-campus job, competing for a second-year scholarship, choosing a summer job opportunity, or applying for an internship. Preparing for an interview begins the moment you arrive on campus because, as a first-year student, the interview will be about you and how college is changing you. Luckily, the chapters in this book have begun preparing you for the interview process.

The purpose of the interview is to exchange information; the goal is to assess your abilities and competencies. For you, the interview is an opportunity to learn more about the employer and whether the position would be a good fit with your abilities and preferences. Ideally, you want to find a match between your interests and abilities and the position or experience you are seeking. It is important to research the organization and the people you may be working with prior to any interview. Doing so will help prepare you for the interview and help you know what questions to ask. The following explains how you can go about doing this research:

1. **Start with the company website.** This is usually the single best resource. Scroll through the entire site. Note details you can use to

develop good questions to ask in your interview and prepare relevant answers to anticipated interview questions. If the company does not have its own website, go to other sites, such as Hoovers.com, which provide extensive information about companies and industries.

2. **Ask for advice.** Ask your instructor or a staff member in your college career center about the organization.

3. **Note the employer's goals and values.** This tells you about the organizational culture. Use this information to decide whether you would be a good fit.

4. **Research details on the employer's products and services.** Being able to talk a company's language shows that you have prepared yourself.

5. **Take your research with you to the interview.** It is recommended that you show how you have taken the time to find out about the company prior to the interview.

After you've done your research, the next step is to practice interviewing before the actual interview. Check with your career center to find out whether you can participate in a mock interview. Mock interviews help students feel comfortable in real interview situations. Your counselor might ask you for a position description, your résumé, and an organization profile before the interview. Career counselors use these materials to create a situation similar to an actual interview. Many career centers also have practice interview software such as InterviewStream, which is a popular program that allows you to record answers to interview questions asked by the computer for replay and review. You can record your answers multiple times as you try to perfect your response; you can send your recorded interview to instructors or others for feedback; and because the interview is recorded using a webcam, you can review not only your words but also your body language! Nonverbal communication is often more important than what you actually say in the interview. Even if a mock interview

‹ First Impressions

A critical step on the way to any job is the personal interview. This is your chance to put your best foot forward. Remember to be on time, dress professionally, offer a firm handshake, look the interviewer in the eye, answer questions honestly, and smile!

session is not available, the career center can offer tips on handling an interview situation. Check your career center's website for sample interview questions so that you can practice before an interview.

If you are changing your career and have some experience with interviewing, make sure to think about the best and worst interviews you have had and try to avoid repeating mistakes you made in the past; more important, build on the positive interview strategies you used in previous successful interviews.

In an interview situation, any of the following might be a deciding factor in whether you are hired for the position:

- **Dress appropriately.** First impressions matter, so always dress neatly and appropriately. You can be somewhat casual for some types of employers, but it is better to dress too professionally than too informally. Some colleges have outfits—suits or dresses—to loan to students who cannot yet afford to buy expensive clothes for an interview.

- **Arrive on time to the interview.** If your interview is off campus, carefully estimate how long it will take you to travel to the interview site before the day of your interview. Be mindful of traffic volume at certain times of the day, and if you are driving, make sure you know where to park. The interviewer expects you to be on time, regardless of the weather or your commuting time.

- **Follow up.** It is important to follow up any interview with a thank-you e-mail. Many times, the person to whom you addressed your cover letter is not the person with whom you actually interview. Prior to leaving the interview, ask for business cards of the professionals you met with so that you have their contact information. Send a thank-you to every person who interviewed you. In your follow-up, you can once more highlight how your skills and experience match with the organization's goals.

SKILLS EMPLOYERS SEEK

One of the many important purposes and outcomes of your college experience is gaining a combination of knowledge and skills. Two types of skills are essential to employment and to life: content skills and transferable skills. **Content skills** are intellectual, or "hard," skills you gain in your academic field. They include writing proficiency, computer literacy, and foreign language skills. Computer literacy is now a core skill like reading, writing, and mathematics. You can apply content skills to jobs in any field or occupation.

Certain types of employers expect extensive knowledge in your academic major before they consider hiring you; for example, to get a job in accounting, you must have knowledge of QuickBooks or of Microsoft

Excel's advanced features. Employers will not train you in basic applications or knowledge related to your field, so remember to be prepared to speak of your qualifications during the interview process. Remember that for most college students, it's sufficient to have some fundamental knowledge. You will learn on the job as you move from entry-level to advanced positions.

Transferable skills are general skills that can be applied in a lot of settings. Transferable skills give you flexibility in your career planning. For example, volunteer work, community service, involvement in a student organization or club, and having hobbies or interests can all build teamwork, leadership, interpersonal skills, and effective communication abilities. Internships and career-related work can offer you valuable opportunities to practice these skills in the real world. Some transferable skills are listed and described below:

Skills	Abilities
Communication	Being a clear and persuasive speaker
	Listening attentively
	Writing well
	Communicating with individuals inside and outside the organization
Presentation	Justifying
	Persuading
	Responding to questions and serious critiques of presentation material
Leadership	Taking charge
	Providing direction
	Making decisions and solving problems
Teamwork	Working with different people while maintaining control over some assignments
Interpersonal	Relating to others
	Motivating others to participate
	Easing conflict between coworkers
Personal traits	Showing motivation
	Possessing technical knowledge related to the job
	Recognizing the need to take action
	Being adaptable to change
	Having a strong work ethic
	Being reliable and honest
	Acting in an ethical manner
	Knowing how to plan and organize multiple tasks
	Being able to respond positively to customer concerns
Critical thinking and problem solving	Identifying problems and their solutions by combining information from different sources and considering options
	Analyzing quantitative data
	Obtaining and processing information

STAYING ON THE PATH TO SUCCESS

Because so much research has been done on first-year students like you, we can confidently tell you that successful completion of this course is a good predictor for overall success in college. When you finish any of your college courses, take some time to step back, think, ask yourself the following questions, and perhaps even record your answers:

- What did I learn in this course?
- How can I apply what I have learned to other courses or to my current job?
- How will I use what I learned both in and out of class?
- What did I learn that I am most likely to remember?
- Do I want to stay in touch with this instructor?
- Did I improve my basic skills?
- How do I feel about what I accomplished?
- Did I do better than I thought I would?
- What did I do that helped me progress, and how can I repeat those kinds of successful efforts in other courses?
- What challenges do I still face?

Whether you are finishing this course at the end of your first term or first year in college, you have learned many success strategies that can help you throughout your entire college experience. For many students, the first year is by far the most challenging, especially in terms of adjusting or readjusting to college life. Once you complete your first year, you will have made many decisions and encountered many opportunities, and you need a set of strategies to succeed beyond the first year.

> **Celebrate!**

Before you know it, you'll be a college graduate, equipped with all the knowledge and skills you have acquired and on your way to a successful career and a bright future.

© Ariel Skelley/Blend Images/Corbis

CONDUCT INDUSTRY RESEARCH

In the world of business, anything older than six months is considered ancient. Today, information about industries and the companies that represent them is essential for anyone who wants to get a sense of how careers are trending, what the most innovative sectors are, which college majors are in or out, where the money is, and who's hiring.

THE PROBLEM *You have no idea where to begin your industry research—all the options leave you dizzy.*

THE FIX *Start with a tried-and-true comprehensive resource.*

HOW TO DO IT

STEPS TO DOING INDUSTRY RESEARCH

Step 1. Figure out what industries interest you:

1. Visit O*NET OnLine (**onetonline.org**) and use the Find Occupations option at the top of the page to begin your search.

2. Search occupations by keyword, or choose from the occupational categories:

   a. **Career Cluster.** These are occupations in the same field of work that require similar skills.

   b. **Industry.** These are broad groups of businesses or organizations with similar activities, products, or services.

   c. **Job Zone.** These zones group occupations into one of five categories based on required levels of education, experience, and training.

   d. **Bright Outlook.** These are occupations that are new and emerging, are expected to grow rapidly in the next several years.

   e. **Green Economy Sector.** These are occupations in fields related to environmental protection and sustainable energy.

   f. **Job Families.** These are groups of occupations based on skills, education, training, credentials, and work performed.

   g. **STEM Disciplines.** These are occupations that require education in science, technology, engineering, and mathematics (STEM).

Step 2. Continue your research to identify your desired role within your chosen industry.

Step 3. Identify companies or organizations of interest within a larger industry. The federal government, for example, has approximately 575 departments and agencies! With so many choices, your research will depend on your expectations and wants.

Step 4. Do research on each individual employer of interest. How well does the organization pay compared to others in the same industry? Does this employer require long hours or frequent travel? Set up an informational interview to talk to people who are already working within the organization.

OTHER HELPFUL RESOURCES

Market Research	marketresearch.com
Wall Street Journal	executivelibrary.com /Research.asp
First Research	firstresearch.com /Industry-Profiles.aspx
Market Watch	marketwatch.com/tools /industry
Hoovers	hoovers.com
Occupational Outlook Handbook	bls.gov/ooh
Job.com	job.com
Job Bank USA	jobbankusa.com
USA Jobs	usajobs.gov
Yahoo! Hot Jobs	hotjobs.yahoo.com

GO ONE STEP FURTHER

Create an Online Profile on LinkedIn.com. Your online profile should be professional and include your résumé and only the information you'd like potential employers to know.

THINK

As a first-year student, you do not have to know exactly what you want to do when you graduate from college. What is important, however, is to take advantage of the resources and support available. Think about strategies that can help you make the right career choice.

WRITE

Choosing a career can be a challenge. Of the topics covered in this chapter, which would you like to learn more about?

_____

_____

_____

_____

APPLY

1. Almost every college has a career center where you can obtain free counseling and information on different careers. A career professional will help you define your interests, interpret the results of any assessment you complete, coach you on interview techniques, and critique your résumé. Schedule an appointment with a career counselor who is responsible for your academic major or interests. Ask about opportunities for internships and interview practice. Find out as much as possible about the education and training required for a specific career in the field. Ask about the skills that are necessary to succeed and the outlook for the future. In the following table, list what you need to do each term to prepare for your job or career of choice when you graduate:

Time Line	To Do
First Term	
Second Term	
Third Term	
Fourth Term	

2. Now that you have a better understanding of your possible career, identify a person whose job you wish to have in the future. Make an appointment with this person to interview him or her. Create a list of questions you would like to ask during the interview. For example, you can ask about college degrees, training, and previous jobs. You can also seek advice on how to prepare for a job similar to the one this person has.

USE YOUR RESOURCES

Below are suggestions for resources that are available at many colleges and the online resources that are available to everyone.

AT YOUR COLLEGE

VISIT . . .	IF YOU NEED HELP . . .
Career Center	learning about specific jobs and careers, how to prepare an effective résumé and cover letter, and how to prepare for an interview.
Academic advising/First-year counselors	finding supportive networks to connect academic learning to co-curricular and extracurricular learning.
Instructors	connecting your academic interests to careers. Instructors can recommend specific courses that relate to a particular career. Some instructors have direct contact with companies and serve as contacts for internships.
Library	finding information on careers.
Upperclass students	navigating courses and finding important resources. Many two-year colleges have established peer mentoring programs that connect you to upperclass students for one-on-one guidance. Upperclass students might also have practical experience gained from internships and volunteering.
Student organizations	finding leadership development opportunities.

ONLINE

GO TO . . .	IF YOU NEED HELP . . .
Occupational Information Network: onetcenter.org	getting information on occupations, skill sets, and links to professional sites for selected occupations.
Mapping Your Future: mappingyourfuture.org	exploring careers.
The Riley Guide: rileyguide.com	finding tips for interviewing and job search strategies.

MY COLLEGE'S RESOURCES

_____

_____

 **LaunchPad** macmillan learning

LaunchPad for *Understanding Your College Experience* is a great resource. Go online to master concepts using the LearningCurve study tool and much more. **macmillanhighered.com/gardnerunderstanding**

Glossary

abstract A paragraph-length summary of the methods and major findings of an article in a scholarly journal.

academic calendar Calendar that shows all the important dates that are specific to your campus such as financial aid, registration, and add/drop deadlines; midterm and final exam dates; holidays; graduation deadlines; and so forth.

academic plan A list of the courses you need to take and complete in your program of study to graduate with a degree.

acronym New words created from the first letters of a list or group of words you are trying to remember (a category of mnemonic).

acrostic A verse in which certain letters of each word or line form a message (a category of mnemonic).

active learning Learning through engagement and participation—talking with others, asking questions in class, studying in groups, and going beyond the lecture material and required reading.

active reading Participating in reading by using strategies such as highlighting and taking notes that help you stay focused.

adjuncts Instructors who teach part-time at your college.

annotate To add critical or explanatory notes in the margins of a page as you read.

annotations Notes or remarks about a piece of writing.

appendixes Supplemental materials at the end of the book.

aptitude Your natural or acquired proficiency in a particular area, which makes it easier for you to learn or to do certain things.

argument A calm, reasoned effort to persuade someone of the value of an idea.

attention disorder Officially termed attention deficit/hyperactivity disorder or ADHD. Is characterized by an inability to be attentive or to control impulse and activity.

balance A state in which different things occur in proper amounts.

biases Some tendencies against or in favor of certain groups or value systems.

Bloom's Taxonomy A system of classifying goals for the learning process, now used at all levels of education to define and describe the process that students use to understand and think critically about what they are learning.

budget A spending plan that tracks all sources of income (financial aid, wages, money from parents, etc.) and expenses (rent, tuition, books, etc.) during a set period of time (weekly, monthly, etc.).

cheating Acting dishonestly or unfairly in order to gain an advantage. Different colleges define cheating in different ways. The following activities are often included in definitions of cheating: looking at the work or test of a classmate for an answer, using a calculator when it is not permitted, purchasing term papers, or copying someone else's lab notes.

citation A reference that enables a reader to locate a source based on information such as the author's name, the title of the work, and the publication date.

cognitive learning disability A disability related to mental tasks and processing.

collaboration Working with others.

computer literacy The ability to use computers and related technology efficiently.

content skills Intellectual or "hard" skills you gain in your academic field that can include writing proficiency, computer literacy, and foreign language skills.

co-requisites Courses that must be taken in conjunction with other courses during the same term.

Cornell format One of the best-known methods for organizing notes, which uses two columns—one column is used for note taking during class, and the other is designated as a "recall" column where you can jot down main ideas and important details.

credit score A single number that comes from a report that has information about accounts in your name such as credit cards, student loans, utility bills, cell phones, car loans, and so on.

critical thinking A search for truth that requires asking questions, considering multiple points of view, and drawing conclusions supported by evidence.

cultural literacy The ability to understand and participate fluently in a particular culture.

culture Those aspects of a group of people that are passed on or learned.

database An organized and searchable set of information often organized by certain subject areas.

deep learning Understanding the why and how behind the details.

discipline An area of academic study.

diversity The set of differences in social and cultural identities among people living together.

emotional intelligence (EI) How well you recognize, understand, and manage moods, feelings, and attitudes.

encyclopedia A book or an electronic database with general knowledge on a range of topics.

engaged students Those who are fully involved with the college experience and spend the time and the energy necessary to learn, both in and out of class.

episodic memory A category of long-term memory that deals with particular events, their time, and their place.

essay exams Exams that include questions that require students to write a few paragraphs in response to each question.

ethnicity The identity that is assigned to a specific group of people who are historically connected by a common national origin or language.

evidence   Facts supporting an argument.

experiential learning   Learning by doing and from experience.

extrinsic motivation   Motivation that comes from the hope of an external reward or the fear of an undesirable outcome or punishment.

fill-in-the-blank   Test questions that consist of a phrase, sentence, or paragraph with a blank space indicating where the student should provide the missing word or words.

financial aid   Sources of money that are available to support education at a college or university.

fixed expense   An expense in your budget that does not change whenever you pay it.

foreword   An endorsement of the book written by someone other than the author.

forgetting curve   The decline of memory over time.

freewriting   Writing without worrying about punctuation, grammar, spelling, and background.

glossary   A list of key words and their definitions.

GPA or grade point average   The average of the points you receive from the grades in your courses.

grants   A form of financial aid provided by the government or private organizations that does not have to be repaid.

grit   A combination of perseverance, passion, and resilience.

humanities   Branches of knowledge that investigate human beings, their culture, and their self-expression, such as philosophy, religion, literature, music, and art.

hybrid course   A course that uses both face-to-face and online instruction.

identity theft   A crime that occurs when someone uses another person's personal information.

idioms   Phrases that cannot be understood from the individual meanings of the words.

independent learner   A learner who does not always wait for an instructor to point him or her in the right direction.

interlibrary loan   A service that allows you to request an item at no charge from another library at a different college or university.

intrinsic motivation   Motivation that comes from an internal desire.

introduction   The part of a book that reviews the book's overall organization and its contents, often chapter by chapter.

keyword   A word or phrase that tells an online search tool what you're looking for.

knowledge   The bottom level of Bloom's Taxonomy, which refers to remembering previously learned material and includes arranging, defining, memorizing, and recognizing.

learning disability   A condition that affects people's ability to either interpret what they see and hear or connect information across different areas of the brain.

learning objectives   The main ideas or skills students are expected to learn from reading the chapter.

logical fallacies   Mistakes in reasoning that contain invalid arguments or irrelevant points that undermine the logic of an argument.

long-term memory   The capacity to retain and recall information over the long term, from hours to years.

major   An area of study like psychology, engineering, education, or nursing.

mapping   A preview strategy of drawing a wheel or branching structure to show relationships between main ideas and secondary ideas and how different concepts and terms fit together; it also helps you make connections to what you already know about the subject.

marking   An active reading strategy entailing making marks in the text by underlining, highlighting, or making margin notes or annotations that helps you focus and concentrate as you read.

matching questions   A type of exam question that is designed with terms in one column and descriptions in the other, and you must make the proper pairings.

media literacy   The ability to access, analyze, evaluate, and create media.

mind map   A visual review sheet that shows the relationships between ideas whose visual patterns provide you with clues to jog your memory.

mindset   What you believe about yourself and about your most basic qualities, such as your personality, intelligence, or talents.

mnemonics   The different methods to help with remembering information.

motivation   The desire to do things.

multiple-choice questions   Questions that provide any number of possible answers, often between three and five. The answer choices are usually numbered (1, 2, 3, 4...) or lettered (a, b, c, d...), and the test taker is supposed to select the correct or the best one.

multiple intelligences   A theory developed by Dr. Howard Gardner that suggests all human beings have at least eight different types of intelligence: verbal/linguistic, logical/mathematical, visual/spatial, bodily/kinesthetic, musical/rhythmic, interpersonal, intrapersonal, and naturalistic.

multitasking   Doing more than one thing at a time.

Myers–Briggs Type Indicator (MBTI)   One of the best-known and most widely used personality inventories to describe learning styles. It examines basic personality characteristics and how those relate to human interaction and learning.

nontraditional student   Someone who is not an eighteen-year-old recent high school graduate and may have a family and a job.

office hours   The posted hours when instructors are in their office and available to students.

outlining   A method for organizing notes that utilizes Roman numerals to represent key ideas. Other ideas relating to each key idea are marked by uppercase letters (A, B, C, etc.), numbers (1, 2, 3, etc.), and lowercase letters (a, b, c, etc.) in descending order of importance or detail. Also called listing.

overextended   Having too much to do given the time and resources available to you.

peer-reviewed   A term meaning that other experts in the field read and evaluate the articles in a journal before it is published.

periodical A resource such as a journal, a magazine, or a newspaper that is published multiple times a year.

perseverance Continued effort to achieve a goal in spite of difficulty or failure.

personality The combination of qualities that combine to form your character—how you think, feel, and behave. Your personality makes you who you are.

plagiarism Taking another person's ideas or work and presenting them as your own.

preface A brief overview near the beginning of a book that is usually written by the author or authors and will tell you why they wrote the book and what material the book covers; it will also explain the book's organization and give insight into the author's viewpoint.

prefix Part of a word that comes before the root or base part of the word.

prerequisites Courses you must take before enrolling in upper-level courses.

previewing The step in active reading when you take a first look at assigned reading before you really tackle the content.

primary sources The original research or documents on a topic.

prioritize Putting your tasks, goals, and values in order of importance.

procedural memory A category of long-term memory that deals with knowing how to do something, such as solving a mathematical problem or driving a car.

procrastination The habit of delaying something that needs your immediate attention.

punctuality Being on time.

race The biological characteristics that are shared by groups of people, including skin tone, hair texture and color, and facial features.

religion A specific fundamental set of beliefs and practices generally agreed upon by a number of persons or sects.

research A process of steps used to collect and analyze information to increase understanding of a topic or an issue. Those steps include asking questions, collecting and analyzing data related to those questions, and presenting one or more answers.

resilience Not giving up or quitting when faced with difficulties and challenges.

returning student A student returning to formal education after being out of the educational system for some period of time.

reviewing The process of looking through your assigned reading again.

review sheets Lists of key terms and ideas that you need to remember.

root The base part of a word.

scholarly journals Collections of original, peer-reviewed research articles written by experts or researchers in a particular academic discipline.

scholarship Funds provided for a student based on his or her academic performance or need.

self-assessment The process of gathering information about yourself in order to make an informed decision.

semantic memory A category of long-term memory that involves facts and meanings without regard to where and when you learned those things.

sexual assault Any type of sexual contact or behavior that occurs without the explicit consent of the recipient.

sexual harassment Any kind of unwanted sexual advances or remarks.

short-term memory How many items you are able to understand and remember at one time.

sisu A term from Finnish culture that means going beyond one's mental or physical ability, taking action even when things are difficult, and displaying courage and determination in the face of challenge and repeated failures.

social sciences Academic disciplines that examine human aspects of the world, such as sociology, psychology, anthropology, economics, political science, and history.

stacks The area of a library in which most of the books are shelved.

stereotype A generalization, usually exaggerated or oversimplified and often offensive, that is used to describe or distinguish a group.

student loan A form of financial aid that must be paid back with interest.

suffix Part of a word that follows the root or base part of the word.

summary Provides the most important ideas in the chapter.

summary paragraphs A note-taking format in which you write two or three sentences that sum up a larger section of material.

Supplemental Instruction (SI) Structured opportunities outside class to discuss the information covered in class.

syllabus A statement of requirements for a given course.

synthesis An activity that involves accepting some ideas, rejecting others, combining related concepts, assessing the information, and pulling it all together to create new ideas that other people can use.

thesis statement A short statement that clearly defines the purpose of the paper.

transferable skills General skills that can be applied in a lot of settings.

true/false Questions that ask students to determine whether the statement is correct or not.

values Those things you feel most strongly about that are formed through your life experiences.

variable expense An expense in your budget that may change every time you pay it.

VARK Inventory A sixteen-item questionnaire that focuses on how learners prefer to use their senses (hearing, seeing, writing and reading, or experiencing) to learn.

vocabulary A set of words in a particular language or field of knowledge.

wellness A healthy balance of the mind, body, and spirit that results in an overall feeling of well-being.

work-study Part-time jobs on campus available to students who are receiving financial aid.

Index

Note: Figures and tables are indicated by *(f)* and *(t)* following page numbers.

T